D1602448

The Future of Intelligence
Biological and Artificial

The Future of Intelligence
Biological and Artificial

by
Victor Serebriakoff

The Parthenon Publishing Group
International Publishers in Science & Technology

asterton Hall, Carnforth,
ancs, LA6 2LA, U.K.

120 Mill Road, Park Ridge
New Jersey, U.S.A.

Published in the UK and Europe by
The Parthenon Publishing Group Limited,
Casterton Hall, Carnforth,
Lancs. LA6 2LA, England — ISBN 1-85070-133-4

Published in the USA by
The Parthenon Publishing Group Inc.,
120 Mill Road,
Park Ridge,
New Jersey, USA — ISBN 0-940813-02-5
Library of Congress Catalog Number: 86–063 806

Typeset by H & H Graphics, Blackburn, Lancashire

Printed in Great Britain

Contents

Foreword

by Isaac Asimov

When I was very young, I read the myth of Narcissus. Narcissus was a handsome youth who rejected all the young women who were dying for his embraces. One of them prayed that he, too, would feel the pangs of unrequited love, so, of course (since the gods are always eager to answer unkind prayers) he did.

He spied his reflection in the water, thought it was another youth, fell in love with its beauty, attempted futilely to embrace it, and finally drowned when he tried too hard. The myth has made such an impression on people that the word "narcissism" is a recognized psychiatric term for morbid self-love.

I did not like the myth at all. To my childish self, it seemed incredibly stupid. How could Narcissus mistake his own image for another youth? (I was also more than a little puzzled that he should fall in love with another youth, rather than with a maid, but the problem of the image overrode that.)

No one bothered to explain that point to me. They were only interested in explaining the moral: that if you are unkind to others, then others will be unkind to you; that if you are too fond of yourself, you will find life unpleasant.

I saw the moral, of course; it was obvious. What I wanted, though, was a technological explanation, and I never got it. I had to work it out for myself as I grew older.

The point is that in primitive times, it was perfectly possible for a person to see the faces of those around him with perfect clarity (assuming eyesight was normal.) He (or she) could tell, at sight, the identity of every human being with whom he was acquainted. He would also tell at a glance that some person he encountered was a stranger to him, someone he had never seen before.

There was one exception. Under primitive conditions, no person could see his (or her) *own* face. If, through some form of magic, his own face were

1

presented to him, he would have no choice but to consider it that of a stranger.

To see your own face without magic, you need a smooth, reflecting surface. A piece of smooth, unflawed glass will do, rather dimly, for it lets pass much more light that it reflects. A piece of glass backed by a smooth layer of metal, will do it with near-perfect efficiency. That would be a "mirror" or a "looking-glass' (for at what glass would we look more eagerly than at a mirror.) However, in primitive times, smooth unflawed glass, with or without metal backing, was unavailable.

One could simply polish a flat piece of metal. That would do well enough till it tarnished. However, in primitive times, a piece of polished metal large enough to see your face in was not an easy thing to get.

That left the surface of water, which was usually so broken up by waves, foam, and (even in quiet ponds) ripples that a reflected face was too disturbed to make much impression. If, then, Narcissus had come upon a pool *so* quiet that he could see a clear impression of his own image, you can well imagine that it was the *first* time he had seen it and, of course, it would seem like a strange youth to him, one who was hiding under the water.

Once you understand the tale of Narcissus in its true light, then you may come across a sudden analogy. Human beings try to understand the universe little by little. They look at this aspect and at that aspect and learn to analyze the appearance and characteristics and begin to understand it. We can be very proud of the fact that all through our existence, our understanding of the universe has grown enormously. But, then, why not? We are looking at every aspect of the universe with one chief tool, the human brain and the intelligence with which it is associated. Since the human brain is by far the most complexly interrelated piece of matter that we know of, we are using a complex tool to understand the much less complex objects which we are observing. Given enough time and thought, we *must* understand.

But then comes a point when we wish to contemplate the human brain and the intelligence with which it is associated. Now we are attempting to understand something extremely complex by making use of a tool that is no more complex. The situation is analogous to that of someone using his eyes to see his own eyes. As soon as we face the problem of the human brain and human intelligence we are in Narcissus's case – faced with our own image; and therefore doomed, perhaps, to misunderstanding and death.

But there are solutions. Narcissus's solution would have been familiarity with a mirror.

Our solution is that we are not using a human brain to study the human brain and human intelligence. We are using *many* human brains to do so.

It is not a scientist who is studying the human brain, it is, rather, the community of science. It has a complex structure of its own, with published papers, with frequent conferences, with communications in which different

2

thinkers present different pictures, different interpretations, different observations. In kaleidoscopic fashion, these all melt together and grow almost without the volition of any individual, so that understanding increases at a speed and to an extent that any one person would find amazing.

What we (who are intelligent but who have done no work on intelligence) need is someone who has followed the work being done on all the aspects of science that impinge on intelligence to present them to us in orderly fashion and, if possible, with his own thoughts and ideas added to the mix.

This is precisely what Victor Serebriakoff has done. Himself a person of monstrous intelligence, he has obviously read, studied, and thought about every aspect of human intelligence, and here it is for us to share with him. He comes to rescue us from Narcissus's fate.

Isaac Asimov

3

Preface

I have written twelve books and eleven of them have been published. All except three were written to fit a market; I wrote what I could sell. One slim volume of light verse was written out of love and joy. The other two were written from deep conviction and a desire to communicate a set of ideas that have always haunted me.

This is one of the two, and is my second attempt to communicate what is most difficult to communicate, thoughts about thinking, ideas about ideas, intelligence about intelligence. There are a number of loosely bound theses that seem to me to hang together but not necessarily for mutual support. Some of the package of ideas I present may be overstated or plain wrong without there being a need to reject the entire parcel.

My hope is that the ideas or some others on similar lines may prove to be seminal. I say that because of my grave fear that that central and distinguishing aspect of our race, mankind, is being devalued and, worse, demeaned by a trend in modern thinking that is as genuine and compassionately motivated as it is dangerous. I refer to the trend to reject, despise and devalue excellence and especially the most important kind of excellence, cognitive excellence.

This book is one man's attempt to examine what he sees as the most important phenomenon in the universe, intelligence in all its many forms.

Acknowledgements

As an autodidact I am, much more than other writers, indebted to my friends and the people I meet for encouragement, advice, help and valued criticism. I have a problem that professional scholars do not have, that of clambering over the presumption hurdle. I had to find the chutzpah to expose such innovative ideas without having been subjected to the appropriate academic discipline. Without these people this book would not have been written. But they are not responsible for my errors or my presumptions.

Especially, I want to thank those who have read the manuscript through and made very helpful detailed comments. These are Dr Graham Cairns-Smith, Professor Iann Barron, Dr Richard Bird, Laurence Holt, Dr Madsen Pirie, and that most literate barrister Johnathan Causer.

Dr Jack Cohen, Sir Clive Sinclair, Christopher Frost, David Tebutt, Dr Douglas Eyeions, John McNulty and many others read and commented on earlier drafts and were equally encouraging and helpfully critical.

Alexandra Merle Post encouraged me and helped to direct my reading.

The initial interest that encouraged me in the pursuit of my enquiry was taken by Professor Bob Green, John McNulty, the late Professor Kapp, Clive Sinclair, Professor Stanislav Andreski, Dr David Feign, the late Professor H. Ross Ashby, Professor Gray Walter, Professor John Good and some others in the Philosophy of Science Society and the British Sociological Association whose names escape me.

I also thank the following people who have worked on progams to test the ideas: James Cherrill, my son Mark, Seymour Laxon, Ashley Niblock, who wrote most of the drawings on his keyboard, Vincent Corbin, Paul Johnson, Laurence Holt and many other members of the Mensa Artificial Intelligence special interest Group. Dr Nigel Searle helped me with the mathematics.

The non-software drawings were done by Michael Moore.

My world-wide contacts in Mensa have at many times and in many places been a source of guidance, help, encouragement, interest and education. Mensa has been my university.

1

The continuum of life and intelligence

If this book is to succeed in its purpose it must change the way you think, which is a presumption. I want to change the way you think, about the most difficult thing to think about, thinking itself.

Intelligence, the word, is from the Latin *intelligere,* to choose. 'Optimising choice' is shorthand for the set of meanings I ask you to look at. Only living things choose. Intelligence is a biological phenomenon, an aspect of life. I intend to use the word intelligence in this extended sense, because that is the best way to pass my message.

Wherever there is behaviour, or activity, which comes within the meaning 'optimising behaviour in the light of information', I see intelligence.

But if we start our inquiries by looking for beginnings we do so in vain. We find no starting points or borderlines. We see a continuum, a smooth stepless transition from that vastly preponderant mass of lifeless matter which Karl Jung called the Pleroma, the inanimate material universe, to that insignificant smudge in its great array, Jung's Creatura, the Living. The world of physics and chemistry merges imperceptibly into the world of biology. And there is a similar spectrum of stepless change in the Creatura themselves. Just as there is a smooth slide up to life there is a smooth slide up to intelligence. We see intelligent behaviour in animals, some intelligent learning in insects. We even see plants and bacteria *choosing* which molecules to bind to and which to avoid. We see an optimising, choice-like process in the evolution of life itself. We find no borders where we may pause and say 'Beyond be the living', or 'Beyond be thinkers'.

Intelligence, in a more usual and narrower anthropocentric sense, cognitive or conceptual intelligence, mankind's biological speciality, has become almost unmentionable in some academic circles in the Western world. There has been an academic fashion to denigrate and devalue it as a field of study and even as a reality.

I am not concerned here with psychometric intelligence, scalar human cognitive ability, as I have dealt with that controversial art and science elsewhere. It is with a much broader view and meaning for the word and concept that I hope you will be concerned in these pages.

What I invite you to is an intellectual adventure in this disregarded and neglected field of speculation. Having a profound and life-long interest in the concept I have arrived at the view that there *is* a useful and important reality behind the classification of behaviour and behavers along a spectrum of intelligence, that intelligence in its widest sense is an enormously more complex, strange, uncomprehended and important phenomenon than it has been the recent fashion to suppose and that to deny it, denigrate it and deplore it is very dangerous for mankind and even for the future of life on this earth.

The comprehension, preservation, protection, fostering and development of intelligence in all its forms but especially in its advanced forms is the most important task in the universe. That is my creed and thus I throw my hat into the ring. I have stood up. I hope to be counted.

From the above it is clear that my meaning for intelligence is not the semantically central one. So, although I doubt the communicative usefulness of definitions in this field, I shall start with one. I feel that it is only by broadening the concept and then analysing it that it can be properly understood.

'Intelligence', like most words, has around it a semantic connectivity envelope which gives us the chance, like Humpty Dumpty, to have it mean what we choose. There are numerous disputed definitions. Most attempt to confine the meaning to the small ambit of psychometrics, intelligence testing. I shall find a much broader meaning useful. Here is my definition: 'Intelligence is the name we give to the data-processing activity of entities which respond to information with behaviour which appears to be intended to be optimal with respect to preset goals'. Be it noted that 'information' includes both that which is immediately sensed and that which is stored.

Scalar intelligence varies positively with the amount, variety and complexity of the informational input, the storage capacity, the number and complexity of the goals, the degree of optimality achieved thereon, the amount and complexity of the output instructions involved in the response and the position on a scale strategic/tactical of the activity involved. These many elements are not equiponderous. The last carries the heaviest weight.

The weakness of definition as a comprehension tool is revealed. This one calls immediately for several further contextual definitions: data, process, optimal, goal, etc. My choice among the range of meanings for all these will appear in time. My meanings for these words and for the word 'intelligence' will emerge from the context of the book in the usual way. But a hint of the extended meaning I intend is exemplified when the word is applied to species other than mankind or used in the expression of 'artificial intelligence'.

LIFE KNOWS, CHOOSES

Intelligence involves knowing and choosing. Behaviour which is to be labelled as intelligent must have an information store, data bank, memory and an informational input. The intelligent entity, cell, animal, social assembly, artefact, must have received some coded information about the state of the world and it must have behaved appropriately, acted in some way that it would not have done without that information and without the information store, genome, memory or other forms of data bank. An entity has a choice and chooses on the basis of information. The very form of even a bacterium implies a 'knowledge' of its world, its usual environment. And its behaviour is selective, it makes choices.

So first, what do we know about knowing and choosing?

COGNITIVE KNOWING IS MODELMAKING

For humans there are two kinds of knowing: knowing like a good billiard player and knowing like Newton. The first sort of knowing, psychomotor knowing, involves the same field, simple mechanics. The laws of motion, acceleration, impact and friction must be understood in some sense by the player but he cannot easily formulate or verbalise them, they are not socially transmissible. Newton created a model, paradigm, symbol system, which was transmissible and which could therefore be applied more widely, very much more widely indeed. The knowing jumped off the billiard table and exploded into engineering, technology and space travel. Yet the data processing problem in dealing with the laws of mechanics is minute relative to that involved in the billiard player's skill. Robot spacecraft are commonplace, a robot billiard player is not yet feasible.

Intelligence in the extended sense given here is manifest at the level of the cell, again at the level of the animal and thirdly at the social level. Organised communities of animals and people behave intelligently. But before we consider conceptual or socially communicable intelligence in ourselves we should look at what we usually see as a lower level intelligence, psychomotor intelligence, like that seen in learning skills.

Since we have begun to think about making thinking artefacts, artificial intelligence, A.I., we have begun to realise there is a lot more to the tacit, inexpressible, psychomotor knowing than we thought. In human beings, for instance, an astronomical amount of data has to be received at the 130 million receptors in the retina of each eye. It must be sorted, filtered, processed and transduced into messages to a million or so muscle fibres. All this happens several times a second. Seen this way it is the psychomotor understanding which is the higher, more miraculous achievement than the comprehension and use of the simple Newtonian equations. There are lots of creatures that excel man in psychomotor intelligence. Watch any bird. Yet we feel that human intelligence, conceptual, transmissible, symbolic knowing, is more important. I think we are right and want to explain why we are. We need to revise our models of knowing. (I assume that knowing is the business of making useful internal models of the world.)

HOW NEW MODELS APPEAR

Thomas S. Kuhn showed (in 'The Structure Of Scientific Revolutions') what is really held in common by those tight, inward-facing élites which constitute the scientific communities in each discipline. It is, he argued, the science textbooks with the carefully selected exemplary models that they contain. It is these examples, paradigms, thought-moulds, perspectives, rather than defini-tions and laws of the discipline, that underlie and inform the common mind-set and way of thinking of the group.

Kuhn showed that the history of science is the story of a succession of revolutionary new paradigms, each of which takes a generation to establish its pre-eminence. New paradigms usually come from the young or from those new to the field. They arise when ad hoc adjustments to the accepted paradigm get too messy. The anomalies within the theory or between theory and prediction become too great and, from somewhere, strongly resisted at first, a new paradigm emerges and gradually takes the place of the old one. The science then proceeds to refine and perfect the new model until the increasing amount and accuracy of observation reveals the inevitable anomalies which are to be the irritant that generates another new paradigm.

I see in the field I have chosen a pattern, model, paradigm, modality, which seems new and helpful. I use the word paradigm in Kuhn's special sense.

During the last 100 years there has been an accelerating cascade of change and an overwhelming advance in scientific knowledge and understanding. Almost all the accepted paradigms have been changed in just a few genera-tions. Nothing like it has ever happened before and though much of the change has been improvement, many people do not feel comfortable with a rate of change which looks as if it is dangerously exponential.

A line of generalist speculation and a personal perspective that started in my youth has led me to closely follow the scientific revolutions in all fields, during this age of change. It is the persistent and advancing appropriateness of the analysis and resynthesis that arises from my idea that emboldens me to make this fresh attempt to express it.

Communication at this high and strategic semantic level is possible only from the widest perspective. The best a thinker can do is to paint a preliminary, generalist picture with a broad brush, on a vast canvas, in crude colours. You are asked to stand off and look for pattern. If you peer too closely and nitpick at the brushstrokes, I fear you may miss something which is worth attention.

It has long been impossible to reach the old ideal of an educated person, one who knows everything of something and something of everything. Today's professional, institutional, scholars and scientists are running on the spot to keep up with the relentlessly rapid advances in every specialist discipline. The most they can hope for is to keep up with the other treadmillers until they tire. The handful of presumptuous generalists still around are therefore usually enthusiastic amateurs like the early scientists. Perhaps they should be given the tolerant hearing that a good judge will always give to the self-represented litigant.

PERCEPTION, CLASSIFICATION, TAXONOMY

I hope you will agree that the primary task of an advanced intelligence is perception. The next task appears to be (but is not) classification, putting inputs into classes which require different responses. With the species called primitive the classes of input pattern are hard wired, built in. But even with them there is a process that must have preceded classification, taxonomy, finding the useful way to classify observations, the perceptual input. In simple creatures taxonomy must have been learned genetically, by evolution.

Work on computer pattern recognition is transforming ideas about this. Traditional philosophers and psychologists have taken the perception of complex patterns and objects as given, the starting point of their discipline. We now know that the mere primary act of observation is a highly complex skill that has, in human beings, to be inductively acquired. The mere act of seeing or hearing meaningfully is impossible to the unprepared perceiver. The baby's brain has to be trained to see the patterns that are useful to it, it is deaf-blind to truly novel or ephemeral data.

It is only a highly selected special version of reality that can penetrate the complex, intricate multi-stage sorting, abstracting, filtering and refining network of the brain and get through to the consciousness. We are all half drowned in a torrent of data, an incessant cascade of terabytes from many millions of inputs. The primary problem for aspiring comprehenders like babies is *taxonomy* (I use the word in an extended sense), how to classify experience, how to abstract those patterns which help mind or brain to simplify, sort and order data. The baby has to find the most useful brainable (brain compatible) understanding. The survival tools are predictive, subjective models of the world.

The main job is filtering, rejecting the irrelevant without knowing what it is, trying and scrapping models. We have only about one and a half kilograms of the complex spaghetti, the grey fibrous felt called brain, to work with and there is an awful lot of universe out there to be simulated or modelled.

What is learned from attempts to simulate simple perceptual and learning skills on today's linear, deterministic (Von Neumann), computers makes it necessary to modify the philosophy of science.

Like the animal, the scientist, too, can now be seen to be swamped with data. His main job is to do systematically, in groups, with instrumental aids, what the individual does in perceiving and predicting his world. Science is sorting needles of relevance from haystacks of facts, condensing, refining, abstracting and then checking the congruence with a succesion of models to find the most useful. Relevance, I argue, is the property of being potentially useful to some entity, individual or social.

We now know that messages cannot be sent to an unprepared brain and (from Kuhn) that facts cannot be perceived by an unprepared science. We have to start from where we are. New understanding has to key into and start from previous understanding. When we have a sudden insight we often feel we have something wholly new. But if we look at it we shall find that it is not. It is a new arrangement of the old. We can perceive new constellations but they are of the old stars. There is an evolutionary aspect to knowledge, as well as the revolutionary one Kuhn suggested. Knowledge is constrained to relate not only to the new data and the new arrangement of it, it has to follow from the track of its own development in the past, like animals and all other life forms.

Sir Arthur Stanley Eddington warned us that knowledge cannot be cleaned of its epistemological connections, it is designed as much to suit the mind of the knower as it is to suit the data known. We can further say that like a biological species it must be constrained by its former state and its line of development. There may be sudden leaps but there is a thread of continuity.

ARGUING FROM ANALOGIES

This brings me to the special problem of communication. How to start? Which of the thought-tracks in your mind is the best for our purpose?

In the 'fifties the fashion turned against arguing from analogy, because all analogies break down somewhere. No-one explained that there is no other way to argue. If I am to convince you of something new I have to find the system in your mind into which the new pattern fits with least anomaly.

Analogies never became respectable again, we followed the usual path of reform by euphemism and began to talk of models. Analogies are dead, long live models. We are all making and testing models of reality, whatever that is. Seeing an analogy or model is an act of taxonomy, the creation of a new class in the mind, that class of which what is modelled and the model itself are members.

Astronomers arrange a model sun and planets in an orrery, because Nicolas Copernicus had conceived the new class 'Copernican planetary systems', of which the solar system and orrery are both members.

In seeing the relationship we have created the new super class, that of systems which behave like that. What is happening in a brain or mind is the building, testing and constant inductive amendment of models of interesting bits of the world. For this purpose a model can be seen as an understood system of some kind that behaves congruently with an external system whose behaviour we need to comprehend or predict. The elements of a model may be material, as in an abacus or any other analogue computer. They may be symbolic, words or other symbols. They may be mathematical or they may take the form of computer hardware or software. They may be strings of words, sentences, propositions. All these enable us to comprehend new relationships via old, already comprehended ones. That is the power of the paradigm. It helps us to perceive new members of classes whose members have similar relationships.

Therefore, the most primary and elementary knowledge, that involved in sound and visual perception, must be of the same nature. No-one in the computer pattern recognition field seems to be able to do without something like subject comparate, a mask, an internal model of the pattern or pattern element sought. The brain's cognitive business appears to be creating, then improving the congruence of subjective models of the repetitive and significant (life aiding), aspects of its objective input from world. What the brain does for the person science does socially. Both have the same task; comprehension, which aids prediction, which aids survival.

I shall therefore start my quest for the essence of intelligence by looking at the anomalies that intelligence cannot deal with. I shall start by trying to abolish miracles.

GOOD SCIENCE ABOLISHES MIRACLES

People before the age of science needed the concept 'miracle' to fill in hiatuses where prediction and expectation failed by too wide a margin. A miracle is an extremely improbable event, one which is grossly contrary to experience and expectations. Kuhn's anomalies are miracles, observations which do not fit in with preconceptions. A paradigm, hitherto successful, ceases to serve because in the light of fresh data it challenges credulity. A new paradigm is needed to demote miracles, to reduce them to the status of explicable, expected events.

A fruitful territory for hunting new paradigms is therefore miracle country. Let us look at some miracles which are still left in the world of science. Where is our credulity under most stress?

Miracle One

A friend who is the editor of a biology journal once told me that almost every post brings a paper from some biologist who is disturbed by the astronomic improbability involved in the origin of life, the assembly of the original genome.

Even the simplest living thing, a virus, has a genome, a program, instruction set or prescription, in the form of a string of information consisting of 1300 np (nucleotide pairs) letters from the four-letter genetic alphabet).

This genome is a long, fragile, aperiodic crystal, as Irwin Schroedinger called it, and is highly unstable. It has to remain in a very narrow, improbable range of environments and survives only in a temperature slot where its fragile components are under a heavy bombardment of threat from the thermal agitation of the molecules. It needs constant repair. Yet it is practically immortal.

The probability that such a thing could rattle together from the most favourable environment by chance is so absurdly low that there is a better chance of drawing the right ticket from a hat where the ticket is one particular fundamental particle and the hat is the whole universe of particles. There are 10^{80} of them in all (100000000000000000000000000000000000000000-000000000000000000000000000000000000000).

Some biologists have given up as scientists by suggesting that the origin of life is so improbable as to be truly miraculous. The myth of divine creation seems as likely as any other origin for life to those who look at the figures that way. Others like Frances Crick, who first deciphered the genetic code, push the miracle further away by relying on the concept panspermia. They think the earth was 'seeded' with life from elsewhere.

Further, the paradoxes and conceptual difficulties involved in epigenesis (the science of the development of organisms) are much like the contradictions that began to arise in physics when Albert Einstein, Max Planck, Paul Dirac and Werner Karl Heisenberg came to the field. We do not really understand how a simple linear string code, even if it is billions of characters long, can prescribe organisms as complex as an Einstein, Planck, Dirac, Heisenberg!

Miracle Two

The miracle of brain. Very detailed, tactical understanding of the function of brain elements, nerves, has been acquired. But no-one has the remotest notion of its functioning at the overall strategic level. More investigation has made perception, taxonomy, classification, memory and cognition seem more, not less, miraculous. Consciousness, mind, memory, attention, learning, sleep, and many of the processes of cognition and data recall are far beyond the realm of explanation, modelling in physical terms or comprehension, as things stand today.

We have no credible hypothesis as to how the input from a hundred million receptors is processed and transduced into the appropriate instructions received by a million motor neurones. It is a miracle which has been tucked out of sight in a 'black box'. Attempts to simulate even simple psychomotor-type intelligence artificially have only brought out the enormity of the problems. I hope to show this.

Miracle Three

We have very little idea how complex societies work. Professor Stanislav Andreski is just one frank sociologist who has admitted that sociology is not yet a predictive science (*The Social Sciences as Sorcery*, Pelican).

In *The Wealth of Nations* Adam Smith created a successful paradigm for the working of an economic system governed by the concept of the free market. His model was that it was a kind of autonomous 'engine' (today he would have said computer). His system was not a predictive one, it was one in which the model was autonomous and unpredictable in detail. However, it remains much more predictive and explanatory than any other in the field, which is saying very little. None-the-less it has informed the work of the most regarded pundits in the field, not excluding Marx.

Recently, determinist theories of economics have been increasingly abandoned and there has been a return to Adam Smith's ideas, through thinkers such as Ludwig Von Mises, Friederich Hayek, Milton Friedman and Madsen Pirie and the whole school of followers. But Adam Smith described rather than explained the working of the market. From the selfish actions of millions of individuals comes a better pattern of the adjustment of supply to needs and demands than by any other method. Smith had to resort to the idea of a miraculous 'hidden hand' which ensured that the polycentric pooled selfishness of the market produced more general satisfaction than monocentric patrician altruism, as in aristocratic and Leninist communist systems. More recently, Hayek has looked to theories of information for a miracle-abolishing paradigm in economics and I suggested (in a previous book, *Brain*, 1976), a similar idea which I develop here. Hidden hand, black box, ignorance, anomaly. We need a new paradigm.

Miracle Four

Understanding of the universe vastly expanded and improved in the last couple of centuries and the most important contributions to that improvement were the basic paradigms of modern science. Central were those of causality and determinism, the underlying belief that the universe is an ordered system with comprehensible and unbreakable causal laws. This led to the obstinate disciplined search for such and the rejection of the easier options, mysticism, animism, divinity and other such dogma barriers to improved understanding. Determinism and strict causality became the permitted dogmas of the scientist, belief in them their one faith.

But some philosophers were less happy. Determinism came from Calvinistic religious roots but proved fruitful in the world of science. However, the incompatibility of strict determinism with the daily human experience of options and free-will to choose between them remained unresolved.

Many scientists had difficulty with the contradiction between the determinist dogma and their experience of freedom of action and learning. How can any entity *learn* in a universe which is preordained, which is unrolling, frame by frame like a film show? How can any creature whose least action arises from inflexible causes create a working model of things that are remote from it, even of itself? How can a celluloid character in a film create an image of the camera and the photographer?

Here is a miracle. An entity finds out that the world is determinist and by the way it did and the fact that it did shows that it cannot be.

The paradigms I propose indicate that my perception that I have options and choices between them need not be false and that my options need be neither illusory nor miraculous.

In what follows, these speculations venture gingerly into more hazy realms of philosophy or religion, I cannot be certain which. The ground here is weak and treacherous and cautious scepticism is required. Yet there is a persistent idea from many sources that seems worthy of some attention. The cost of attention if these ideas are quite wrong is much less than the cost of inattention if they happen to be right in any sense.

Miracle Five

Except as a cult-figure the unfrocked priest, Teilhard De Chardin, carries little weight today but he has pointed to a miracle. He described the overall tendency of evolution, divergence and the competitive elaboration of variety of the species. All was explained by Darwinian theory backed up by modern genetics. But he also noted a contradictory *convergence* and symbiotic combination at a higher level. He was puzzled by the apparent symbiotic stability of the biosphere and especially the emergent coalescence of human societies. All these were contrary to expectations from evolutionary theory, where divergence is the trend. It is this anomaly with which the newer discipline of ecology seems to be concerned. He also spoke of the noosphere as a supervening world of knowledge uniting mankind which unexpectedly exists and is not accommodated by evolutionary theory. This is echoed by the concept 'World III' elaborated by Karl Popper and John C. Eccles. Herbert George Wells had a similar thought in *World Brain*, while Bernard Shaw's 'life force' was not dissimilar. I have written of that inexplicable, emergent phenomenon, our present world culture, which has miraculously appeared within a few hundred years from the informational coalescence of the societies of a species which was bred for 20 million years to be a network of mutually repelling hunter gatherer tribes.

These are the anomalies that I address in these speculations. I shall advance an epistemological hypothesis, one of mentality, of brain function, which I hope will advance understanding of what I believe to be the most important aspect of the universe, understanding itself.

LIFE IS WHAT?

Imagine a very durable extraterrestrial intelligence which visits earth once every million years. What changes would it note on successive inspections?

The inspections of the geological and geographical details would cause the intelligence to say with Heraclitas 'Everything flows, nothing abides'. Looking at what we ephemeral creatures see as the durable things, the rocks, stones, mountains, valleys, coastlines, rivers and streams, it would find little that was unchanged between visits. All would be grossly changed.

But if he chanced to look again at certain soft, unstable, ephemeral, moving, constantly changing, excrescences that he finds down in the mud, dust and rubbish of the planet; if he looked at the moving and growing *creatures* that had been clinging to, swimming, flitting, wriggling, creeping, dodging and just growing on and under the surface of the changing rocks or in the restless waters; if he looked again at the quick, the Creatura; what then? He would find an anomaly, a contradiction, a miracle. Peering again, however closely, at a stickleback, a bee, a pine tree, or the pattern on the wing of a butterfly, he would find that within close margins they had not changed at all, despite scores of thousands of generations of replication. Absurdly, the stable would have proved to be unstable, only the changeable would be unchanged.

Defining Life

About such a broad term as 'life' there is little general agreement among scientists but one thing is common ground. They are agreed that there is no agreement about a satisfactory definition of it.

The august pages of the *Encyclopaedia Britannica* complain that 'life' has no generally satisfactory definition (much like our subject, intelligence).

Various manifest functions, ageing, metabolising, excreting and reproducing are mentioned as aspects of life but objections can be raised to any definition in such terms because things that are not alive have some of these aspects and some things that are have not.

Some things that are undoubtedly living remain dormant and without metabolic activity. For instance, the tobacco mosaic virus can exist in an immutable crystal form, but applied to a leaf the crystal becomes active and reproductive. Life remains, like many real and useful concepts, perceivable, understandable, understood, but undefined.

The Life Miracle

It is unscientific to use the word 'miracle', which is merely the word for an event so very improbable as to set us seeking new paradigms. Dobzhansky estimated the probability that anything as miraculously unexpected as a genome should appear on this earth. He calculates that the coming together of the human genome with its 3.5×10^9 nucleotide pairs and its 3×10^4 genes is rather unlikely. If any odds are low enough to merit the term miracle these are. He puts them at one in 10^{10000} (ten to the *power* ten thousand) (plus or minus a few hundred orders of magnitude, I dare say). This is, as I have said, about the chance of picking the right electron in 10^{80} universes like this one.

Now the distinction between the appearance of something so improbable and a miracle might be hard to establish, so we must not blame Jaques Monod when in the light of similar reflections he calmly talks of the miracle of life. We should not over-react.

I am not making a religious argument or uttering fruitless 'Ooh!s and Ah!s' in the above. The need to labour the point will emerge. Monod seems to be right. It seems to be true that there are features of living systems that are incompatible with the very methods of science. He feels we need a new paradigm and proposes 'teleonomy', a neologism for an internal autonomous determinism which, he posits, guarantees the invariance of living things.

Karl Popper and John Eccles, in *The Self and its Brain*, made a similar point when Popper says, 'It is incredibly improbable that life ever emerged but it *did* emerge. Since it is incredibly improbable, there cannot be an explanation to say how it emerged in probablistic terms because . . . an explanation in probablistic terms is always in terms of high probability.' Any explanation based on a very low probability simply is not an explanation in the normal meaning of the term.

We must start from where we are. There are over a million species of living things on the earth and each of them is so improbable as to seem unexplainable, miraculous in the normal meaning of the term. Let us make an attempt to abolish this formidable miracle.

Morphostasis (Formholding)

Here I recapitulate. In the book *Brain*, I explored the concept of morphostasis or formholding as the fundamental essence of Jung's Creatura, the living.

By definition, morphostasis is the process by which the form taken by a physical substrate system or succession of them acts as though it has the purpose to preserve itself (the form) through time with minimum change.

A simple example of morphostasis might, except for one thing, be a river. In Zimbabwe there is a Shona tribal saying that we never step into the same river twice. I deny it, we do step into the same *river*. We do *not* step into the same *water*. The water changes, the river remains. What we call a river is *form,* not *substance*. It is not material. It is the form taken by a succession of snakes of material water.

Any living thing is the same. You are not a lot of molecules, you are the form successive lots take. The molecules come and go like the water. You stay on.

The one way in which the quality of a living thing is distinguishable from that of a river is this. Living things are forms, patterns, which behave as if they were teleonomic, had the *purpose* of preserving their form with minimum change. Actively and improbably they are homeostatic.

Homeostasis (the tendency for the internal environment of the body to be maintained constant) is an aspect of all life. All living things, morphostats, are homeostatic on many parameters of possible variability. They are actively homeotastic, using feedback signals and corrective action. They are not stable passively, like a river or a fountain. They strive actively, using triggerlike information, to retain their form on a succession of substrates.

Richard Dawkins, a founder of sociobiology, in his book *The Selfish Gene* says Darwin's survival of the fittest is really a special case of the more general law, 'the survival of the stable'. It was just such a thought in my youth that gave rise to the series of speculations and enquiries that led me to write this book.

Life forms, all of them, *seem* actively to *seek* to preserve their form with minimum change through time. They can do this only because they carry coded information stores forward with them through time. All life forms, without exception have some sort of *memory,* a data bank, a coded, symbolic, representational copy of their survival form. These, technically, are called their phylogenic or memory form and their ontogenic or survival and replication form.

I know the expressions 'seem' and 'seek' are suspect. To whom do they seem? What is it that seeks? I mean simply 'seem to us to behave in a purposive manner'. At this point the evasion is to convey meaning without ascribing purpose in a wrong sense. Later when we discuss *purpose* I think this will be clearer.

Change and Stability

The idea that stability, unchange, is the primary aspect of life and its distinguishing characteristic is counter-intuitive at first glance. The living, the quick, the animate, seem to be in a state of constant, restless flux. We see the inanimate as unchanging. But the parable of the infrequent earth visitor warns that things are not that simple.

What the Creatura are restlessly reaching, growing and scurrying about for is to *ensure* the persistence of their particular form through the aeons. The creatures as physical objects, collections of individual particles do *not* persist. My body spends its time transmuting bread, meat grain and vegetables into ever new physical things, all of which are called Serebriakoff; all, sadly, in the same form. The physical object with that name which was at this keyboard last week is gone for ever. It is not, I repeat my molecules, but the *arrangement* of any old set of them, that I am busy to preserve. My obsessive activity to preserve my form cannot be used as evidence against the fact that I am basically a form preserving entity.

The words 'change' and 'stability' are broad and imprecise in meaning. They are blunt tools for such a profound discussion. But if we look at a world with this crude analysis we see things which are not so clear otherwise. We see that the universe cannot help selecting stability. In a contest between stable systems and unstable ones we can predict without risk that there will be a greater proportion of stable ones left at the end of any substantial time than there were at the beginning. Among the infinity of possible changes to unstable systems there must be some towards stability and some towards extinction. Stable systems not only last better themselves but are more immune to second-order changes, those towards instability. But systems which change towards being more stable will become more frequent. Thus imperfectly stable systems tend to become more stable. In any late sample there will be more of those which have changed towards more stability than there will be in any earlier sample. Some of those that changed away from stability will be unrecognisable, will have moved beyond some class boundaries (wherever they may be set), or they will have become extinct.

This is the solution to the strongest objection to morphostasis as the key to life. Here is the second strongest.

The False Paradox of Evolutionary Change

Evolutionary change, adaptive and diversifying changes have been sited as counter-examples to the concept of morphostasis. There are two kinds of adaptive change. Evolution is an intelligent learning process, it is *genoplastic* change, that between generations. Some vertebrate learning is *ontoplastic* change, learning-type change in an individual animal. Both can be called meta-change, a small class of changes which morphostats accept, nay seem to seek, those towards higher order stability. Those which make them *more* morphostatic. Even diversification into sub-species which are fitted to eco-niches preserves the basic form better and increases its numbers more than if it did not happen.

The class of second-order (meta-morphostatic) changes is usually so small that it has led to the pragmatic saying of geneticists that 'All mutants are lethals'. This is the experience dealing with drosophila (fruit flies). The thousand or so known mutations have no examples of advantageous ones, but in the rather larger sample of the biosphere evolution has thrown some up now and again.

Another definition of morphostats to bring in this idea could be 'morphostats are a class of entities which are organised to minimise irreversible changes in their form other than those which increase their power to resist changes'.

Here is one of many quotations I could give. It is from C. H. Waddington in *The Strategy of the Genes.* 'All living organisms, except possibly some of the simplest, though even that exception is doubtful, are characterised by possessing a characteristic form or shape.'

Heraclitas, with support from the Second Law of Thermodynamics, was right when he said that everything is in a state of flux. But as to an infinitesimally small proportion of the world, he was in error. Everything *does* flow, nothing *does* abide, with one exception, an exception as infinitesimal in size as it is infinite in importance. *Life forms abide.*

Entropy

You might have thought that the introduction of Boltzmann and Maxwell's law in the last sentence was somewhat abrupt. I shall deal with it in more detail later, but for now I need only remind you that when life forms seek to preserve themselves they are in breach of the very heavy statistical weight of the Second Law of Thermodynamics.

This law establishes that all ordered or organised systems tend to break down, disperse, scatter, become disordered, randomise with time. Entropy, disorder, increases inexorably in every known, closed, physical system. The Creatura have to struggle upstream against a fierce universal current in order to do their difficult thing. They have, constantly and incessantly, to make decisions that enable them to climb entropy slopes, past and against the pressure of everything else that is sliding down them.

I have talked of the miraculous improbability of the origin of life forms. The point I return to and emphasise is that all life, even now, is overwhelmingly improbable. The universal trend to the increase of the degree of entropy in any free system as predicted by the Second Law is statistical.

A paradigm textbook in this field is Barton's *Heat.* He says 'so we see that the Second Law of Thermodynamics is true, and so very certainly true, merely because we are dealing with systems of very large numbers of individuals. It

owes its validity, to this fact. . . . It is definitely not true for a system consisting
of a small number of individuals.' (By individuals he means molecules.)

In any one sample of a substance, solid, liquid or gas, the molecules are
equipotent, they have equal mutual effect. The assumption behind the statistical
laws governing the Second Law is that the elements of the system are equipotent.
If they are not equipotent the laws do not apply. But the molecules of living
systems are not equipotent, they have unequal effect on each other, there are
catalysts and trigger-like or relay-like effects at all levels. The elements of
living systems are, we could say, 'heteropotent', of unequal mutual effect. We
must not expect the heteropotent elements in a system to obey laws which do
not apply to them.

So there *are* systems (albeit immaterial ones, ones of transducible form)
which defy the overwhelming weight of probability which establishes the
truth of the Second Law. They subsist on substrates with extremely large
numbers of molecules. The systems *do* defy the Second Law. Living things do
that, all of them. The monstrous accumulated improbability calls urgently for
a paradigm shift.

Death is Change

It takes practice to see the lively as stable and the dead as changing, mutable.
Even the pioneer of this field, the towering Norbert Weiner, committed the
error of saying *(Cybernetics)* 'The stable state of any living organism is to be
dead'. How wrong! The stillness of death is deceptive. It is the beginning of an
irreversible runaway change.

I propose a test for my hypothesis against Norbert's. Take two horses and
kill just one. The living one will act as the control. Keep them in a stable or if
you have not got one in a spare room. Supply feed and water to both. Treat
them exactly alike. Check up which changes the most over the next few years.
I am bold enough to predict that the living horse will change its form less than
the dead one. It works with mice but is more odorously and assertively
convincing with horses.

Death is resumption of change, the final surrender to the Second Law, the
reluctant return to what is overwhelmingly normal in this universe. The decay
of death is the end of the rebellion against the universal trend to dispersal,
randomisation, disorder. It is the return to probability from the highly erratic
and utterly unlikely behaviour of those rebels against the Law, the Creatura.
However, the *cycle*, birth, maturity, reproduction, senility and death *is*
morphostatic. It has a higher order stability. This brings us to replication,
another such higher order stability.

Replication

I touched on replication earlier. The Creatura have many techniques for perpetuating form or pattern. The two main ones are survival and replication. I said that morphostats behave 'as though they had the purpose' of preserving form through time. I put it this way because teleological explanations are rightly suspected. But I have to convey meaning by context and this is the best way to put over my meaning. But I do not suggest that a genome has a conscious purpose as men do. It is just that those creatures that 'appear to be purposive' increase in numbers and spread. It is easier to understand the behaviour of living things if, as a tool of understanding, we attribute the 'purpose' to survive to the *form** itself rather than to the individual member of a species. Richard Dawkins is doing just this. The 'selfish' (therefore, by implication, purposive) gene is form, not substance (it is a flux of changing atoms, it is under constant repair). It is a form and a form prescriber, it is information. Richard Dawkins, Edward Wilson and their colleagues have shown clearly that it is 'as though' the gene itself, the form, the everchanging, mutable complex of unstable molecules with its incredibly immutable *shape*, seem to be motivated to endure and multiply.

IN THE BEGINNING WAS THE WORD

The concepts behind the two words 'life' and 'information' have a close semantic connectivity. There is nothing that lives which is without an information system if for no other reason than that the genome itself is clearly one. (No known life is without a genome.) Conversely, there is nothing within the semantic envelope of 'information' which has no biological connections. It can also be argued that no information passes without there being in some entity, some purpose (in the loose sense). So information systems and living systems are bound together by a teleological aspect also.

The Homology of Information Systems

Here is something that transdisciplinary generalists might better see. Specialist scientists seem to have taken something odd for granted. When Crick and Watson found the pattern of the genome and enabled us to look at the very source of our creation in a speck of nucleus, in a microdot cell, they revealed an information system astonishingly like that we have found most convenient for social communication. Long before men learned what the genetic pattern

*It might be argued against the foregoing that, though the surviving *forms* are negentropic and designed to preserve form, they are material as well. The answer is philosophical. If a material *thing* is an entity made of material we mean that it is the form taken by a particular set of molecules of matter.

   Living things are the form taken by *any* of many successive sets of molecules. The form of the entity is the *essence*, not the substance. I suggest it is confusing to think of the two classes of entities as if they were of the same type.

was they reinvented it. Speech, writing, and the random access memory which holds information in a computer all take an unexpected simple form, a one-dimensional string or vector. Complex information is stored as a very long linear array of coded units. The units, symbols, alphabets, are in all cases highly specified units of low variety, nucleotide base pairs, sound phonemes, letters and ASCII symbol strings. The genome precognitively plagiarised literacy and computer technology. 'In the beginning was the word.'

The important thesis here is that the information systems that we find at various levels may be found to throw light one on another, that these systems are more than simply homologous, they belong to the same class of phenomenon. They have similarities, shared invariances and limitations. We may learn about all by examining those that are easy to probe. We may find models where the explorable will help us to comprehend the unexplorable, even though it works in a different way at a different level.

MORPHOSTASIS: THE LIMITS OF THE CONCEPT

The similarity of information systems found in tiny cells and those which serve social communities of man leads to my next point. Why did I need the neologism 'morphostat'?

We see that protozoa, unitary cells and metazoa/metaphyta (co-operating groups of cells, otherwise known as animals and plants) fall within the semantic envelope 'morphostat'. We may ask what other members of the class there are.

The behaviour of groups of animals that live in communicative co-operation is also morphostatic. Such groups, tribes, nations, firms, all have intercommunication systems, and they use and exchange information. They all appear to be purposive, they act to survive, to preserve form through time. They survive not by welcoming but by resisting all but beneficial change (the rare sort). They are all characterised by conservatism. A cell, an animal, a society is a continuity of form through time. It is a change-resisting machine.

I remind you that the word 'morphostat' does not describe entities which are passively unchanging but the class of all those entities or systems which *actively* resist change, the set behaves as if the members had the intention of preserving their form as little changed as possible through time. I may legitimately include human institutions, groups, societies and nations within this class without being accused of drawing false analogies.

Another False Paradox*

We have to deal here with an objection that has been advanced to the paradigm proposed, that of morphostasis. There are aspects of living systems

*A false paradox is a seeming paradox.

which seem to contradict the thesis that they behave as if they seek stability. There are risk-taking propensities in animals, such as curiosity, adventure, exploration. There are mechanisms such as sexual reproduction, and the gene-shuffling process of crossover which seem like invitations to change. In a special way the creatures seem to seek change.

The contradiction is simply resolved. Creatures with these experimental, probing, risk-taking mechanisms and propensities turn out to be more stable, to survive with less change through more adverse environments and traumas than those without them. Evolutionary mutation, recombination, and exploration turn out to be better strategies to achieve minimum change than over-conservative ones. Optimum stability of form comes from the offer, at second order, of a limited amount of change for selection by the environment.

This factor has arisen quite separately at the various levels of life: mutation, sex and crossover in the cell, curiosity in the animal, exploration, migration and experiment in social collectivities, adventure, research and experiment in human groups.

The approach is indirect but the apparent purpose is the same, to avoid the gross change of extinction by accepting smaller changes and keeping those to a minimum. Death is change. Life is minimum adaption.

Morphostats can be distinguished in many ways. They are very different indeed from the rest of the universe. They are so different that we shall be at a loss to understand them via the physical laws which prevail among the Pleroma, the things of the inanimate material world. There are good reasons why we should seek what amounts to a different set of natural laws, those which apply to the immaterial forms which are the continuing aspect of the living. These, I shall show, are other than those statistical laws which apply to the inanimate. I have to develop the argument more before this is manifest so I shall not defend it further here.

Morphostasis: Recapitulation

A morphostat is a miraculously improbable platform of unchange, an ordered functional arrangement organised principally to resist changes in its form, structure, pattern, which would normally result from the effect upon it of the forces and entities in its environment.

Most of the activity of any morphostat is consistent with an intention; that of resisting, countering, avoiding, or adapting minimally to changes within its boundaries or threats thereof, which arise from things, forces or entities outside them.

It is perhaps no accident that the word used for the concept of my field of enquiry, 'intelligence', has another sense, 'information'. We see that intelligence in the loose sense of optimising choices has connections with the Creatura at many, if not all, levels.

We see 'the miracle' of life. The highly complex, durable, ordered forms which constitute it appear to be forbidden or made overwhelmingly unlikely by the physical law which commands order to disperse. So we shall be wise to look more closely at the concept 'order' which is associated with the *pattern* or *form* of our paradigm. The next chapter goes more deeply into that concept.

Protozoa, Metazoa, Sociozoa

Now that we have the concept morphostat, what can we do with it? We can seek to clarify aspects and invariances of the class and we may seek new ones. These may help us in understanding and prediction at all levels, chemical, morphological and social. I now look at the concept of social morphostats, societies of creatures. I have suggested that these, too, are morphostats.

A concept which has come forward several times is that of a social meta-creature, one which comprises a collectivity of separate co-operating creatures. A metazoon comprises a number of separate, co-operating cells (which resemble protozoa). Ernst Heinrich Haeckle, the recapitulationist philosopher, talked of this concept as a 'corm'. The philosopher Henri Bergson, one of the last of the animists, talked of the beehive community as being more like a simple dispersed animal than like a colony of them.

There are protozoa, single-cell creatures, and metazoa, co-operating, inter-communicating combinations of cells. There is another stage, co-operating, intercommunicating collectivities of metazoa, of animals. We could call these *sociozoa*.

There is even a creature which sits neatly and squarely on the semantic borderline between a metazoon and a sociozoon. Slime moulds spend part of their time as a colony of tiny, mobile, wormlike creatures which live and feed independently. But to spread their spores they swarm together and merge to form a single, much larger, worm which crawls to a suitable position, turns vegetative and grows like a small plant so as to produce a sporing pod.

The whole language of human organisation and politics is based on the simplistic Roman paradigm of the State made up of parts related to each other like the parts of a living body: the head, organs, organisation. It was an immensely powerful and effective paradigm even if it was oversimplified and increasingly inappropriate after a time.

One of the uses of the concept 'morphostat' is to make a more sophisticated paradigm to consolidate the apparent unity that underlies this perception.

It is very clear that many social colonies and communities of creatures behave in many ways like complete animals. We can now see that such social collectivities have a non-genetic method for passing information between members. They can thus co-operate to preserve their form, their social organi-sation, their culture and customs (and thus their individual lives). They have invented another kind of heredity, a non-genetic one, to add to the genetic one. Such collectivities fit perfectly within the meaning envelope of the concept 'morphostat'.

If they do, they open the door to improved understanding of the whole class. Sociozoa have the same problem as metazoa and protozoa, that of preserving and replicating their form. We may therefore expect to find ways in which their systems echo each other. Since some are easier to probe than others this may improve understanding of all. For instance, the communication systems of cells and brains are complex and very difficult to unravel, but the simple communication systems of animals and those of human beings, being patent, are easier to probe.

THE ROLE OF INTELLIGENCE

Intelligence, a form of data processing and the phenomenon we are seeking to understand, appears only in morphostats (so far) and it seems at least on the surface to have an important role in the vital morphostat task, survival, formholding.

2

The nature of order

The physicist and philosopher of science, Professor David Bohm, advances the view that there may be a large or infinite number of levels of reality in the world or levels of inspection in science, one below the other, from astronomic down to the physical and on further. Seeing the bad fit of science observations at one level to those at other levels, I borrow the idea in simpler form. I see the levels as being, like most observations, partly epistemological in nature, as much to do with the brainability of useful concept systems at the various levels as with anything about the way the world is.

I suggest it will be useful and helpful to make a mental dissection and to talk of three principal levels. The lowest level is the *microcosm*, the world of fundamental physics, of particles, radiation, the strong, weak and other forces. This is the weird, Heisenbergian, quantum world which is so incomprehensible when viewed with our vastly larger sensory and cognitive apparatuses. These eyes and brains were built for and adapted to the *mesocosm*, the second level, which I define as the familiar world of things about mansize (within a handful of orders of magnitude). The top level in this simple analysis is the *macrocosm*. That is that vast otherworld of space-time, stars and galaxies. Here too, mesocosmic perception and cognition are inadequate when trying to deal with relativistic Einsteinian astronomy, for instance. Our mathematical models of the two unbrainable otherworlds do work, are predictive, in the big and little worlds but our mesocosmic brains get very fuddled, stretched and confused.

I ask thought for the thesis that the Creatura are mesocosmic entities that have the power of reaching down through the interface between microcosm and mesocosm, dipping down and scooping out quantum indeterminacy from the microcosm. They draw upon and amplify that indeterminacy to provide *choices*. Choices are needed to build, gradually by trial and error, by stability selection, preservation and replication, the mesocosmic structures that decrease local entropy to build ordered systems in the mesocosm.

Living systems are entropy pumps. They pump disorder out of themselves into their environments. First, then, what *is* order? Let us examine that variously defined concept. Definitions seem to be confined to the mesocosm as above defined.

THE MEANING OF ORDER

In the exposition of the Second Law of Thermodynamics use is made of the concept 'order'. We also seem to need it in thinking about living systems and their derivative and our theme, intelligence.

Comprehension here is not made easier by the fact that James Rudolph, Julius Clausius, James Clark-Maxwell and Ludwig Boltzman have conspired to get it upside down in pointing to and naming the negative property of disorder rather than the positive one, order. The reverse semantic polarity would have been better. (Benjamin Franklyn got it the wrong way round when he named that charge 'positive' which turned out to be the *absence* of electrons.) In both cases the mathematics were made to fit but the ideas are less brainable.

Thermodynamics, as well as life and intelligence, is deeply concerned with order. So what *is* order? The curious thing about the concept is that although it first obtruded itself into science in the pragmatic business of engineering heat engines, it seems to be largely an epistemological concept.

Order and Intelligence

Order has an apparently subjective anthropomorphic connection with our central theme, intelligence. The *Oxford Dictionary* contains three pages on the word. The original meaning was 'rank, grade, class,' the pecking-order* of people in a community. The sense we have in mind comes thirteenth among the array of meanings of a very fuzzy word: 'formal disposition of array'; 'regular methodical or harmonious arrangements of the position of things contained in a space or area, or composing any group or body'. These ideas seem a curious basis for such down-to-earth, pragmatic laws as those governing the engineering of heat engines and refrigerators, the research that started the pioneers. (Later thermodynamics *did* find a place in explaining the behaviour of matter and energy throughout the universe.)

*Many social animals have a strict dominance ranking system which is seen by biologists as advantageous. It was first noticed in chickens by observing which pecks which.

What part can entropy or 'decrease in the degree of regularity, method or harmony arrangements' play in universal laws? The answer is, a very important part indeed! There appear to be two main senses, one in which we talk of constrained arrangements of similar things, and the other where we talk of functional or purposive arrangements of many different things. Let us take them in order.

Order as mental constraint

Let us look more closely at this simplifying sense of order that life and intelligence defend and build.

We speak of order in this sense in connection with a plurality of similar entities or parts thereof. Semantically, we could not order the ideas 'love', 'hat', 'eat' and 'thick' (except as members of the class 'word').

One or even two points or particles cannot be either ordered or disordered. But the closer a group of three points are to lying on a straight line, the more ordered we should think them.

With sets of four points (or similar things) we would consider the set most ordered that lay closest to a single plane, but that would not work for three points.

Set theory was evolved to bring rigour into our thinking in this context but it is deficient in its axiomatic approach. It works only in an abstract, ideal world which does not exist. In it, entities can be exact copies, one of another. Set theory lives in a fuzzless world where members of sets can have zero variety and events are precisely repeatable. It has its uses and its limitations. It is a useful brain tool in some spheres.

In this real world entities defined by a class or set are always varied, changeable and individually unique. So we appear to *impose* order as we impose any (and this is vital) mentally comprehensible constraints on positions or arrangements of similar things. 'Similar' means that there are constraints on the position, aspects, qualities and features of the entities which are said to be so. The entities are specified in some way. The tighter the specification the more ordered they are seen to be. Points randomly scattered in space are disordered, those confined to a plane are more ordered, those confined to a line more so, those at regular spacing on the line even more so, and so on. But in real life they can only be so confined within some tolerance, some permissible deviation, but the smaller this is, the more order we should see.

The positional co-ordinates and their tolerance are constraints which confer order. Atoms are more ordered than their component particles because they have less variety of relative position and momentum. They are under constraint. Molecules are more ordered than the free atoms. Nils Bohr's atom with its constraint on orbits is more ordered and lawful than its conceptual predecessors.

The constraints which confer order seem always to be brainable, easily comprehensible! Why? Straight lines, planes, fixed orbits and distances are limits as to variety, confinement to brainable classes with brainable constraints. These are all purely mental phenomena, ways of comprehending. What are they doing affecting completely objective physical systems outside a mental context?

Clausius, Boltzman and Maxwell showed that systems of low entropy, ordered ones, were less probable, less likely to be found. If they are subject to constraints that makes sense. Adding specification reduces frequency.

It follows that by imposing some constraint, by increasing the specification (imposing a norm) we decrease the membership of a class and thus its probability. Further, if we reduce the permissible deviation of a set of entities or systems from such an imposed norm we shall further reduce the number of entities that fall within the reduced limits and thus the probability, where this means frequency likelihood of occurrence. Recognition and classification, with which we shall deal, show the same pattern. The more highly specified (or constrained) a class is, the less members it is likely to have. There are more men than tall men, more tall men than tall, dark men, and so on. But the constraints of classification are simplifying ones, introduced to help the brain deal with the data mountain. We need to work out what these ideas are doing in a very different context, on that of heat engineering and physics. Is nature trying to tell us something?

Order as durability

It seems intuitively obvious that we should see a durable arrangement in the above sense as more ordered than an ephemeral one, so the idea of constraint does not apply in the time dimension – the less constrained in time, the more orderly the entity. But here the lack of time constraint implies, conversely, a lowered and not a raised probability or lowered frequency in the sense given above. Durable entities, ordered within given constraints, are rarer than short-lived ones within the same constraints.

We should also ascribe more order to repetitive events (within some deviation limits) than we should to less repetitive events. And the more iterations and the less variability, the more the order. Again, more order means less probability, frequency.

Now this concept of order as stability begins to touch closely on the living world to which we belong. The Creatura, the living, are more ordered in all the above senses than the Pleroma, the unliving. They are highly specified, (by the genome) within narrow constraints, they are more durable, have more replicates. In every way they are more ordered and less 'probable' in the sense given above.

Order as function

Now the other sense of the word 'order' *seems* quite different from those above yet is intuitively associated with them. What of order as function? It is truly applicable only to living things and their artefacts. It can be force-fitted to the invariances and regularities of successive observations of inanimate systems but the differences are great and the semantic gap wide. The way magnets attract and repel each other is very different indeed from the way people do.

This sense of the word 'order' is inescapably teleological. It has no application to non-purposive systems. It is that sense concerned with the correct and harmonious functioning of the parts and the whole of some purposive system. A clock, car, person or committee is in order when it and all its parts are functioning correctly to serve some pre-established purpose.

In previous usages, we have been dealing with similar entities and their arrangements. In this sense the order lies in a much more complex idea, that of the mutual 'fitness' or co-operative suitability (related to some purpose, say survival) of many differing parts of an entity.

In his excellent book, *Genetic Takeover,* Dr Graham Cairns-Smith says that orderliness is not a particularly significant aspect of living things, and his definition of order is similar to my first usage: things that are ordered are confined to a small subset of the possibilities. Considering a dewdrop the size of the bacterium *E. coli,* he shows that the gain in 'order' when it condenses is vastly greater than that which could possibly be specified by the 4500000 nucleotide pairs of the *E. coli* genome.

Now, the highly structured bacterium is vastly more specified than the dewdrop. There are an enormous number of molecular arrangements of the water molecules that would still be classed as a dewdrop, it could be rearranged ad infinitum without ceasing to be one. This does not apply to the *E. coli* bacterium, so each of the much smaller set of viable arrangements is much less probable and much more orderly. There seems to have been a paradigm shift from the type of order that I first described and the functional order I dealt with last. Dr Cairns-Smith mentions that there are different levels of order and that functional order is different.

CONCENTRATION AS ORDER

It might be thought that there is no way to unify, to make sense of, these different senses of the meaning of the concept 'order'. The sense used in the Second Law seems more restricted. But is it?

Looking at the beginning, the big bang, we find an underlying sense which links the different aspects of the concept. The classical view of entropy, if applied to recent consensus cosmology, looks odd. On this view the universe exploded out of unknowable void with a big bang 15 billion years ago. For a short period there were no particles, nothing but a vast exploding ball of extremely hot plasma, mixed matter-energy without singularities. It is hard to think of such a chaotic explosion of proto matter-energy as being of low entropy, ordered. But extrapolating backwards through time, this beginning *ought* to have been the first, the most ordered state of the universe, this one from which the ubiquitous running-down process of rising entropy started. If not, how do we explain the decrease of entropy that led to the highly sorted (ordered) array of galaxies and stars.

From this cosmic view we have to include dispersal as a measure of disorder, concentration as an aspect of order. And this seems to be the most important of the various aspects of the concept. The running-down and the expansion of the universe are the same thing, the more space occupied by a given amount of matter energy, the less available the energy, the higher the entropy.

Order and information

Jaques Monod, in *Chance and Necessity*, following Szilard and Brillouin, speaking in terms of information says 'The order of a system, in such terms, is equal to the quantity of information that is required for the *description* of that system. [My italics.] This is why it has been usual to think of information as itself representing negentropy.' This needs to be modified in the light of the above if we are dealing with order as constraint.

My case is that there the uniting paradigm which brings together all the foregoing senses of order is the opposite, it is this. The degree of order of a given system is *inversely* related to the information required to describe it. The points on a line or those on a plane are easier to specify within a given tolerance than those without those constraints. Describing stable, permanent and durable systems requires fewer terabits than an equivalent succession of ephemera.

If the elements in a system were in random interaction it would be described only by giving the position and momentum of every particle. Any constraints, any ordering, reduces the information required to describe it.

The contradiction between the views of Monod, Brouilliard and Szilard and what I say here is resolved by noting that there are two usages for the concept 'complexity'. We use the word to describe the elaborate as well as the uncertain. We would say that complex, ordered system requires more information to describe it than a simple, ordered system but in both cases the less ordered it is the more information will be required for its description. Geography is the pool of information that is needed because the earth is not a uniform sphere but a fuzzy, noisy, disordered one. If it were a perfect sphere it could be described by four co-ordinates. Complex, ordered systems are further along the morphostasis continuum than simple ones and in the sense that Monod was using they are more ordered.

We evidently have to make a distinction between two kinds of complexity, random complexity such as that of a disordered collection and ordered or functional complexity such as that in an animal or a machine. Functional or morphostat order seems to be inversely related to the information needed to describe something multiplied by the complexity. We lack a definition or measure for complexity but we can rank things for it.

The requirements of harmonious function are constraints. Any constraint imposes a limitation on variety and thus on the information required for description. The drawings required to make a watch are very much simpler than those needed to describe a given watch with its billions of separate, agitated atoms.

The information required to describe the universe after the big bang increases continuously with time from the first femtosecond. The original plasma could be described by simple equations of a few unknowns. When the singularities, particles and atoms appeared on one hand and the galaxies and then stars condensed on the other, the information needed to describe the universe became continuously greater. Entropy increased, order decreased, information required increased.

When Claude Shannon formulated the theory of information (to which we shall come) it was thought that the equation takes the negative form of that which describes entropy loss in the Maxwell-Boltzmann Second Law and a connection was sought. But if their paradigm for order was what it seems to be it should have had the same form. Certainly, the degradation of information during communications takes exactly the same form. There has been a constantly renewed speculation on the theme that there is some relationship between the two formulae. It is often dismissed as mystical but always comes back again. It needs an undogmatic re-examination.

THE BIOLOGICAL NATURE OF ENERGY AND WORK

To understand the wholly epistemological concept, order, we must look at its peculiar place in thermodynamic theory.

As I have said, the universe according to Sir Isaac Newton and classical physics had no real direction in time. Classical mechanics works as well forwards as backwards in time, the fourth dimension. If a film of the Newtonian solar system were to be run backwards no-one would be the wiser. But when Lord Kelvin, Clausius, Maxwell and Boltzman really got down to what happens in steam engines they found that real life physics was irreversible. There is a one-way arrow in time and we *can* distinguish later from earlier events. You will not know if a planetarium is being run backwards but if you film boiling water or breaking crockery you will know if you spool wrongly and run the reel backwards. The smashed crocks have lost order and if they were seen to gain it by flying together instead of apart it would be noticed. There would be something funny about steam that shrank and crawled into a kettle spout.

The pioneers of thermodynamics found that time insists on its direction as soon as you begin to do any work or use any energy in the mesocosm where we all live.

In the macrocosmic Newtonian world of classical astronomy we see almost perpetual motion as the planets whirl on, untired, around the sun. The classical microcosmic electron, too, whirls on round its orbit without fatigue. But mesocosmic perpetual motion machines have obstinately been lazier, they run down and refuse to work after a short time. How vexing! As soon as we want to use energy to do something useful we get all these problems.

The teleological nature of thermodynamics

The Second Law of Thermodynamics is, as I have said, an unashamedly statistical law. It is not a deterministic, causal law. It is a gamblers' law that tells us about chances. It tells us only what happens to very large assemblies of equivalent, equipotent entities and nothing at all about the behaviour of a system's elemental entities (molecules) which *must* according to the theory *behave randomly*.Yet, assuming only an overriding but statistical law of large numbers and the randomness rule at the microcosm, it turns out to be the surest law of all. Statistics deals only in probabilities, but a probability which is high enough cannot be distinguished from certainty in the real world. The Second Law was formulated in its first form by Clausius, who invented the term 'entropy'. It arose from the discovery that heat engines and refrigerators were governed by a strange unprovable negative 'law' which limits efficiency. The law governs how much of the available energy can be made *use* of in any thermal system. But 'use' is a teleological term, it implies some purpose.

The Second Law says that if we have a body that is at the same temperature as its surroundings, although both body and environment have plentiful energy there is no way that it can be used. It is only when energy moves from a hotter (more disordered) body to a colder, more ordered one that energy is available to do work upon something, or warm it or cool it. The amount of energy thus available depends upon the temperature difference and not upon the energy contained. Part of the energy can be turned to our useful purposes but part must be given up to lessening the temperature difference.

Everything that we know of what happens in the universe increases the total entropy, the disorder in it, nothing diminishes it. That is, simply stated, the effect of the Second Law. If we extrapolate that rule we see a picture of the universe which will gradually run down from its present fairly sorted, ordered state with very much available energy, towards a heat death as everything warms up and matter and energy (which we now know are aspects of the same thing) slide down the entropy slope towards less and less available states. The final state would be when all particles have decayed into radiant energy of lower and lower frequency, spreading into the void in an eventless world.

We must question some terms which have been used all too uncritically in the formulation above, which is a simplified version of the classical one. We speak of 'doing work', 'consuming', 'useful' and 'available' energy in these contexts and tend to forget that those words are inescapably anthropomorphic (or *biomorphic*) and teleological. They imply purpose. They have no meaning that is not associated with some living thing and its purposes. They are meaningless in the world of fundamental physics. We have to ask "who?". Who finds it useful, available? Who consumes things, does work? Something living, nothing in the Pleroma! It is only when some purposive creature has to make changes in the universe to suit itself that the base concepts of thermodynamics appear. The terms and the laws that appear when the abstractions are made are therefore biomorphic laws relating only to the Creatura and having little meaning apart from them.

So is it true that the Creatura are, by all their actions, simply hastening the universe towards its eventual heat death? The simple answer is 'yes'. There is, however, a 'but', to which we now come.

Seen in the lower levels of the mesocosm adjacent to the microcosm it may seem that life merely hastens the disordering process of the entropy slide. We said that the *total* entropy must increase. We cannot reduce that total but we can *redistribute* it, shift it from here to there, from this system to that so long as we accept the overall increase. Useful work is the process by which the downhill increase of entropy in one place is partly balanced by an uphill climb, a climb towards lower entropy, greater order, lower probability in another. We can dam but we cannot stop the flow of a river. However, we, the Creatura, immaterial form though we be, can divert it and use its flow. The order built up at cost of a lower level increase in entropy is therefore often of a different and (I dare to say) higher, more important, more complex, nature than the order that is destroyed to build it. Chemical level disorder buys morphological order in an organism. At the cost of molecular or even atomic organisation here, we buy structural organisation, functional complexity and improbable order there. The entropy stream drives negentropy mills, order building engines. Things get more disordered and probable here that unlikely ordered things may happen there. Entropy mill-races work miracle mills.

THE SPECTRUM OF PREDICTABILITY

The next few pages are intentionally repetitive. They summarise, vary images, emphasise.

Fundamental particles are not predictable but as I have said they lie on a spectrum of durability and therefore partial predictability. We would rate the more durable and the more constrained as the more orderly, the more predictable. We would see particles as more ordered, more stable than radiation, we would count more durable particles as more orderly than the ephemeral ones. Stable combinations of particles, atoms, are seen as more orderly again, molecules more so, and so on.

The macrocosm, the world of astronomy, on the other hand, behaves, as we would expect, in an even more orderly way than the mesocosm. Indeed the macrocosmic world as seen since Newton was so orderly that it may have led to the widespread acceptance of determinism. More knowledge recently has been changing this idea.

Karl Popper believes that new ideas and visions of the world are creative acts and that we do not really know their source. Hypotheses come from out of the mental 'blue' and are not the result of conscious rational processes.

However, most of our understanding of the world is subliminal, it lies out of sight in what Sigmund Freud would have called the Unconscious. It has to be made conscious for the purpose of communication and to be tested. The semantic connectivity network in our brains influences the serial chain of our speech, but we do not *know* that network. It contains all our wisdom and maybe a lot more that never gets to the point of expression.

The fuzzy collection of associated meanings behind the words 'order', 'pattern' and 'form' are not merely a ragbag. I believe they may have hidden understandings in them. I point to what may be seen as a semantic chasm between the meaning 'physical and astronomic order' as described above and the other usages 'order and pattern' as found in the Creatura, the living. The functional order in a cell, a leaf, an insect or a society may seem to be fundamentally different from the order arising from natural invariances but they may not be so different as they seem. They too arise from constraints though they are of an apparently teleological origin. Our subconscious act of classing the two meanings together may be telling us something.

It is this functional order, pattern, or form that I find myself forced to explore in my search for the origin of that which we call intelligence in this universe. Though this sort of order is found only in connection with the Creatura, I may not ignore its connections among the Pleroma, the unliving.

THE IMMATERIALITY OF FORM

In the first chapter I made the point that the Creatura, the living, are not in essence material and that life can be transduced or transferred to many different material substrates without losing its essential nature and its effect.

Here, I assert that this applies equally when we consider the forms and patterns of the Creatura. Consider the genome, the long, double-helix, chain molecules in the nucleus of the cell. In the pattern of the side-chains they hold the information which enables the cell's machinery to replicate a plant or an animal.

The material genome is an extremely fragile chain with many millions and even billions of nucleotide pairs along its length. But the entity described by the word 'genome' is immaterial. It 'inhabits' or parasitises the constantly changing series of ephemeral *materials* which successively take on the double-helix form. The effect of the genome on that *form* which endures, remains stable and constant. It is the stability of a river's course or a fountain's shape, not that of a physical *thing*.

The genome is replicated, it is constantly being repaired by wandering enzymes and its individual atoms and side-chains are in a state of constant flux. The genome itself preserves its form despite ever-changing content. It is information made durable and replicable.

I have suggested that it may be unwise to try to understand informational systems by looking at the cause and effect laws which apply to the determinist materialist world, as scientists have been trying to see it. We must seek that other set of invariances and symmetries which apply to this different realm of nature, that of unsubstantial form which lives on, in, with and by means of a succession of material, physical substrates.

I emphasise, the form of information systems has a close resemblance to the one we find in every cell of every living thing. A computer memory, a book, speech, these are all different examples of a very long chain of elements from a very restricted and highly specified set (bytes, letters, phonemes, nucleotide pairs). They all have the power to cause, triggerwise, extremely complex and highly specified, energy amplified actions via long, unlikely causal chains working on highly prepared entities. They are all subject to repair, they all replicate with extremely improbable exactitude.

ORDER AND PATTERN IN THE MICROCOSM

A creature capable of comprehending and predicting events would obviously be impossible in a random world, a universe which was truly anarchic, one where any existing state could be followed by any other state, unrelated to the former state in any way. Such a creature would be equally impossible, I assert, in a universe in which strict determinist causality prevailed. Where everything is pre-ordained nothing can evolve or learn.

If these terms have any meaning at all, they require the existence of selectable options and in a truly determinate world there are none. There are many attempts to fudge this, but if they are looked at closely a circularity is revealed.

Cognitive learning involves a succession of models which improve gradually in congruence with the world that is modelled. This trial-and-error approach makes no sense if the world is truly determinate. What is the need for such an approach, why is not the first model perfect or none so?

Without either anarchy or determinism we are left with a mutable and partial order or probabalistic type laws or invariances.

Certainly at base, the universe has invariances, constraints, symmetries, and statistical laws which greatly limit the variety of outcome states from any given state. But the state of the universe at time t_1 does not uniquely *determine* that at time t_2. It limits the range or variety of possible states at t_2. But here where we live, in what I have called the mesocosm, the mid world between the infinitesmal and the infinite, the particles and the galaxies, we find an apparent determinism because we are dealing with such very large samples of the less lawful elementary particles. The laws, the invariances we see can be accommodated just as well in a open, forked, statistical universe containing real options as they can in the closed determinist world where there are none. This is a contradiction I hope to resolve in the next chapter.

MORPHOSTASIS CONTINUUM

If we see life as morphostasis and take a positive view about it, we ought to look at the morphostasis continuum, the stability scale that rules in the universe.

The morphostasis continuum might look at bit like the much criticised Scala Naturae, and it is of course based on the same perception, that which impressed so many earlier biologists, such as Haeckle. The idea is that there is a progressive direction to evolution, an upwards trend towards more complex, more elaborate and more intelligent forms. The criticism arises from the question, "Which life form comes out at the top of the scale?" By a suspicious coincidence it is mankind! So we accuse ourselves of *speciesism* and turn aside. Science rightly suspects anthropocentrism, it smacks of imperialism and racism. (Mind you, if the *Scala Naturae* were valid there would *be* a top, and it would know itself.)

The morphostasis continuum embraces the earlier perception but since it arrives at a different summit, far beyond mankind, one which puts man around the middle of the continuum (the most likely place), the same objection does not hold. I present it for what it might be thought to be worth (Figure 1).

Biophysical dualism

This crude oversimplified picture of the world is frankly dualistic. It is convenient to think of the things and the forms as being touching, but different. On one side, the Pleroma, the physical matter and energy; on the other side, the Creatura, the biota, the surviving, replicating, self-optimising, purposive forms that matter may take in the mesocosm. The forms survive in semi-independence of their physical substrates.

Starting, arbitrarily, at the top, where there is least morphostasis, we have

Increasing
Order
Epistemological constraints
Durability of form
Improbability
"Useful" energy available
Divergence, variety
Amplification of
Microcosmic randomness
(creating mesocosmic choices)
Irrelevance of material substrate
Complexity
Organisation
Symbiosis
Intelligence (comprehension of the universe by the Creatura)

The realm of the Pleroma
Energy (electromagentic radiation)
Low frequency
High frequency

Matter (stable energy)
Particles
  Ephemeral
  Durable

Atoms (stable ensembles of particles)
  Ephemeral
  Durable

Molecules (stable ensembles of atoms)

Gases   Stable ensembles of molecules

Liquids
Solids   Stable crystals, periodic
aperiodic crystals (information carrying)

The realm of the Creatura
(surviving forms, patterns, on pleroma substrates)
Protozoa   One cell life forms. Stable patterns
of periodic crystals DNA, RNA, proteins
Prokaryotes (bacteria, algae)
Eukaryotes (nucleate cells). stable ensembles of prokaryotes

Metazoa   (animals) and metaphyta (plants)
Stable ensembles of eukaryotic
form with internal communications

Sociozoa   Stable ensembles, patterns of metazoa
with external communications
Swarms, herds, flocks,
colonies of animals
Human societies
    Stable ensembles, patterns
of intercommunicating people
Tribes, gangs, firms, cultures,
nations, alliances,

Earth culture.   The intercommunicating pattern
of international communities, e.g.,
commerce, industry, the market

Interplanetary cultures?

Figure 1   The morphostasis continuum

pure energy, electromagnetic waves. Those of lower frequency have the lowest order, least available energy. Higher frequency radiation comes next.

Moving down, we enter the realm of matter, frozen (or stabilized) energy. We start with the least energetic and most ephemeral particle and work down to the most stable and durable, the electron and the proton. Next along the continuum we meet the *combinations* of particles, atoms, with rising orders of complexity, available energy and durability. We now enter the more complex world of combinations of atoms, of molecules.

All the time we are moving on a *descending* scale of entropy and probability* and an *ascending* scale of order, constraints, permanence, increasing and diverging variety.

Next we reach the great junction. The line between the two realms. We cross the frontier into the realm of the Creatura, the forms, which parasitise the things, the Pleroma. They are like information, they cannot exist without their material substrate, but they are not constrained by it in the usual way. Their laws are different. They can seem incompatible. The Creatura seem to have choices and can move from one substrate to another without loss of form. They can pump order and energy in and out of their substrate systems.*

The continuum continues among the Creatura. All aspects change in the same way. Increasing order, complexity, organisation, symbiosis, larger combination and informational rather than physical interaction, greater comprehension and control of the Pleroma by the Creatura. The probability of what is found, relative to physical laws, descends out of sight. The independence of those laws, choices and the power available to those choices increases.

At the limit of the known, we have the earth's ecological overcoat, the balanced and stable interacting biosphere and its most recent manifestation, the present world culture.

As we reach the extremes of the continuum the picture passes beyond the conjectural horizon to possible contact between life forms on different worlds. The picture here is wildly speculative and 'impossible' to state-of-the-art astronomy but it is one that seems to have an imaginative appeal, to judge by the art form science fiction. A hypothesis that ruled out contact between astronomically separate life forms might be risky. But so might too much conjecture about it at this stage. I shall develop this theme later.

*The word 'probability' here is used in a special sense. The probability of any arrangement of matter, in this sense, is the reciprocal of its frequency of occurrence in a posited system where all the elements are assumed to be equipotent.

3

The universe, interactive game or movie?

If we now provisionally concede that we cannot explain the miracle of life and intelligence without the interlinked ideas of options and choice between them, we cannot be in a really optionless determinate universe. We find these awkward miracles. So now, in the hope of abolishing them, we venture on speculation about causality, determinism, and uncertainty.

Evolution, learning, and intelligence in a universe without options is too big a strain on our credulity, not to say gullibility. Descartes, a towering figure in the history of science, is among many sages who was a strict determinist. Bishop Berkeley, David Hume and Jeremy Bentham and, despite the statistical nature of the laws of fundamental physics to which he contributed so much, even Albert Einstein believed the world was governed by strict deterministic causal laws. We are witnessing a film show where the future is waiting for us, every frame of it, on the reel.

Calvinist predestination was probably the precursor to scientific determinism. It implied strict causality. This as a paradigm was probably a product of monotheism. Pantheism allows for contention between different gods, and unsettled outcomes. The Pantheon had an open forking future but one God makes an all-embracing set of rules valid everywhere for all systems. So everything is settled. The celluloid characters have the illusion of choice while the universal movie reel unwinds.

Whatever its origin and however hard for wilful, striving creatures like men and women to accept it, deterministic causality is deeply embedded in the roots of modern science and it is so for the best of reasons. It works. This is what we ask of each of the succession of paradigms before we are forced to abandon them.

45

It is not too much to say that determinism has been decisively effective and productive in every field of science. Before the causality paradigm, the scientist could sweep all sorts of puzzling anomalous phenomena under the table of animism or entelechy. Now, determinism is rightly, fully and firmly established as the central *strategy* of science, almost its hallmark. The obstinate, obsessive, pursuit of determinist, materialist, invariances that *explain* has produced almost the whole of modern science. Even where uncertainty and indeterminism cannot be disentangled in the microcosmic world of fundamental particles, down in the Heisenberg region, to continue the search for causal law is the best course for science.

But the determinist paradigm leaves us these troublesome miracles.

Even some scientists find it difficult to believe that their actions were all set parts on the universal actors' script. Their thoughts, desires and will were all part of the play! It was a severe trial for the faithful. For a faith is what determinist dogmatism is. It is fairly common ground since Werner Karl Heisenberg produced the uncertainty principle that causality, or indeterminism, cannot be distinguished from uncertainty, which *is* compatible with determinism. This makes dogmatists of both camps in the dispute that has raged ever since.

However, our day-to-day certainty that we have freedom to choose between different actions is central and fundamental to our lives.

VERBAL BELIEFS AND BEHAVIOURAL BELIEFS

There are two kinds of belief, V or verbal beliefs, which affect only what we say, and B or behavioural beliefs, those which affect what we *do*. Words written by Descartes, Hume, Berkeley, Einstein and Bohm can give us the V belief that all our striving, contriving and efforts to change outcomes are an illusion. We will dutifully verbalise this view. But our B belief that we have options and can choose will still be seen in all our non-verbal behaviour. In their words, many scientists are determinists. In their actions they are unanimously indeterminist.

There are cults, religions and other belief systems which show that there is no sort of crazy farrago that will not attract passionate, devoted, but inoperative verbal belief. Watch what they do. Do not listen to what they say, is my advice. On this ground I may say that whatever you, my patient reader, may say, you are not really a determinist. If the next page is destined to be turned it will be, so why do *you* bother? If you really believe in strict determinism (and what other kind can there be?) you take it easy and see what your fingers do.

ANTHROPOCENTRISM AND SOCIOCENTRISM

Scientists often warn us against the error of anthropocentrism, of making the world in the model of man. Perhaps we should be warned against socio-centrism. The monist view of the universe and the concept of unbreakable laws may be a reflection not of man, but of society. Human societies were governed by chiefs or kings who ruled through laws. As larger social units, this paradigm can be idealised and 'perfected' into a single God with a universal set of infrangible laws which must be obeyed.

The actual observations of modern science give no reason for belief in a universal system of strict causality. Things are much fuzzier. Without excep-tion, the match between what law predicts and observation is statistical in nature. Laws can tell us of the variable probabilities which connect observa-tions of events called causes and events called effects. Some of these prob-abilities approach unity, but they never get there. The congruence between observation and what is predicted from any law of science is never perfect, if only because of the imperfections of observation.

Heisenberg established, at base, down in the microcosm, that we could account for what we see only by using statistical laws. It follows that the hypothesis of causality was an entity 'multiplied without necessity', as Occam put it. Where there are just two mutually exclusive hypotheses there is a problem in cutting either of their throats with Occam's sharp razor. Causal law, statistical law, which is least necessary?

Uncertainty/indeterminism: the default hypothesis

I submit that the safest course and the practical one is to scrap the most restrictive law. This will avoid errors from assuming undemonstrated con-straints. Since causality is infinitely restrictive it is the one that should go.

The latest discoveries in fundamental physics tell us that the laws of nature, as far as there are any, are prohibitions rather than commands. Physics is getting cautious and telling us more what may *not* be than what *must* be. There are invariances, constraints, certain aspects of matter that are conserved, mass/energy, parity spin, etc. We can tell what cannot happen, there are no inflexible musts.

But man is an animal that knows, at the deepest centre of his being, that he survives only by choosing between real options. Nothing is more vital and obvious to him than that he has the power to make decisions which affect what will happen, that he can change the world. His B belief, credulity, would be strained to the limit to believe, really believe, in deed as well as in word that he has no such power, that he is a puppet dancing on causal strings. Try selling B determinism to plants. You have a better chance.

As for myself, I can only discuss life and intelligence which seem to make choices, on the assumption of a forked world with options to optimise.

My final kick to the crutch of determinism is the argument of a one-time industrialist businessman who is used to making action decisions without enough information or time to get it. It is an argument akin to that advanced by Blaise Pascal, who was Christian, 'to be on the safe side'. His policy was right even if, in the instance, he was wrong. (Maybe in those days of atheist-bashing not so very wrong.)

In business we make fail-safe decisions when we can. Which, I ask, of the hypotheses, determinism and indeterminism, does best in the fail-safe test? Which carries the most severe penalty for error? In a determinist universe the very ideas *penalty* and *error* are nonsense. *Nothing* can affect outcome. But in an indeterminate forked world there would be severe penalties for those who acted on the belief that striving and effort were *really* irrelevant to outcome. Determinism has the highest error cost.

To summarise, nothing is more manifest than that we are intelligent, if only because the fact that something is manifest to a creature implies intelligence in the creature. The concept 'intelligence' makes no sense unless there are options, choices between alternatives and means to optimise outcomes. None of these things can exist in a truly determinist world. So if any intelligence, including our own, informs us that the world is determinist, it undermines its authority to tell us anything by doing so. It sends us a message which cannot be both meaningful and true. Information is either surprise or tautology. If the world is determined there can be no surprises. The message of determinism fails Karl Popper's falsifiability test.

QUANTUM WEIRDNESS

If you are familiar with quantum wierdness, the incompatible things that observations and calculations in the microcosm try to tell us, you can skip this section. If you want to be reminded, read on.

Once Nils Bohr, working from the data from Max Planck, had elaborated the first version of the modern atom, quantum weirdness appeared. Electrons leave lovely straight tracks which show that they are point-like particles in one experiment, but behave like dispersed waves in another. Photons of light which are just as obviously wave-like, behave like particles when looked at another way.

From 1925 to 1927 Werner Heisenberg, Nils Bohr, Paul Adrian Dirac and Max Born struggled with these intractable problems. The whole world of physics, not to say philosophy, was put into a turmoil. In 1927 everyone seemed to give up the attempt to 'understand' in the normal sense of the word. The odd idea that reality was somehow changed by the way it is observed came to be accepted as the best that could be done by way of comprehension.

Bohr's lecture at Como in 1927 is still accepted as the last word. In what has come to be called the Copenhagen Interpretation, he closed a fruitless discussion in a most unsatisfactory way. Statements of his interpretation differ, but the effect is that while in mesocosmic 'classical' physics particles behave like clockwork, in the microcosm the interaction of the observer and the particle system is such that the particles do not behave independently of the way they are observed, and that it is useless to try to *understand* this in the normal sense of the word.

The effect of the interpretation was that there is a quantum world which can be predicted (statistically), but it cannot be understood. The equations could cope but the mind could not.

Later, in 1935, Einstein, Podolsky and Rosen wrote a paper which proved to be an even bigger bomb of weirdness thrown into the disordered house of microcosmic physics. They proposed a thought experiment which undermined the fundaments of science altogether. It showed that the known results of physical observations must falsify Bell's inequality. I shall not recount the story, which is prominent in any book on fundamental physics. The point is that the only rational 'explanations' of such a falsification were either the overthrow of the principle of local causation or the acceptance of influences that moved faster than light. To accept either of these was to admit that the very foundations underlying physics were built on dust.

In the macrocosm of astronomy there were other unbrainable discoveries. Einstein showed that the experiments on the speed of light and Heisenberg's work proved that measuring rods, clocks and weights were different for different observers according to their relative speed. He showed that there must be unsimultaneous nows, differing rates of time for different observers. These absurd conclusions were infuriatingly confirmed as being true whenever checked.

One remark by Nils Bohr should be etched on the mind of anyone who aspires to be member of the world culture. He said, 'Anyone who is not shocked by quantum physics does not understand it.'

My view? So What? What would *you* expect of brains built for a world a score of orders of magnitude bigger or smaller? Is quantum weirdness simply an expression of the unbrainability of these other worlds to mesocosmically evolved and trained brains? How well would a molecule-brain or one built of galaxies do in comprehending our world? We can try not to be sexists or racists, we are born mesocosmists.

WHAT WOULD A FORKED WORLD BE LIKE?

Let us therefore posit a forked world, an indeterminate one where the apparently inflexible causal laws in the mesocosm, where we live, are really statistical in nature. The inhabitants of the mesocosm in such a world would develop brains based on the laws of cause and effect. Such brains must learn by induction based on the expectation that the future is going to be like the past. How else? Because the weight of large numbers makes statistical laws very predictive in beings that consist of trillions of particles the laws they observed would be falsified very rarely. These laws would prove an excellent guide to life and prediction. Those creatures who discovered and acted on them would do very well, survive, thrive. They would rightly be very hard to convince that the laws were marginally false in the mesocosm and quite false in the microcosm.

Indeterminism amplified at hierarchical stages

At the Heisenberg level, the microcosm in such a world, the laws are not so much laws as constraints, low probabilities. The smaller the assembly of atoms, the greater would be the chance that some rare microcosmic event could have a margin effect upon it, triggerwise. So the variety of form of very small assemblies of matter and energy that could happen would become very great indeed, because the envelope of constraints, statistical, not lawlike, would be opened by the indeterminism amplified from a lower level. Small systems would be under a constant rattling bombardment of randomness just as tiny particles are by agitated molecules in Brownian motion.

It is safe to assume that some of this wider variety of forms would be such as to have a non-equipotent (heteropotent) amplified, triggerlike effect on larger systems and some of these again would have a marginal effect on those above. But the chance of such quantum level effects reaching the entities in the mesocosm would be infinitesimal because, relatively, the mesocosm is so huge. Well and good.

With long ages, vast numbers, replication?

However, what would be the effect of immense tracts of time on very large assemblies of such a set of systems? What of that infinitesimally small group of them that fell into self-perpetuating and self-replicating configurations?

Earlier I suggested that collectivities which are stable in form would increase their frequency simply because they are durable and the others are not. It is also certain that if they were metastable, stable within some variability envelope, there would be an increase in the frequency of the more stable kinds within the envelope. Among the vast variety of such form-stable collectivities which are increasing in frequency there are bound to be some that are both metastable and self-replicating.

This is the crucial step. But the substrate system which takes a form or shape and has the quality of growth and division while retaining it produces an energy problem and a choice problem. The substrate system has to be such that its elements bind selectively to those bits of the world around them that increase their size without altering their form. For the growing assembly to split is no problem. (Crude entropy-type splitting will evolve towards the more stable precision of a reproduction system.) In the enormous variety of things that can happen in the hugeness and variety of an indeterminate universe we know that the energy problem must be, was, solved in some array somewhere.

THE ORIGIN OF EVOLVING FORM

When it does happen, something new has come into the universe, a new entity, a self-replicating immaterial *form*. There are now continuing entities which, not being of matter, are not bound by its mesocosmic laws. (This simply means that they will not be bound to have the same astronomically high probability relationships between succeeding events as those of normal cause and effect in unbiological physics.)

The advantage of access to randomness

We aspiring softsmiths (and hardsmiths) who are playing on the fringes of 'artificial intelligence' know one thing well. Optimisation or trial-and-error systems need a source of randomness, or at least irrelevance as in pseudo-randomness. I suggest that the variety of true indeterminism must, for any finite system, be greater than that of any system for producing pseudo-randomness.

It must be true that developing life forms would find that access to an input of randomness is an advantage. The best source for such must be the levels below, those nearer to the quantum world.

With time many stage amplification systems must evolve as long as each stage remains stable and replicating. Thus we might expect the evolution of the primitive Creatura. Such long trigger chains would promote microcosmic indeterminism in stages up to the mesocosm. This would offer a wider range of options for selection by proto-life forms. Those early life forms which are more various have more options, are less bound by the statistical-type 'determinism' of the mesocosm, and must from their greater variety have more chance to throw up metastable forms (entropy pumping forms) than those with less of such options. Indeed, it would be surprising if no such long, dice-throwing, option-selecting, chains were to arise. Such chains can reach down into the quantum world, to evolve the long unlikely chains, the means to defy the statistical laws that seem to forbid the life we know.

PHYSICAL LAWS AND BIOLOGICAL LAWS

The chains of variety-offering triggers, or relays, which I posit, would, among many effects, open another door. They would make it possible for a different kind of triggering chain to be built up by selection over time. Indeed, they could evolve into such a chain. The sort of chain I refer to is the long chain of chemical actions and reactions involved in cell chemistry. This is a story which is gradually emerging as the study of ontogeny proceeds.

These long chains of processes are initiated by the genes. They are immensely long, complicated and miraculously improbable on the hypothesis of random assembly. Their effect is that the reactions we observe in developing cells are as Jaques Monod explained, so improbable as to be almost an infringement of the laws of physics. We can say they conform because they happen, and of course the *material* substrates are 'legal', but that they should *happen* is not. It is like any other physical illegality, improbable to the miracle level.

Physical realm, heteronomous biological realm

If this speculation is fair we would expect in its later evolution and enlargement, that as this new aspect of existence, form-existence, grows up into life forms it will be found to have a set of laws that are no longer based on the mass-action statistical invariances of the material world. It would be another set of laws, or invariances, those of the biological world, which applies to this new immaterial universe of *forms*.

The laws of forms would be different from those of material because elaborate probability-defying systems (forms) have been imposed upon the material substrates. These have made its material immune from the laws that apply to all other material. Those laws assume that the elements of any system are equipotent, of equal effect, like the molecules of gas which obey Boyle's Law. But biological systems are full of triggers, heteropotent effects. There are many relays and triggerlike amplifiers by which small biological subsystems have unequal effects on larger ones in highly specified, unstatistical ways. What is lawlike, very probable, for material, is not lawlike for biological forms; they have their own different legal systems. They are heteronomous (ruled by other laws).

A parable of observation

It is against the laws of the world for which our brains were designed that we can *observe* an electron and know which of two slits it goes through. But we have put together a complex array of instruments which enable us to do so. The existence of such an array in this universe is overwhelmingly unlikely (physically illegal in a purely physical material universe). Why be surprised if we get incomprehensible observations?

MIRACLES OF WRONG PARADIGM

Paradoxically, we must *expect* miracles if it is true that living forms have arisen by amplifying and using microcosmic quantum randomness, amplified at many stages, offering variety for selection. But those are the 'miracles', or disobediences to mesocosmic laws that I want to abolish. They are the miracles of wrong paradigm. They arise from the unwise expectation that systems that can tap the indeterminism of the microcosm and amplify it into effects in the mesocosm will behave like those that cannot. If by many successive amplifications at many levels over aeons of time what has been called quantum weirdness has crept up into our familiar world, the mesocosm, we must abate our surprise at the apparent improbability and weirdness of the result.

INTERGALACTIC CREATION?

The Russian Professor of Chemical Physics, Vitalli Goldanskii, made a relevant report in the *Scientific American,* Jan. 86, ('Quantum chemical reactions in the deep cold'). His researches show that chemical reactions that are 'forbidden' according to classical (mesocosm) physics are possible at very low temperatures.

At temperatures in the range we are used to, many reactions need an energy input to allow them to climb over the entropy barrier between one stable state and another. In conditions near zero degrees Kelvin, quantum uncertainty seems to apply to whole molecules, not merely to particles, and when this effect comes into play they are able to tunnel through the energy barrier without the energy input required by classical chemistry. The effect can be seen either as due to quantum uncertainty of position or as an aspect of the wave/particle duality of all matter energy. This very low temperature effect is, like the other strange effects we find at low temperatures, another example of the way knowledge seems to get out of joint at the fringes.

The significance of this report is that it has a demoting effect on the miracle of life. Biologists have thought that the environment favourable to the development of very complex incredible molecules is a very small temperature/pressure/conditions slot found only on Earth-sized planets. If over aeons of time there has been a slow, progressive development of complex molecular chains, anywhere in the endless stretches of cold galactic and intergalactic dust, then a variety door and a time door have been opened to the polypeptides (among countless trillions less viable forms). The Creatura seem to have had more tickets in the Great Lottery than we supposed. Life needs only a seed. There were more chances to create one than was thought.

TWO REALMS; TWO LAWS

The ideas set out here can be seen as a form of dualism which avoids the oddness of psychophysical dualism, which asks us to believe the miracle that mind and world work in unison without connection.

Biophysical dualism is the view that there are two realms each with their own differing but compatible laws. I intend no mysticism. The laws of nature are brainable conveniences, made to fit the world optimally to the brain. Other brains, other laws. Both sets of laws are obeyed but since one applies only to the ever renewed and ever repaired, physical substrate of the other and not to the surviving non-material essence, there is no call for the two laws to be compatible. Both are obeyed within the appropriate realm. Both produce awkward miracles if misapplied.

The two realms contain entities which are in opposition. They are going opposite ways. One towards order, combination, symbiosis, comprehension, intelligence, the other towards dissolution, random disorder and the final hot or cold death of this universe. We, the choosing Creatura, might be expected to have preferences, prejudices, purposes. I shall say more on these lines in the last chapter.

THE ORIGIN OF PURPOSE

Assuming agreement with the proposition that purpose can find no place in a determinist world but that it does appear in this one and is an aspect of both life and intelligence, I now explore the idea.

Teleological explanations of phenomena, those implying purpose to some unseen entities such as gods, are unscientific, but the phenomenon, purpose, does appear to exist and it is not unscientific to speculate on its origin.

Since I have found it impossible to do without the concept 'purpose', in formulating my paradigm for life, I need to give a better account of my view of how it arose.

I have resorted to the somewhat evasive description of morphostats as entities which *behave as if* they had purpose. This was done as the simplest way of conveying my meaning, it is a model you know. It did not imply that the purpose was immanent, or that all morphostats have anything like human conscious purpose. I have tried to show that the sensible, practical hypothesis, the default hypothesis, in the determinism debate is that the future is open, not closed; there are options in it.

It is now my thesis that granted a universe that is only statistically causal it is inevitable that the phenomenon which we call purpose should arise. Why do I insist that *purpose* will arise in such a universe?

Some of the surviving forms will, given time enough, produce mechanisms, systems, which enshrine behavioural preferences, prejudices about what to bind to, and how to behave. Those of such mechanisms which improve stability will survive, replicate and spread. Unspecified purposiveness has good pay-off in stability because only *viable* purposiveness survives. Purposive beings with unviable purpose do not last. Purposeless beings have no such chance. There may be some universal God with a purpose for us. We cannot know.

But if our universe is indeterminate then purpose had to appear in it, God or no. I cannot see what purpose is, or is there for, if the universe is determinate. There is no mystery here, it is simply that when choice mechanisms arise, some proto-creatures fall into a state that has choices (borrowed from the microcosm). Then purpose, preferences, among those options opened a stability door. What is stable survives and endures, so at later times there are more of them around than at earlier times.

LIFE FORMS ON OTHER SUBSTRATES

If biophysical dualism, as presented here, has any truth, which is to say if it is biologically useful, it might throw some light on Fermi's question. 'Where are They?' There has been time in the fifteen billion years since the beginning to develop at least one intelligent form capable of sending messages across space. There is a lot of space out there. Where are the others? Why have they not made themselves known?

The one life form we know, our own, is based on a four-letter alphabet genome, in an extraordinarily confined scale, chemical, space, time, duration, cosmic level, temperature slot. Our sensory equipment, vision, hearing, smell, touch sensors and the brains that receive their input, are all designed for the task of time defiance in just and only that slot, the carbohydrate substrate life slot.

But can we be sure that this is the only such environmental slot that will support the metamorphostatic evolution I have tried to describe? May there not be, indeed is it not likely that there are, other tracks towards morphostatic evolution of types, scales, durations, cosmic levels and based on physical substrates so foreign to our whole cognitive system and equipment that they are unperceived and perhaps unperceivable by creatures like us?

Within the apparent chaos of plasma and gases within the sun and stars there may be other kinds of form-preserving and replicating entities. Such entities might build up their kind of preserved order on the substrate of hot plasma, triggering order and growth from solar energy. Or there may be undetected replicating and evolving stable patterns in the frozen dust clouds of space between the galaxies.

Maybe the very forms and patterns of the galaxies and galaxy groups involve triggerlike control centres which use information sensed and coded in some quite alien way to preserve their form through life spans inconceivable to us.

These are unfalsifiable and unnecessary 'if's and 'maybe's. And if such other life forms are forever unknowable we can happily forget about them or their possibility. But my last 'if' remains. It is this. If we start actually looking for other types of platform of improbable stability in the universe we may even find out where They are, some of Them.

4

Morphostasis requires intelligence

From the foregoing the proposition is that there is no borderline at which intelligence as a phenomenon starts to be manifest within the Creatura. The proposition is that all living forms have, in some form, options, and preferences about them, purposes, and a tendency to optimise their actions on the basis of their information in support of the purposes. I propose that any useful meaning of the word 'intelligence' must cover that kind of activity. If not, there will appear a completely arbitrary dividing line at some point, one which will create more difficulties than it solves.

But the proposition is new and peculiar. The view that the optimising-choosing of the lower life forms is a manifestation related even distantly, to intelligent behaviour is contrary only to usage, it is not contrary to logic. We often have to revise the meaning boundaries of words as we improve understanding of that to which they refer.

INTELLIGENCE IN ITS EARLIEST FORM?

What is the simplest creature to which we must ascribe some intelligence? The simplest life form is the virus, which acts like a parasitic nucleus in a host cell. It cannot live independently.

Viruses have a genome or design manual, in the form of a random access memory, a ram, 1300 to 20000 np (nucleotide pairs) long. An np is a two bit information element.

The simplest and numerically most successful independent, *self-supporting,* life forms known are prokaryote cells (bacteria, some algae). They are simple but the oldest, they have had longest to adapt. However simple they may be relative to later forms, they have had a much longer period of evolutionary-type learning, adapting, refining than more elaborate biota like ourselves.

We, the Johnny-come-lately primates, should doff respectful caps to such perfect viability. Also, as we have been learning recently, bacteria and algae are much more complex than they looked when first observed. They were around billions of years before us, they are likely to be around a billion years after us.

Bacteria have a 4m np prescription string (more information than this book) and their own cytoplasm factory, which acts on design prescriptions. In bacteria a tighter, more efficient genome is free of the long stretches of 'scribble' that infects eukaryote genomes.

Eukaryote protozoa have 10–20 million np (including scribble) and a much more advanced cytoplasm factory. Metazoa or metaphyta, multi-cell animals and plants, have several billion np, a millibook library of book equivalents.

Haeckle's intuitive idea orders the 'higher' and 'lower' life forms and puts the mammals at the top and the viruses at the bottom. It is borne out by the simple test of genome riches. The genome affluent are, by and large, at the top, the genome deprived are at the bottom, for all that they are the immortals. So far. But there are always exceptions. Salamanders, some ancient ferns, psilopsida, and one humble amoeba are all in the decabillionaire genome class.

THE EVOLUTIONARY TIME SCALE

Before we are entitled to be surprised at an event we ought to know what were the chances of it happening. How long has the miracle of life had in which to come about and what were the chances?

Earth has existed for about 4½ gigayears. It took about 2 billion years to get the eukaryote stage and all the nucleate protozoa and metazoa have developed in the last billion years. 2×10^9 years is probably 10^{13} generations (for such simple creatures as prokaryotes). Ten trillion replications when multiplied by the number of bacteria-sized entities that might subsist in the Earth's biosphere comes to an extremely large number of trials. (6×10^{26} or so, even if we allow the average of only one cell per m^2 as the mean population.) Many trials, many errors, but many chances of success too. We would expect a hundred trillion, one in a trillion chances to come off in such circumstances. If selected long shots which come off are replicated by the billion, the population open to experiment changes and the odds change with it. The miracle of life looks less miraculous.

SIGNALS

The nature of a signal has emerged. It is a low energy event which can trigger more energetic events and thus permit Maxwell demonry, climbing entropy slopes.

Triggers, relays, are observed in all manifestations of life from the simplest chemical level. Catalysts are triggers.

Triggers defy statistical laws

We have little idea what early biochemistry was like. Possibly, as Graham Cairns-Smith has suggested, there was some kind of simpler scaffolding substrate, like the clays which served in building towards present life forms. He has argued that these could have been information-carrying and information-replicating templates for carbohydrate forms.

The central problem is the energy problem and there seems to me to be but one way this could be solved. There must be a source of latent energy, there must be a trigger event that can release it, and that trigger must be pulled in a selective way. Morphostatic triggers, demons, are pulled by 'favourable' events, those which favour the morphostasis of the form in question.

When this amplification happens there has been vital change that takes the system out of the normal mass action laws of the Pleroma. The elements of the system are no longer equipotent, having equal mutual effect. Inequality of influence is present. The elements are *heteropotent,* of unequal effect. The assembly of material can no longer be expected to obey statistical laws because the essential condition of such laws is broken.

Chains of triggers and trigger-trees

The trigger effect described above with a single heteropotent effect would not be noticed but, as must inevitably happen, such trigger actions can form chains, with one event triggering another. Further, they will inevitably form hierarchically diverging triggering reactions, trigger-trees, so that the trigger effect spreads its influence through a system cascade-wise.

The word 'inevitable' here may seem unjustified, but when a trigger chain or cascade becomes self-replicating it becomes more prevalent. More of the material of the universe is converted into that set of forms. As this happens there are more instances for chance to work on so as to provide the next stage of the chain or cascade. From then on the modified chain is more prevalent and the chances of the following stage increased. If we threw a barrell of dice, then stuck together all the adjacent sixes, the proportion of doubles sixes would grow. If we now stuck third sixes on whenever they fell together with the double sixes we should soon have an improbable proportion of treble sixes. Continue on these lines and we soon get miracles of improbability.

The order explosion

It is not fanciful to suppose that among the great variety of such hierarchical, heteropotent systems built from quantum indeterminism over the 10^{26} trials some will chance to be morphostatic and autocatalytic, stable and self-replicating.

At the end of any period there will be more of these around than there were at the beginning of it. And this increasing population of 'illegal' or improbable systems is by its nature a cascade reaction in itself, it is an *order explosion;* there will be more of the universe like this as time passes and the morphostatic systems will get more so as the chains and trees get longer, more ordered, more complex.

We can therefore demote the miracle we saw in such effects throughout the Creatura today. Trigger chains and trees make statistical laws inappropriate to heteropotent systems.

Those like me, who try to keep a finger-tip, precarious hold of comprehension on the tail-board of the speeding lorry of advance in microbiology recently are increasingly impressed by the length and complexity of the processes that are being uncovered. Very long, complex, catalytic chains of trigger-like reactions are involved in biochemistry at the atomic level. They show us a world deepening, complexity which threatens to become impenetrable. An article which gives the flavour of this is that by J. E. Rothman in the Scientific American 1985 pp. 88–89. The title is "The Compartmental Organisation of the Golgi Apparatus". The diagram shows just seven out of a long chain of serial catalytic reactions. To represent what is going in tiny sample of the busy complexity contained within the minute span of a cell nucleus Rothman needs to show a chain of eighty boxes in a complex linking.

Even in this small section of a long chain there are numerous exits and entrances to other connected chains so that I begin to compare the complexity of the whole process with that of the neural linkage of the mammal brain and to wonder whether it will ever be open to scientists to comprehend the system as a whole.

It is a parallel to the situation in a vastly larger system; the set of neural connectivities which mediates the typing of these pages. We can comprehend the functioning of a single component, and painfully we can unravel long complex individual causal nervous chain reactions. But we cannot even begin to guess how the whole engine works when all these things are functioning in parallel, concurrently.

Now it might be argued that science is not limited by this complexity. Boyle's Law tells us very accurately the behaviour of gases despite the fact that we can never hope to know the details of the billions of individual interactions of the gas molecules. But the gas molecules are equipotent, of equal power. We can make an enormous comprehension economy because statistical laws, those of large numbers apply. In the biological system this is not so. The elements are catalysts. They are heteropotent. One event of minute energy can trigger a chain or cascade of following events. Comprehension requires an understanding of every link of the process. Laws of mass action are inappropriate.

Rothman shows that the Golgi apparatus, a multi layered structure which lies between the genome and the cell wall, acts as a compartmentalisation system. He explains that this is vital to the functioning of the cell because without it there would be a random mixture of thousands of enzymes and reactions would be chaotic. Each of the vast number of proteins produced by the ribosomes has to be sorted and delivered to the correct compartment of the sorting office by the macromolecules of the many layered Golgi apparatus. In order to be modified correctly each protein must pass through the many stages in correct sequence.

This is all familiar enough to a past Production Director. The modern industrial factory has rediscovered the same system of organisation. We did not know that we were making a system of which we had billions of models within us.

The sociological level echoes the molecular one.

Returning to the theme whatever the primitive proto-creatures were like they must have been able to do something to 'sense' their surroundings. They must have had means of selectivity, to bind to this kind of neighbouring molecule or radical and avoid binding to that. To engulf what is appropriate and eject what was no longer so means selection, which means evidence, information. This involves climbing entropy slopes instead of sliding down them, it means something as odd as falling upwards.

Maxwell's infamous demon, the doorkeeper between two gas chambers, acted as an energy valve, choosing, letting through energetic molecules and thus making more energy available in defiance of the Second Law. The demon had to be intelligent. He would have to have *information* and base *choices* on it to pump order *into* the system, thus making more energy available. Against the Trend.

It is behaviour something like this that the simplest living systems must have stumbled into, including the way of replicating and preserving.

Despite the hypothetical nature of Maxwell's thought experiment demon, he manages to tell us something. The vital essence is the triggerlike control the demon had. He used a very low energy event, perhaps a few photons of light, to trigger a much more energetic event. If the signal had been as energetic as the door action or the fast molecule itself there would have been no gain of available energy, no entropy pumped.

Using signals in this way, it is perfectly possible to make energy available in defiance of the Second Law. Any gleaner picking up seacoal is using a few picowatts of visual information to trigger a few watts of muscular power that bring together the means of making a fire that will drive a locomotive that he could not push with all his strength.

The only thing that explains how the proto-life Creatura did their Maxwell demonry that they were doing something similar, using information to climb entropy slopes.

Let me show the kind of language that is used to describe the activities within a cell. The sense of sorting, choosing, packaging, delivery is very clear and is easily comprehensible in terms which serve in human organisations. This is at least *like* intelligent behaviour and this likeness should not be lightly rejected as having no significance.

THE MORPHOSTAT PROBLEM

If my thesis is accepted, if life is morphostasis, actively preserving form, rejecting all changes except those toward greater stability, then certain conclusions follow . They follow even if morphostasis is merely an *aspect* of all life forms.

It is manifest that morphostatic creatures will have to classify events. There will be two broad classes of events, threats and promises. Since the creatures are in revolt against the Second Law there will be many more events that threaten disturbance to their form than those which climb entropy slopes to maintain and replicate it.

Such creatures will have to be sensitive to any changes in their surroundings that fall into the two classes. They will have to have means to detect and predict such change-events. These *sensors* will have to produce those trigger events called signals which release energetic action within the morphostat (or rather, its physical substrate system) which will reverse threat-changes and exploit opportunity ones.

With the rapid advance in microbiology we are beginning to learn a lot about the chemical signalling systems which we see are needed. Chemical signals and messengers are the primordial ones and most numerous ones in all life forms.

Protozoan trade with environment is optimising, choosing, the selective admission or exclusion of molecules through the cell wall; pocketing some materials from around them and excreting by emptying pockets of waste outside them as they choose. Much of this can go on simultaneously and without co-ordination.

But much must happen in time sequenced phases. This means co-ordination, control. So biological chemical signals must also have the quality of triggeriness, amplification, heteropotency, non-reciprocal chain and cascade effects. They must have these qualities if they are to climb probability slopes. We know that living systems have many triggery catalytic effects.

Consider the definition of 'catalysis': 'the acceleration or retardation of a chemical reaction by a substance which itself undergoes no permanent change . . . . It lowers the energy of activation'. The catalyst has the heteropotency which I suggest is required for making negentropic energy economy.

It has an effect but is not subject to one itself, like any other *instruction* type signal. It can use energy selectively, cause disorder here to build order there.

It is therefore legitimate to classify the whole genome as a catalyst. It is, to be sure, a very large and complex one, but what it is doing is what a catalyst does, inducing and controlling chemical reactions (by the billion) while retaining its form unchanged. It is an extreme example of catalysis, signalling, heteropotency. This is how it achieves negentropy. It builds morphological order at the price of the chemical disorder in its rejected effluents.

But more elaborate (strategic rather than tactical) morphostasis requires organisation and a control centre office or brain, as we shall see.

THE MORPHOSTASIS CONTINUUM AT LOWER LEVELS

Let us scan the morphostasis continuum from bottom upwards. The prokaryotic genome (its control centre, office, brain) takes the form of a single ring-shaped chromosome which is so long that it has to be scrunched up into a diffuse, unstructured looking lump. The long, tangled torus pulls apart into two toruses at cell division. There is none of the complex mitosis that is needed for the more advanced departmentalised organisation system of the eukaryotes. There is no membrane separating the genome from the cell. We can call this a first-order brain. All communication is by chemical signals diffused via the cytoplasm.

The eukaryote organisation centre is a distinct walled off nucleus, which divides into departments called chromosomes for the tricky purpose of replication at mitosis. This serves as the brain for the·more complex protozoa and its signals and messages are again chemical, catalytic. This is the second-order brain.

Plants (metaphyta) are assemblies of millions of separate cells, each group of which specialises in some function. Their cells co-operate well but they have no federal brain supervising the whole colony of cells, the plant. However, plants must obviously have and do have means of cellular inter-communication. A cell has to know its place in the plant-form if all the cells are to assume the right form and produce the right products. The cell gets chemical information from its neighbours which diffuse through the cell wall and activate and deactivate genes, bits of the genome, the right ones for the cell's place and time in the cycle.

Plants are autotrophs, they have the trick of getting energy directly from the sun and building up their form from simple chemicals. With insignificant exceptions, their only behaviour is growing. They have no corporate *motion*. Therefore, the slow-moving diffusion of chemical messengers via the sap is fast enough for them. So metaphyta, too, rely almost entirely on chemical signals. They do without a strategic control centre.

Creatures whose only complex organisation centre is confined to the minute nucleus, where the only sort of brain is a molecule, are very limited in learning power. The genome can only learn the hard way by trial and error. The penalty for error is capital punishment. Evolution has to use life and death as a teaching method.

Multicellular plants and protozoa that rely on such slow communications can only be genoplastic; they eliminate failure by destroying those brains (genomes) with wrong thoughts.* Such creatures are designed fo the centre of broad eco-niches, they cannot deal with short-term problems or exploit ephemeral sub-niches except by the try-and-win-or-die method.

The virus is a special case, a parasitic brain; an organisation centre that infiltrates a cell and pulls off a putsch, or coup, taking over the control of a host cell body. (Some say the eukaryote nucleus is simply a symbiote virus.)

Nerves: metazoan signalling

Metazoa developed another life-style, a parasitic one. Animals are heterotrophs, life-form predators. They build and maintain their form on the destruction of other life forms. That life-style is more active, more competitive. For predators and browsers much movement pays off, and the faster and the more skilful the better.

Seeping chemical diffusion came to be too slow a means of communication between cells. A faster, more strategic communications network was needed. The next development was that of nerves. Within a nerve the electric impulses flick along a chain of relays in microseconds. Nerves talk to each other across synapses via high-speed neurotransmitters over tiny distances.

The channel of communication, the neural network, is especially designed for communication. A new kind of organisation and organisation centre therefore arose, a *third-order* brain, an intercellular control centre and communications *network*. The whole mobile cell-colony called an animal developed strategic control to supplement the localised tactical control of the minute genome brains.

Ontoplasticity

Animals had a new possibility. They could become ontoplastic. They could adapt much more closely to smaller tighter, more detailed and specific eco-niches, learning *within* a generation.

Having a fast telegraph system, they could benefit from many types of sensor to gather more and more elaborate environmental information. They could move when threatened and to get food. They could be viable in larger

*'Wrong thoughts' are of course any genetic patterns which lower probability of survival or reproductiveness.

wider eco-niches because they had the choices brought by mobility and a better means of information leading to more options and chance of selection between them. They had more choice. They could *find* suitable niches.

I now take a look at the more advanced type of brain, the seat of the highest form of the intelligence that we are examining. This is the outward form of *our* intelligence tool, the one that is trying, presumptuously, to model itself. The description is of the gross visible features. It has little immediate congruence with the model of information flow I am developing, but is a preliminary reminder of the physical form that the topological (or connectional) form must use as substrate. The flow architecture I shall describe exists as a connectivity network within what I shall describe, if it exists at all.

Mammal brain: human brain

In its size, class and fighting weight, the seat of human intelligence, the brain, is the most powerful, dangerous and promising entity in the universe. That much plutonium can make a biggish bang but a single governing, human brain with its heteropotent effect on a social morphostat can trigger many bigger ones, change the biosphere, bust the moon apart, defy the statistical laws of nature or . . . or . . . name it!

It is very different indeed from anything else of its scale. We have to look at something about 9 orders smaller to find something in the same class of wild incredibility. We have to look at the nucleus of the living cell. Are we not looking at something related?

If we probe into the mammal brain we find a level of organisation and incomprehensible complexity which makes it, small as it is, by far the most complex, local, holistically functioning system known in the mesocosm.

Known? Known to whom or what? Known to itself! Here is a recursion to end all recursions. Self-consciousness enters the syntactical paradox world where subject and object, knower and known merge. You can have knowledge of knowing about knowledge about knowledge . . . . Observer dependency and complementarity is not only a problem when we look at the microcosm. It affects epistemology and psychology too.

The accepted paradigm for the material universe (in the mesocosm) is one where effect follows cause in time. Brains reverse this. The brain anticipates, predicts future events, and the prediction of tomorrow's events governs today's behaviour. The effect, the behaviour, precedes the cause, the future event. The birth of baby today caused its mother to knit little vests three months ago. The brain reverses the temporal order of causality. It induces negative causality, time reversal.

Filing, sorting and accessing data is now well understood thanks to computers but there are things that the brain can do that defy the comprehension of the computer scientist. Remembering the brain's slow processing speed (a few dozen Hz), how can we explain a classification system that gives us instant access to long complex memories on the basis of a minute irrelevant signal? A whiff of a smell will bring back detailed memories of a whole forgotten childhood sequence of events.

Consider these crossword clues which many people solved.

Clue: (5 letters). HIJKLMNO

Answer: 'Water'. (H to O thus H_2O)

Or this:

Clue: (9 letters). Leaving us unwillingly

Answer: 'Intestate'

What kind of computer could make the wild changes of frame of reference to get to such answers?

May I remind you what a brain is like physically? Simplifying, a human brain is a Russian doll system of three brains, one within another. The original brain or paleocortex is the deepest layer. This corresponds to the reptile brain, which has been twice overlaid in subsequent evolution. The second enwrapped layer of the parcel is the limbic system or archicortex, which we share with the other mammals and only partially with the reptiles. This part of the brain is probably over 150 million years old. It appears to be the seat of our emotional life. Above it is the neocortex, which exists in other mammals but which has been developed in the primates and massively so in man. The neocortex is credited with the great difference in cognitive (communicable, symbolic) intelligence between man and the other mammals.

The neocortex is divided into the two massive cerebral hemispheres which have an intricately riffled and infolded surface like a walnut only much more so. The two cortices (surfaces) thus have an area of about a quarter of a square metre. The convoluted surface of the neocortex is 3 mm thick and consists of about ten billion intricately intertwined neurones, the communicative brain cells. They are packed in a vast putty-like mass of supportive glial cells. The neurones are very strange cells. Exceedingly complex and variable, they fall into a number of classes. Some types are much ramified at either end of a long, containing, insulating tube called the axon. The intricately intertwined spaghetti of neurones within this shell of the neocortex are very densely packed indeed so that it is a serious problem to make out their pathways and interconnections. The cell body is usually at the input end, and the hundreds of probing dendrites or thin tendrils reach out from it and contact other cells at thousands of synapses or connecting points on the body or processes of other contacting neurones. A neurone can be over a metre long yet 3000 can be packed into a cubic millimetre. The whole intertwined basket of octopuses is packed in like the myriad fibres in the baize of a billiard table. That is a simplified description of a thinking tool, a tiny entity in the universe that can, in some degree, make a model of it and predict its future.

A good deal is known about functions of gross features of the mammalian brain and even more about the human brain. There are specific functions associated with defined areas of the cortex, visual reception areas at the back of the skull, a memory centre in the amygdala, speech areas in the temporal lobes and there has been an accurate mapping of the motor centres of the various parts of the musculature, arms, legs, mouth, tongue, hands, fingers and so on. The archicortex seems to be associated with the appetitive, (instinctive, emotional) functions in the animal and sends streams of excitation to all parts of the brain. Pain and pleasure centres have been found but there is little understanding of how they work. The cerebellum seems to have a very important role in co-ordinating movement.

This crude mapping has been done by careful and systematic observation of the effect of lesions in various parts of the brain on many thousands of patients, many of them First and Second World War soldiers with head wounds.

The brain is, as I said, dual. There is a great cleft between the two halves, which are joined by a thick commissure made of packed fibres at the base. By cutting this commissure it has been shown that in many ways the two parts work separately yet without apparent conflict. There are a lot of left brain/right brain theories and discussions at the popular level but little consensus. The duality of the physical brain may be an essential feature of its function or, more likely, I believe, a contingent effect of the basic symmetry ground plan of the vertebrates. All types of learning, including evolution, have to start from where they are and vertebrates are symmetrical about a spine. No duality is essential in the primitive brain model I advance but, if only because redundancy is essential to the model, duality does not conflict with it.

So much for the most complex and advanced sort of brain we know, that is confined to one contiguous mass. We may now look at a brain that is very much more difficult to see as such, a dispersed and/or intermittent one, the brain of a morphostat that is dispersed in space/time. I speak of a brain in which the only essential feature of any brain, intercommunication, passes through much more space and time to connect its elements. Dispersed and intermittent intelligences are those intelligences belonging to and working to preserve morphostats of which the elements themselves are the morphostats called animals (which are themselves composed of the morphostats called cells). It is of these third-order morphostats that I now draw attention.

THE SIGNALS OF THE SOCIOZOA

Atoms fell into stable forms, molecules. Molecules fell into form-preserving arrangements, crystals and then information-guided morphostats, cells. Cells fell into stable arrangements, animals, with nervous information systems. Did it end there?

If separate animals can fall into a co-operative symbiotic mode, can develop the essential of any morphostat – an internal communication system, is there any reason why they cannot form and be part of even higher level morphostats? As I have defined and illustrated the paradigm 'morphostat', it would be improper to exclude many intercommunicating social groups of animals from it.

Zoology is full of examples of symbiotic colonies of animals which live, feed, grow, divide and thrive as a result of sociality and social communication. Swarms, herds, schools, flights, colonies, nests – there are scores of names for these third-order morphostats, these assemblies, colonies, which 'behave' as though they had the 'purpose' of preserving, with as little change as possible, their form through time.

Mutual signalling, the sign of a morphostasis

I have argued that the visible sign of a morphostat is a *mutual* signalling system or communications system. I have argued that all mutual signal systems indicate the presence of a morphostat. So to call the class collectivities of animals 'morphostats' is not to make an analogy. That act of recognition results from an act of taxonomy, the formulation of a class of entities. We are always entitled to do this. When we do we must try to see if the new class, as a whole, has characteristics which are useful and relevant; characteristics by which what we observe in one subclass can give us predictive hints about another subclass.

It is only in my lifetime that we have gradually seen how very closely plants, animals and micro-organisms are related. Then we found the genome which confirms that all are built on an astonishingly similar plan. It is as though the genome 'program' has a 'menu' (to talk computerese) which allows it to opt for yeast, slime moulds, cabbages or Einsteins at choice.

Important advances in knowledge often come from insights which show that phenomena we thought to be disparate were really different aspects of the same thing. Falling apples and planetary orbits are only one example. (The opposite is, of course, also true. Seeing distinctions which divide a class can lead to better comprehension and prediction.)

The idea that an interacting social group qualifies as a being is not new. Much of the language of politics derives from the Roman analogy of the State with the body, 'organisation' from 'organs', etc. The paradigm was very powerful and it may be no accident that it was one which led to a large and very influential empire. In William Shakespeare's *Coriolanus* (1.1) Menenius tries using a parable to pacify the citizens who were rioting against the rich patricians:

"There was a time when all the body's members rebell'd against the belly; thus accused it; –

That only like a gulf it did remain
I'th midst o'th body, idle and inactive,
Still cupboarding the viand never bearing
Like labour with the rest, where th'other instruments
Did see and hear, devise, instruct, walk, feel,
And mutually participate, did minister
Unto the appetite and affection common
Of the whole body. – – –''

Menenius then goes on to explain how the stomach does its work and distributes the results via the blood stream. The strength and usefulness of the model of the State as a body is manifest. Some such comprehension tool is essential to a developing society which is breaking old habits and ways and urging people into new roles so that a much larger and more complex, more viable social creature, sociozoon, can find ways to survive.

However, the analogy with a human body was too crude and had to break down. It is my suggestion that all morphostats have a similar set of problems and though they may be working at very different levels there may be instructive parallels about the solutions that are found. At all levels morphostats will have aspects that are more open to enquiry. By cross fertilisation at several levels we may raise insight, understanding and the object of these, prediction. By understanding how data processing and intelligence work at the various primitive levels we may, in the end, be able to bypass the genome and develop intelligences which are not constrained by 4 billion years of biological clutter. Some present attempts at A.I. seem like trying to make robot horses to draw carriages instead of making horseless carriages as Herr Mercedes did.

Sociozoan communication is primitive

First, I have to admit that sociozoa, though they may have a great future in the next few billion years, are fairly primitive today. Measured by the actual *amount* of information measured in bits, which passes between most animals in social groups, it is very small indeed compared with the enormous internal exchanges. It is like the exchanges between countries in the Middle Ages. A few million richly interacting people 'talk' to another such group via a single ambassador. One animal with billions of richly intercommunicating cells and nerves utters a one bit warning cry. But it starts a herd into flight and saves lives.

The signals that pass between social insects within the sociozoon called a colony, swarm, nest or hive are quite elaborate compared with the primitive ones that pass between, say, the birds in a flock or the fish in a school. Precise metric, cognitive (symbolic) information about the locality of food is passed by bee-dance, antenna-touch. This is qualitatively different from the imprecise danger squawks of birds, or even the conative (emotional) rather than cognitive cries of many social mammals. Most of the 'higher' animals have little more than the power to express emotions, such as fear, rage, sexual readiness, submission, dominance, and sometimes 'food here' without location information. Yes, the insect sociozoa beat man by megayears in the race towards cognitive communication, but they had an earlier start. Also, their language is hardware, not software, genoplastic, not ontoplastic. They take many thousands of generations to learn each phrase.

THE LEVELS OF INTELLIGENCE

With interesting exceptions like the above, the continuum of intelligence, of brain complexity, seems to run parallel with the morphostasis continuum outlined earlier.

The cell nucleus is one very complex brain-like system, the neural brain is another on an entirely different scale and level. Yet they work in close concert, their activities mesh together perfectly while each works independently at its own level. We have morphostatic nodes within morphostats.

The effects of physical interference with brain, such as by trauma, durgs, etc., tell us this. The activity we are conscious of, our thoughts, are closely bound up with events that are happening to the ephemeral molecules and the more permanent cells in our brain. But we know nothing of the activity of the ten billion genomes of our neurones. And to expect those genomes to *know* about the brain of which they are part would be folly of exceptional purity.

Now let us trace intelligence *up* (just in mass) one further step. Concede that the neural brains in a sociozoon morphostat, a herd, jointly create a co-operative behaviour pattern that helps the herd to survive. The signals that pass from one animal to another modify the internal communications system and the result is herd behaviour which is emergent from and includes animal behaviour. The herd behaviour may be directed by one leader but this is not always so. An enormous school of fish will wheel as a body without visible command.

Either way the total effect, the herd behaviour, is the result of the whole of its set of nervous systems brought into unity by inter-animal communication. This is a primitive version of the system in your body, that by which your cells exhibit unified behaviour based on neural communication. It is a fair parallel of the set of brain cells which are in uncomprehending co-operation to produce your thoughts as you read these words.

HUMAN SOCIOZOA

It is obvious that I have to apply the 'sociozoa' concept to humanity. How well does it fit? If the congruence or fit of the model is good enough it may be useful to see human social assemblies as form-preserving entities.

Certainly my personal experience of many score of organisations and institutions amply confirms the view that they are inherently conservative, none more so than those that label themselves radical or revolutionary. Those that were not conservative seem to have been ephemeral

Apart from personal observation, I have read about and heard of many human collectivities. All those that merit the name 'organisation' or 'institution' were the same. For all, the Principal Name of The Game was preserving the form (a set of role relationships) with as little change as possible through time.

Institutions formed for a specific *purpose* often survive long after it is achieved. Many continue for generations, paying nothing but lip-service to anything but the *real,* but often tacit, aim of all known morphostats, survival.

Human purposive sociozoa, institutions set up to further a group cause or serve an interest are, biologically, a very new idea. Until the last few millennia all co-operating human groups were like those in New Guinea and in the Amazon basin today, *purely* survival groups. They had no purpose except preserving the tribal structure, its growth and reproduction, the elementary requirements of morphostasis.

For almost all of man's history the successful social pattern was this small hunter-gatherer tribe. Only around one thousandth of the life of the tool-making hominids has been post-tribal.

In a book with this title we must naturally be concerned with the last small sample, the one extraordinary thousandth, the miraculously improbable intelligence explosion that started when agriculture arose and made large viable groups possible. This happened only a few millennia ago!

The subsequent coalescence of tribes into kingdoms and republics, and of these into alliances and empires, the emergence of that strange unbiological coalescence, the present co-operating, intercommunicating and interacting world civilisation and culture, is another uncomfortably miraculous event that fits badly with the rest of biology.

It is certainly still true that most human sociozoa such as ethnic, religious and cultural groups, commercial and industrial firms, farming groups, etc., have no real-life purpose other than survival and growth. In this they are the same as any animal or bacterium. The more recent invention the Nation State, is much the same.

However, we also see the astonishing emergence at another level of complex world-scale form-preserving information networks like the commercial and industrial markets, the science, business, legal, banking, maritime, cultural, artistic, entertainments, communications, technological, academic, and many other networks and communities, all interwoven and interacting, nearly all arising spontaneously in the last few centuries. It is mysterious and needs a lot of explanation on accepted paradigms.

I say again, 'How come that creatures which slowly adapted for millions of years to life as small groups of hunter-gatherers on plains or in forests have suddenly swarmed together into an enormous network of tightly organised and highly successful, interacting networks of organisations?''

It may seem odd that I set solid-seeming men and their immaterial associations in the same class. But both are form, not substance. It is hard to hold this in mind. You are not a solid mass of molecules. What you are is the form that may be taken up by any such set. You are a river whose source is your mouth and whose mouth is your anus. You are like a tribe or a limited liability company – immaterial, self-preserving form, not substance.

The miracle of human tribes that suddenly swarm together like slime moulds to form a giant world-scale fourth-order sociozoon, the present world culture, is going to take a lot of abolishing.

Perhaps the first clue to the answer was given by the economist Adam Smith. He posited 'engine', already mentioned, a mysterious hidden hand that worked behind the scenes to arrange that all the autonomous self-interested behaviour of citizens somehow merges and combines to produce a beneficial, stable and autonomous economic distribution system. This happens in any area where individual behaviour is not too much constrained by tribal norms or where law and order are maintained by the evolution of a libertarian government tolerant of free traders and artisans.

The market as a brain

Smith's intangible 'market' is an emergent primitive societal brain which collates and combines all the signals of need and desire from millions of people in their consumer roles, processes them and transduces them into that enormous set of detailed instructions received by the same citizens in their role as producers at the work place.

Result: a closer match between what gets produced and what is required, between supply and demand than has been observed under any other system. Workshops, mines, distribution chains, farms are started and halted, products changed, batches ordered, people move, voluntarily, each doing his or her own thing, yet the total result is a highly optimised balance of needs and desires with supplies. The whole machine works without monocentric control and planning and the whole vastly complex system arose like Topsy, it was not born but 'it just growed'. Out of nothing?

A billion autonomous selfish people interact, exchange information and co-operate unconsciously in a system to preserve the form of unknown institutions by which they survive. The elements of a cell co-operate and communicate (chemically) so that its form shall survive. The cells of an animal co-operate and communicate (neurally) so that its form shall survive. In no case do the elements seem to be under any straightforward central direction. It was this thought that set me on the long track to the writing of this book. It is this parallel, this congruence, which may tell us more than we knew before.

The cell and the brain remain, largely, black boxes. But the communications systems sociozoa are patent, open to view. We can see how well the pattern of information flow we observe in society fits with the pattern we can barely make out at the molecular and the morphological levels. We can (and are) trying out computer models based on the sociological level to simulate the neural level. It seems to fit, so we may hope to find out more about all three levels of what appears to be a single class of entity.

Readers who deplore the patent imperfections of market methods are invited to look round the world at those economies where the market works freely and those where monohierarchic central control is felt to be a better optimiser for the satisfaction of needs and desires. It seems to be broadly true that, in free economies, living standards tend to be higher, even for the poor, welfare better, and freedom greater, including the much exercised freedom to complain. A greater variety of goods and services is more freely available, but there is more envy, politics and general dissent. If there is an example of a centralist government that does better at getting the right amount of goods and services available in a more efficient way, then that economy is keeping its success to itself, because I have not heard of it. Perfect the market is *not*. Something better we cannot find.

The picture of the market as a self-organising system that works in some way independently of the will or thoughts of any one person may seem strange but there are many examples, as Friederich Hayek points out, of similar apparently rational processes which arise unbidden from the interactions of many brains. For a culture, a language is a strange unified communications system, a form that is retained and evolved through time with little or no central intention or planning. It is a morphostat that subsists on the insubstantial substrate of human cognitive intercommunication. There are many human cultural, artistic, religious, business, technological, religious, scholastic and moral traditions that are similar types of entity.

The brain as a control centre?

However much we may be intuitively attracted to the Roman Empire model, the model of the central control system, with a government acting in the role of the control centre or brain, we have to be cautious when we see the above examples of apparently spontaneous undirected self-organisation. The brain itself shows no signs of congruence with a hierarchic control centre paradigm. The cell level organisation is an equally mysterious black box, like the market, that fourth-order brain. This thought is offered as a confirmation of one thing Marx claimed, that detailed central control was inessential. States, he suggested, would eventually 'wither away'. However, the system of social classification by social and occupational class is unpredictive and inadequate. Those vast classes are too large and too fuzzy. We need tighter categories if we are to have hopes of a predictive science of sociology.

But institutions are morphostats. That goes even for communist parties and governments. They will be around for a long time like London's ancient Guilds.

THE CONTROL OF COMPLEX SYSTEMS

I want to suggest that there is a fundamental flaw in the traditional model of organisation which bedevils our thinking about it. The organisation chart which we have in our minds, that of a monocentric hierarchy leading down from a chief executive to a ramified structure of departments and subdepartments is muddled and deceiving.

The central problem of any organisation, in the light of the morphostasis concept, is to counter change tendencies from many sources. There are always many ways in which a morphostat can lose order, many variables to be kept within some sufficiency boundaries (to be kept sufficiently close to some optimum state). Therefore, for any complex entity to preserve its form it must organise; form organs to specialise in the numerous different homeostatic tasks. Nearly all of these have to work simultaneously and autonomously. Many must have their own sensors, their means of detecting change threats or opportunity promises. The whole of the world of autotrophs, the world of vegetation, a vast range of complex forms, survives and flourishes with this kind of polycentric control.

The organisation of all the protozoa and nearly all the activity of the metazoa is tactical, not mediated from one centre but polycentric. Most of what is going on, even in an animal, most of the time is autonomic, self-regulating, the body is kept functioning because all its parts detect and respond to local inputs. The strategic level perceptuo-motor behaviour we see in more advanced creatures, the behaviour mediated by brain-controlled muscles, is more obvious and dramatic but it is, in terms of the volume of data-processing, only minor. Most of the data-processing is tactical, specialist, autonomous and at cellular level. It is only in what are classed as the 'higher' animals that there is anything like central strategic control at all. Setting priorities and *doing one thing at a time* is seen only at the top of the morphostasis continuum.

The strategic level, deciding priorities on multiple goals that cannot be achieved simultaneously, became essential because of the more active life, first of opportunists like predators, and then defensively of their prey. This development drove them to develop brains with a system of priorities, with flexible attention, a strategic control system. Browsing is vital to herbivore life but fleeing from predators takes priority at some times, so does drinking, sex, and breeding at other times. Central data-processing with means to give priorities and emphases is needed. But that does not necessarily mean CPU-type* central control, as I shall try to show.

Konrad Lorenz pointed out that human tribes and even nations have two mental modes, the normal gathering mode and the occasional hunter, warrior mode. He suggested two entirely different types of behaviour, two programs on a computer-like 'menu', which can be selected according to circumstances. In the 'military enthusiasm' role the same person responds differently from how he would in the other one. The man who avoids a scuffle in one role will charge a machine-gun nest in the other.

Man in the hunter/warrior mode must be more leader-prone than as a gatherer or cultivator. Thus the need for two modes of behaviour. The natural pattern in small groups was that of a single leader for hunting and was an autonomous action for gathering vegetable food.

The same central leader pattern served very well even when tribes began to coalesce, there were warrior leaders who, because of informational constraints grew instructional, (motor) hierarchies with several strata beneath them, commander, officers, sergeants, etc. This leadership pattern is deeply engrained in our traditions and possibly in our genetic nature because it was very suitable for our long stint as small hunter-gatherer groups. So our much larger and more complex institutions are built round a monocentric mental model.

However very large institutions cannot, for data-processing reasons, work in monocentric mode except intermittently in very exceptional circumstances such as war. The problem is very simple. In a monohierarchic system over a certain size, where all information has to be channelled to a single apex, the upper strata and especially the apex itself become overloaded and cannot cope with the rate of data flow. Organisation, forming specialist departments (both on the afferent and on the efferent side of the apical leader) becomes necessary. Eventually these 'organs' need and get less and less input from the apical figure. They become autonomous and the system is transformed into another form.

If we examine the actual flow of information and instructions in a large organisation I suggest it would not look remotely like its monocentric authority or organisation chart which is supposed to be the guide to the thinking of those in the network (see Figure 2).

I do not think we are going to be able to understand the various levels of intelligence or create artificial intelligence on a monocentric model. I shall propose another model which has a better congruence with reality and which may be a better ground plan for an artificial brain.

* = Computer central processing unit.

EVOLUTION AND LEARNING REQUIRE RANDOMNESS

Philosophers, so far, have been people. But recent work on computer pattern recognition shows that in taking perception as their starting point, a simple 'given', they have failed to see its vital importance or its complexity. They have modelled in ignorance of the fact that for people, including philosophers, perception is largely ontoplastic not genoplastic, a learned skill, not a given, hardwired propensity. Learning involves trial and error, trying models and rejecting or improving them over many of trials. The very act of seeing is an inductively acquired skill. Adults do not remember that primary baby learning, the hard-won skills in learned taxonomy and pattern recognition are taken for granted. People, philosophers among them, are too familiar with their adult world to see all that was involved in entering it.

Trial and error require experimental variety

It is obvious that trial and error in the completely unsophisticated beginner must involve an input of penny-toss randomness. Complete ignorance must try anything. Options for trial must be created, just as genetic mutations must arise before they can be selected. In evolution it is widely accepted that mutations are random. I suggest that at first all and later at least some of the activity of learning involves an input of true randomness. A baby which has very few genoplastic behaviour patterns, almost no preconceptions about what is the right behaviour response, needs to experiment with as little constraint as possible if it is to hit on the right combinations of instructions to muscle fibres.

In this context randomness could be defined as complete absence of constraints on options. Therefore the desirable source of the options required should be as close to being truly random as possible. To see this clearly we have only to look at the enormous range and variety of human skills. Skaters, acrobats, jugglers, artists, all produce a vast range of complex, intricate, incredible behaviour patterns, many of which seem to be unbiological in that they cannot be necessary to survival. How can all the required option doors be kept open if there are many hardwired constraints?

True randomness is microcosmic

In the heavily statistical world of the mesocosm the only source of pure randomness is the world of quantum weirdness in the microcosm. To draw on this in the mesocosm it must be amplified enormously. Such amplification is possible. A Geiger counter does it, it produces a mesocosmic click for a microcosmic electron or photon. The British Post Office savings lottery system uses a computer called ERNIE which draws on quantum randomness

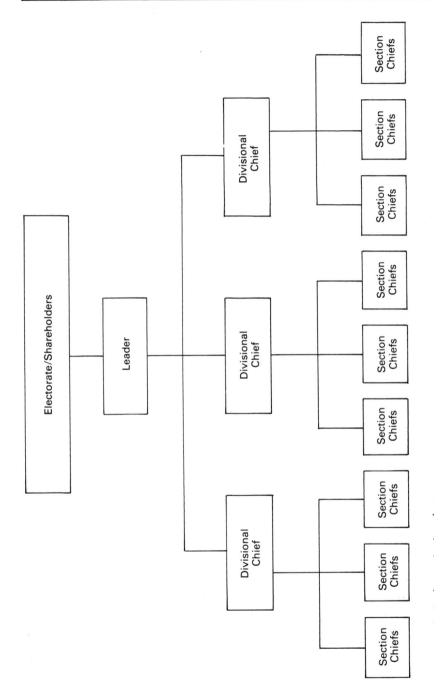

Figure 2 Typical organisation chart

to award prizes. The very great electronic amplification factor is based on complex technology.

Microcosmic events can change a cell

A single cell such as a receptor is an enormously large system compared with an electron, so the statistical laws of large numbers ought to apply fully. It would seem to be impossible for the minute remote impact of a fundamental particle to be amplified so enormously as to make detectable changes in a human nerve cell.

But they do. Experiments have shown that, marginally, a human eye can score better than chance expectation at detecting a few photons of light. Further, we know that radiation can convert a healthy cell to a cancerous one or cause a genetic mutation. Radiation is a quantum effect, a step function, there must be a step difference between a cancer-causing amount and an amount less than that.

The amplification of quantum events

Quantum level events, therefore can indeed trigger changes in cells. Further, we may reasonably posit that cells, being heteropotent and intercommunicating, may, must form trigger-trees and cascades by which an event in a single cell can trigger a much larger action in a brain and then in a musculature. The action thus triggered in one person's brain can be sent by hierarchical social cascades to a society where that brain commands or influences many others. A marginal quantum event in a particle can trigger the movement of an army!

RANDOMNESS AND PSEUDO-RANDOMNESS

Nearly all computers have a means of generating pseudo-random numbers. It is claimed that when these are used in learning programs they are indistinguishable from true randomness. I beg leave to doubt the claim. Firstly, I have too often found that I am in a highly constrained recursive loop when I have used pseudo-random numbers in learning programs. Secondly, as I have said, quantum randomness is without constraints, while pseudo-randomness must, in any physical system, have some constraints if only those of computer time.

Take for instance the time intervals between gamma ray emissions from a radioactive substance. This is a truly random magnitude which can have any real number value in femtoseconds between some upper and lower practical limit. An infinite number of such real numbers would be required to represent the possible variety. As I have said, any practical system for producing pseudo-random number must impose some constraints on the real numbers it could produce between these intervals. Merely expressing them in any conceivable number system would be an important constraint. There would be too many decimal places after the zero!

Pseudo-randomness is fully constrained in that it is deterministic. The reason it can be used in learning programs at all is that its input is *irrelevant* to the particular process in hand and so can produce previously untried options. However, being determined, pseudo-randomness has limits to the variety of untried options it can offer. True randomness has, by definition, no such constraints and where can it be found, in mechanical terms, except in the microcosm?

RANDOMNESS IS PROMOTED TO HIGHER LEVELS

What I suggest must happen in animal and especially human learning is that as learning advances and becomes more sophisticated the *randomness applies to more and more complex and developed systems*. It moves up into the network, affecting areas at a more strategic level. That may seem strange at first sight but consider this.

The learning baby needs trial and error to learn the simplest basic skills, how to move groups of muscle fibres in unison, then a limb to the left, to the right. As these subskills are assembled into skills they become more repeatable, more deterministic, less random *at that level,* but at the higher level where subskills are being combined into skills there is still trial and error and the need for random input. Later, with skills having gone hardwired as it were, the randomness input needs to move to more senior, more strategic levels still as skills are assembled into behaviour patterns. Until these are learned there is still a need for random input but now it affects penny-toss choices among much more developed behaviour trains. The random input moves distally, inwards, away from the peripheral and tactical zones towards the central and strategic ones as the learning process goes on.

The baby makes tiny behavioural elements deterministic, as it learns, then assemblies of them become so, then assemblies of those and so on. After a time the child has a large and growing repertoire of fully determined skills, abilities, whole temporal trains of behaviour.

But where is the random input now? It is now offering options about prolonged periods of skilled activity. Random, experimental trial behaviour now applies to these. Can we falsify this? Is this stage observable in babies? We cannot falsify it. We see such a stage. It is called play. The randomness now applies to what role the child takes and what game is played, no longer to which muscle fibres are moved and how much.

Does this process finish with childhood? Not in man. In adults, sport, pastimes, hobbies, games, gambling, whole life schemes with no direct biological benefit continue. At that age the random input is given other names. Free-will, autonomy, whim?

Free-will, whim, perversity

Consider free-will. If our behaviour is the sensible and proper response to the informational input, the data store in memory and appetitive needs all the time, it is not free. It is deterministic, the only possible output from the input. It is only when it runs counter to the obvious, where there is an element of self-will, whim, perversity, that it can be called really free. This is unachievable by an automat. Yet we cling obstinately to our power to be whimsical, to behave in spite of indications and not because of them. Is not this precisely the freedom which we are ready to die to preserve?

Do we die to preserve our right to behave illogically? Yes, and rightly so because the whole business of learning is itself illogical, trying options randomly rather than because we know how they will turn out. Lose whim, lose learning, lose progress. Logic is a determined chain. Learning is necessarily indeterminate.

The random input moves up the scale and into the network from the tactical level at muscle fibres, to skills, and then longer and longer term strategic behaviour trains.

Where does the process finish? At the limit, whole policies which may last years come into the region of arbitrary choice. Our whole mind set and path through life may have started as random choices. Really free choices. Those which could have been different.

The perception of free-will

Let me come straight out with it. Let us look at what is so much disputed between philosophers, free-will versus predestination. Following the reasoning above our perception of free-will is the last vestige of the random function at the end of its journey up the tactical/strategic ladder. Can my treasured free-will be just quantum weirdness borrowed from a senseless particle?

This is a hard pill to swallow and I obviously balk at it myself. But I have to show where the argument leads. There is a difficult question. If free-will is not this, how could we tell? What is free-will but the desire be free to do the unobvious? The obvious, a computer can do, must do. A Von Neumann computer is the least free thing of its size and complexity in the mesocosm, designed to be so. Is that what we want to be like?

When we see free-will operating it is impossible to say that we are not seeing a microcosmically generated event, like the click of a Geiger counter. Only bigger.

Caveat. An *apparently* free choice is often much constrained by unseen things below conscious level; there are usually only a few *true* options. To the extent that our will is influenced by these unconscious inputs it is determined, not free, the true freedom remains only at the last most strategic level. Here we plump for one among a small number of highly favoured, strongly indicated options. At this point the randomness that used to offer options to muscle fibres as a baby will now operate on decisions that affect the rest of our life. Whom shall I marry? Which job shall I take? Which book or invention idea shall I work on?

It would be disturbing if our will free turns out to be free alright, but not ours, just borrowed microcosmic randomness.

The alternative involves something like Julian Huxley's idea. Mind, sapience, he implied, is immanent, it is a hidden aspect of the material of the universe. My argument here shows how it might penetrate the mesocosmic material world. But this is an unfalsifiable and unnecessary hypothesis which offends both Popper and Occam!

Without it, if we follow the morphostasis continuum, we have a world in which more and more of the universe is making larger and larger experiments with random options commanded by events at the lowest level.

AN INTERPOLATION ABOUT PSYCHOMETRICS

For a book about intelligence we seem to have got a long way without mention of psychometrics, the art (rather than the science) of mental measurement.

In the context of this book it is obvious that the life of every morphostat depends on its perception of its environment and its judgements about how to respond to it.

For autonomous people in unforced social association a vital part of perception is that of the other people in the association. Individual and group success for human beings depends deeply on complex co-operation. That requires that they all make adequate predictions about the behaviour of fellow members. Making judgements about each other is of first importance and that is why there has grown up an immense language of description applying to personal differences in temperament, character, behaviour, personality. In order to communicate judgements about behavioural probabilities there are such words as brave, lazy, curious, inquisitive, miserable, enterprising, dull-witted, aggressive and many thousands more like them. The need for this language is obvious. It improves social co-operation and makes it possible for people to work together, to know whom to trust for what and how much, whom to help, whom to oppose, etc.

I am labouring the obvious for a reason. As I mentioned earlier we seem to have been, for a few dozen years, in a strange new intellectual climate in which some thinkers express the verbal belief that making judgements about each other is not, as previously thought, absolutely essential to group survival but in some way harmful and divisive. The fruitful and valuable idea that societies work well when each member has relatively equal legal rights and opportunities has been extended to the extraordinary notion that they should and can be treated as clone-mates rather than as the unique individuals that they are.

This is a book about intelligence and in the field of individual differences all B-believe and all but the above mentioned group V-believe that there are very marked differences between people in the quality to which we give the names intelligence, sapience, cleverness; the ability to see relationships, to make effective and predictive mental models, to deal with data and solve problems.

This group, from the best motivation and with real sincerity (of the verbal belief kind), claim that the manifest differences in thinking power between people are explained by environmental factors such as poverty or are an illusion, a reification, or false model. Luckily, such beliefs are purely verbal. They affect only what is said and written and never what is done. Even the most ardent human 'clonist' (as we might call them) decides who is to be appointed, trusted, employed, or consulted without the use of dice or a random number table. They visibly and rightly make judgements about people and act on them.

The art of intelligence testing is an obvious target because it reveals what is thought to be immoral to know, the differences in ability and potential among people. It is because there has been a sustained and damaging campaign by the clonists against the very concept intelligence (in this narrow sense) that they merit this parenthesis. The V-belief is beginning to make the vital task of fitting people to roles more difficult and is causing much misapplied human effort in trying to do things without available information.

There are known to be genetic factors which partially decide, other things being equal, how tall people are to be. This does not mean that anyone claims there is such an objective reality in the genome as 'tallness'. 'Intelligent' is a description of a position on a rough judgement continuum about thinking power which has been reached by a very widespread consensus.

An intelligence test is simply an early example of what, since Edward Feigenbaum's book *The Fifth Generation,* is called an expert system, a way of improving, grouping and standardising expert human judgements and there-fore making them more universal, less partial, fairer.

As I have pointed out in previous books, the sort of intelligence that we are trying to measure in our social judgements (and that formalisation of those judgements, intelligence tests) is social intelligence, verbal or cognitive intelli-gence, the sort of strategic level conscious intelligence that is more a social than individual phenomenon. It is that very special kind of symbolic coded intelligence that is communicable between the units of that special kind of sociozoon, a human institution.

The limitation of intelligence tests is that they depend largely on language. Even the so-called Culture Fair tests involve the comprehension of such artificial conventions as diagrams. These are good when you have been exposed to them but are less predictive or unpredictive when used on subjects who are unfamiliar with the conventions. This means that there are two banal stupidities which are repeated endlessly about IQ tests. One is that because they are not fully valid except on the language/cultural group upon which they were standardised they are of no value at all. The other is the false circularity, that what we call intelligence is only 'what intelligence tests measure'. It is quite clear that within a culture group, tests do, more fairly and systematically, what we are all doing all the time anyway, judging how bright people are. It is equally clear that the further a subject is from the culture and language of the standardisation group the less useful and predictive the test is for him or her. However, my long experience in this field convinces me that the brighter the subject is the less the cultural differences matter in psychometric measurement. The higher the flyer, the more you can trust the mental test.

5

The nature of information

The meaning of the word 'information' given in the *Oxford Dictionary* is 'formation or moulding of the mind or character; training, instruction, teaching; communication of instructive knowledge'.

However, the development of modern communications together with what emerges from studies of the brain and the cell have caused a gradual extension of the meaning envelope of the word. I have pointed out that the systems that communications and data processing engineers had to invent for social communication proved to have uncanny echoes in those two entirely different spheres. Brain, cell, computer, telephone network; they are utterly different in every way. Yet in spite of greatly differing origins, scales, dispersions and materials, they fell naturally and immediately into a common linking paradigm. This was the new extended meaning for the word 'information' which has been developing and elaborating all this century. Terms, concepts, algorithms, modalities, from all these disparate levels were exchanged and found to be applicable and predictive. What is nature trying to tell us? Let us see.

Nothing can live without information systems (in this extended meaning). Men know of no information system without biological connections and purposes. Information is a biological phenomenon.

THE COMMON FEATURES OF INFORMATION SYSTEMS

What are the common features which unite these different systems? The first and most obvious point of resemblance between life systems and information systems is that the essence, the message itself and the life itself, is *not part of the material universe*. In all cases they are form, not substance. Life, at cellular, neurological and social levels and all forms of information, they are all *form*. They are forms that can occupy a succession of material substrates unchanged.

They must have a suitable substrate but it does not much matter which. That is to say that all are transducible and replicable. They are only temporarily dependent upon their often ephemeral substrates.

The second feature is that all those we know have strangely one-dimensional, monolinear *memories*. Data are stored as strings. Genome, ram, speech are all one-dimensional strings. Our own memory, even, follows this pattern; it can be seen as a long, stored string of events.

The third feature may be less well known. Such memories are under constant repair. Form cannot be long preserved through time without regeneration. The genome, the information centre, or brain, of a cell is under constant repair; special proteins are constantly running along the strands of the double helix of DNA and repairing breaks, mismatches and errors.

In the world of data processing, digital computers won out over the analog computers that were their early competitors because the digital pulses get cleaned and squared up at each stage. Computer hardware and software also contain many mechanisms, such as parity checks, to clean up and correct noise. Telephone and cable systems have numerous relay stations where messages are regenerated.

Much less is known about the brain but Lashley's and Penfield's experiments with many others revealed equipotentiality. When brain cells are removed or die others often take over their function.

The fourth feature has already been mentioned. The pattern of coding, symbolism, and data storage is stratified, it has hierarchic levels which are surprisingly similar, a simple 'string' of 'words' made up of 'letters' from a highly specific and very limited 'alphabet'.

In the cell read 'genome', 'gene', 'np'. In the computer read 'ram', 'address', 'alphanumeric (or code) characters'. In the brain, conscious thought has the same linear sequential presentation, one word after another, and the same hierarchic form, e.g. phonemes/letters, words, phrases, sentences, paragraphs . . .

Social communication is in sequential linear strings, speech and writing. It also has the same hierarchic structure, a close parallel of conscious thought.

We did not copy the genome when we invented speech and writing. Nor did we go to it for our model when we laid cables, and built computers. We came independently, by trial and error, to the same pattern. Where we find the same solutions we expect to find similar problems.

NON-SEMANTIC INFORMATION THEORY

Before we explore the paradigm I have suggested let us look at the classical information theory. The accepted theory was right for its time. It deals only with the problems of passing signals through channels and avoids semantic considerations. The channel-capacity problems were difficult enough and it was right to solve them first.

Information theory as such probably started with Lord Kelvin's work on transatlantic cables. He was the first to sense that the limit of the information-carrying capacity of a cable was set by the frequency band-width that a channel could accommodate. Between 1934 and 1928 K. Keumfuller, H. Nyquist, and then R. V. L. Hartley gradually developed the formal theory. It was Hartley who first saw the underlying principle that coded information flow via strings of pulse-like signals involved the formalisation of a limited set of signals and that the distinction between the members of the set had to be as sharp as possible. This is the first step towards the reduction of variety and so of ambiguity. He noted that the selection of s pulse signals to represent semantic information, (dots/dashes, low/high pulses) from a repertoire of n possibilities gave a variety of s^n and that the informational 'value' of a string of such signals could best be represented by a logarithmic measure. His formula was:

Where H_n = the *quantity* of information.

$$H_n = \log_2 s$$

Base 2 logarithms were shown to be most convenient for the purpose.

Why was the logarithmic measure important? The essence of the idea of information is surprise. If you are told something you know already, no information has been imparted to you. It is only when what you are told is unexpected that you have learned anything. It follows that the more unexpected, the more surprising a piece of information is, the more its *value* as information, so improbability is a measure of the value or weight of information.

The convenient measure of probability is a fraction where certainty is equal to one and low probabilities are represented by small fractions. This was the insight we got from Claude Shannon's theory. We have to deal with probabilities by multiplying them. If event A and event B in a time slot have a probability of ½ then the probability of both events together in that slot is the product ½ × ½ = ¼. The logarithmic measure is obviously best since the informational value can thus be obtained by adding instead of by multiplying.

Claude Shannon and Norbert Weiner brought the theory to its present general form with the formula for a long sequence of signals:

$$H_n = -p_i \log p_i$$

SIGNALS AND NOISE

Philosophers since Plato have speculated about perception and knowledge but it was not until the development of telecommunications that a concept vital to comprehension, noise, was introduced into the field. Even now it seems to be unimportant to most philosophers. 'Noise' was the term chosen by Claude Shannon for the uninformative fuzz that is inseparable from the act of communication in every instance. Whenever a chain of signals passes from one entity to another it has to suffer the fate of everything that is ordered in this particular universe, it has to take its chance of being disordered, of having its degree of entropy increased. Whenever information passes through a channel, it is subject to this process. The remedy is, as I have said, repair, regeneration. The receiving system must have some aspect of expectation, some internal model of what it should receive, and it must be able to recognise a version of this that is imperfect and correct its imperfections before passing it on further. The whole business of perception is bound up with this problem, but our brains are such efficient automatic noise filters that we find it hard to understand that the problem is there at all.

As a simple demonstration of your own power to abstract meaning in spite of distortion I suggest this experiment. First make a guess. Roughly what proportion of a pattern can be obscured before you fail to recognise it? 10 percent, 20 percent?

Experiment 1
Take a piece of paper and place it so that it obscures one line of the type that you are reading. Slide the paper downwards revealing the tops of the letters to find the least amount of type you need to see in order to read them. You will probably find that you have underestimated yourself as noise filter, you need much less than half the line to understand it. You can read through 60 or 70 percent noise.

(True noise is not that systematic and can better be described as fuzz. You would find a similar result if the letters were gradually revealed through a fog of distortion.)

Experiment 2
Look at any caricature. The information you are receiving is far less than 1 percent of what you normally need. Can one explain in terms of information theory how you can recognise the person depicted?

Seeing pattern through fuzz is much more of a problem in the world of classical information theory because the internal models of the receiving system there are so much more primitive; pulses high and low, bits, bytes. So it was in that field that the problem was first understood as a result of the collaboration between Claude Shannon and Norbert Weiner.

Shannon's great contribution was to quantify noise in a way suitable to his own non-semantic paradigm. His formula was as follows:

> The greatest quantity H of information that can be transmitted
> through a channel with a bandwidth W over a period of time T
> though a mean fuzz of noise D and a mean signal P is given by
>
> $H = WT \log_2 (1 + P/D)$

While this powerful concept is completely correct, predictive and the
engineering basis of all telecommunications, I suggest – and I think our
programs prove – that Shannon's Law does not apply to semantic information
systems. Patterns of great complexity can be detected reliably through very
much more noise than would be allowed by the Shannon formula. This was
proved by the two experiments above, as will become clear later.

We now have to look at a much more difficult area: the data-capture
problem and the fuzz problem of an animal.

INFORMATION NEEDLES IN DATA HAYSTACKS

David Hume said that human knowledge starts with impressions (to him of
unknown origin). We would call them sense data and say they are an input
from receptor nerve cells to our brain. But what we take in from 10^8 nerve
cells is nothing like the picture we see or the sounds we hear and even less like
the symbols and sounds by which we tell each other our impressions. Since
we cannot communicate sense impressions the starting point of science,
philosophy and epistemology has this century been taken to be 'propositions'; statements in words or symbols which are supposed to be approximately congruent either with some observation of the world or with some
imagined axiom system. Such statements are composed in some mutually
comprehensible language such as speech, mathematical statements or some
similar symbolic system.

But the words from which speech is made up are symbols for classes of
entities, actions, ideas or concepts which have fuzzy, often very fuzzy,
boundaries. Words have many overlapping meanings which greatly depend
on context. Mathematical symbols are less fuzzy in meaning but they represent
quantities and operations which are never in exact correspondence with their
object comparates, the things in the outside world with which they are
cognate. There is always a margin of observational error.

The early problems of science arose from the fuzziness of the common
words they used for communication. Precision was introduced by using the
technique called definition. Words were borrowed unceremoniously from
the common stock of language and redefined to be less fuzzy in the scientific
context. But the words used for the *definitions* were themselves semantically
fuzzy. (Neologisms based on Latin and Greek proved useful because they had

an understood semantic background but less of the semantic haze which, I suggest, is *necessary* in everyday language if social intercourse is not to become prolix and pedantic.)

New paradigms call for new language but comprehension comes more from contextual practice than from definitions. The same words are used in different fields, but they have quite different semantic connectivity networks in different usages. In many cases understanding comes only inductively with constant exposure and cannot be achieved at a stroke.

Although defined and therefore more precise meanings were an advance, there was a continuing problem because of various subtly different interpretations of the new language. Many of the disagreements and arguments in science are semantic in origin.

There is also another problem with definition as a tactic, with which I shall deal later. Sir Arthur Eddington, in *The Nature of the Physical World*, introduced an important new idea when he said that the primary informational input of the community of scientists is a vector or profile of meter readings.

Eddington could well have said more. He could have said that the primary input to the brain, perception, was the same, an array of events like meter readings, a very large one. The accepted view, based on recent neurology, is that all sensory information comes to us as a very large array of signals each of which tells us of change in the intensity of some externally caused phenomenon at some small point in space-time, a sensory (input) nerve ending. The atom of knowledge and intelligence is a point-intensity in space-time. We learn how strong some tiny action is somewhere, somewhen. The informational input *element* is a magnitude/pixel/microsecond.

A receptor nerve input is a meter reading where the position of the meter needle is represented by the amount of change of frequency of neuronal firing. You read this page because you are receiving many millions of such meter readings in the form of trains of pulses from receptor neurones in the retina at the back of your eyes. Sounds you hear come from the increased firing patterns of the miriad hairs in the conch-like whorls of the cochleas in your ears. You 'read' the sound vibrations as the patterns of intensity of the hair movements as expressed by the rate of firing of many hair-vibration receptor cells.

Touch and all the other senses, including many of which we are not conscious, all work the same way. We get a large array of signals representing the point intensities.

MODEL SEARCH

I suggest that what we need here is a single model which is brainable enough and has enough elementary fit with the facts we know to be useful as a structure upon which a family of developing paradigms can be built. The

Bohr-Rutherford model of the atom has been superseded and elaborated but the whole family of successive models could not have happened without that simple original.

Let us look at one attempt at such a brain model (Figure 3) which comes from Karl Popper and John C. Eccles in *The Self and Its Brain*.

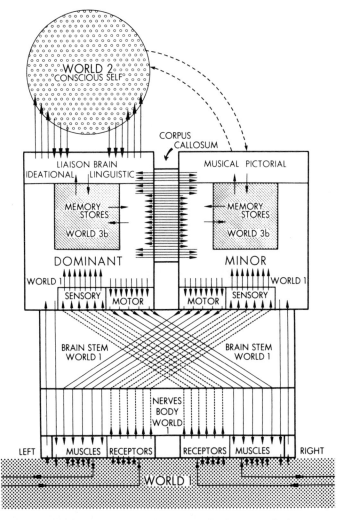

(From Popper, K. R. and Eccles, J. C., *The Self and its Brain,* p. 375, Springer International)

Figure 3   Communications to and from the brains and within the brain

You will see that the model shows the receptors grouped in the centre and the effectors outside them at the bottom of the drawing. That design does not correspond at all to the spatial arrangements in a brain but it is a permissible topological distortion to make what happens in the brain more brainable. A connective system is a topology and it is possible to distort such spatially without destroying that topology. A wiring diagram does not tell us where the wires go in space, it tells us how they are connected, their topology.

Let me suggest another such model, the one I first suggested in 1958 and which is creating interest now. Take a box and call it a brain. It has many afferent inputs sending in information (in-pointing cones), and many efferent outputs (outward cones) sending out instructions to muscle fibres and organs. These may enter anywhere and emerge anywhere (Figure 4).

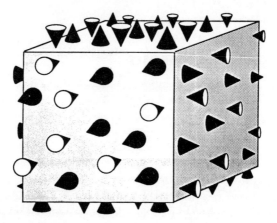

Figure 4   The black box brain

Let us now look at the whole set of inputs. These are the nerves from receptors in the body, the receptor rods and cones in your retinas, the receptors at hair roots in your cochleas, the touch sensors in your skin, the proprioceptors on every muscle fibre, and those that are monitoring your bodily functions. Let us give a name to the whole set, the entire input knowledge interface of a brain with the world. Let us call this vast array the *sensorium*. Let us do a permissible topological distortion and draw all these input nerves to one face of our black box.

Now let us take all the efferent (output), instruction-giving nerves to the opposite face (Figure 5). Let us call this the motorium; (the entire set of motor neurones). This is a simplification which I believe will aid the sort of strategic level comprehension that we shall need for such an intensely difficult field of speculation. The hope is that this simple structure may have enough strength to bear a later edifice of development.

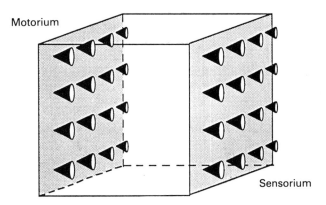

Figure 5   The black box brain topologically distorted

SEEKING FEATURES IN BLACK BOXES

What can be done with brain model based on a 'black box' with input and output interfaces? How does it help our thinking?

We can see that it is going to be a daunting problem but in the light of the more general class morphostat of which our black box is the information centre we can expect to get clues at several levels if the class is a valid one.

All morphostats receive and act on information from their environment. The information arrives as a constant array at numerous input ports at an afferent interface. All morphostats transduce this information into complex actions at a very large efferent interface. These actions are purposive, intelligent, and uncausal in the sense given earlier.

To start with the simplest case, the surface of a cell is its sensorium. It has the means to detect the presence of nutrients in its environment and can respond either by forming a bubble to engulf them or by allowing its diaphragm to become selectively pervious. Further, the cell surface is covered with many complex protein 'receptors', vast molecules, scrunched-up balls, made up of strings of amino-acids. The sensor proteins have sites on their surfaces which bind to and thus detect very specific chemical messengers which may be signals either from other cells or from the environment. These are used to trigger the cell's response. The signal passes through the cell wall in many ways we are beginning to understand, then passes via intermediary proteins to the genome (the cell's central control level). In some way these messages activate or inhibit specific genes or gene combinations on the genome in the correct sequence. The result is that the genome peels off and sends appropriate RNA and mRNA messengers to the layers of mitochondria, and thence to where the ribosomes are building proteins. Thus the cytoplasm generally and the ribosomes especially represent the motorium in the oversimplified picture I have drawn.

In metazoa the whole chain of ontogeny, cell development, is mediated by the immensely complicated signalling system by which each cell at a given location learns where it is and by that 'knows' which parts of its program to activate and in what order. It knows which pages of its instruction book to read and which to ignore. The 'book' is the genome of which every cell has an exact replicate. So the cell's motorium is instructed what commands to obey and in what order as a result of the perception at the cell surface of quite complex classes of informational input.

Figure 6 shows the information flow in very simplified form.

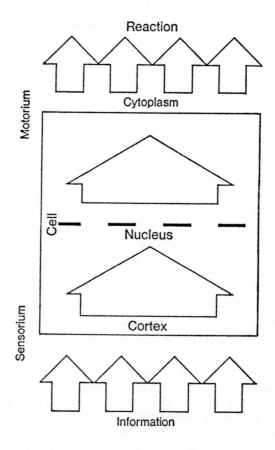

Figure 6   Helpfully distorted view of information flow in a cell

Figure 7 schematically shows the same cell at different times receiving different input patterns of information and causing this to actuate specific genes. In the 4th diagram we see all systems working concurrently, as they must do in real life.

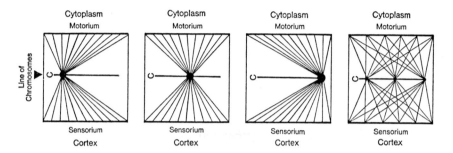

Figure 7   The surface of the cell has been separated conceptually in respect to its two roles: 1) sensing environmental conditions, sensorium and 2) reacting to them, motorium. Information activates different genes (chromosome loci) according to the information from the sensorium, the cell surface.

It is my point that the whole animal, a relatively enormous system of which the cell we have discussed is an infinitesimal part (less than a trillionth), has an echoing system. A neural brain, too, gets signals from its sensorium, deals with them and produces the required behaviour at its musculature.

Figure 8 represents the information flow in a simple metazoon such as an insect. Complex patterns of events in the environment are detected by an array of receptors, patterns of events significant for the creature are detected and each triggers its own specific response pattern of behaviour at the muscles and organs instructed by the motorium. (This expositionary picture takes no account of time.)

The case is different but the pattern of information flow is much the same as that we see in every minute cell of the same insect.

Let us now look at the human case, because we have a specially privileged position in this respect. We have an internal inspection system. We have, each of us, some small power of introspection. Behaviourists preach that we should ignore such evidence, but I have never quite seen why. So I shall not.

The human brain has a quarter of a billion receptors at the sensorium, the ingoing interface. The flow of information moves into the system and eventually has a great influence on the set of instruction signals that are sent out at the motorium, the set of about a million motor outputs which command muscle fibres and organs.

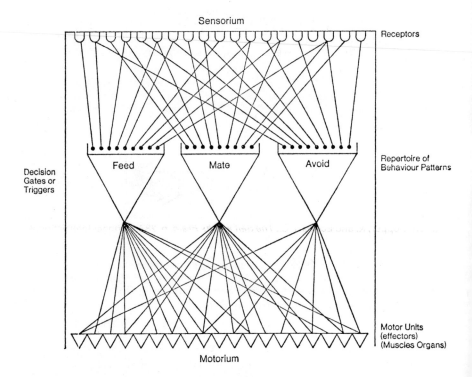

Figure 8   Information flow in a simple metazoon

Let us look again at the concept 'sensorium', the entire set of receptor nerves in the body, the entire informational input interface with the world. The axons of these nerves connect these receptors with your nervous system, which includes your brain and spinal chord. There is no brainable physiological representative of this sensorium in the physical brain pictured in Figure 9. It is a topological or connective concept. But it is a simplification which I believe is essential if we are to advance the strategic level comprehension in such a difficult field of speculation. Some physical mapping can be made but it only confuses rather than advances understanding at this point.

From this picture of the process of perception we see that the amount and the complexity of your informational input is astronomically huge. If we allow 8 bits for intensity at each point and a view rate of 10 Hz at each of the 180000000 receptors, then from one eye we have a data flow rate of 10 terabits/second (10^{12} bit/s)!

There is a popular view that it is impossible to have too much information. Especially in a managerial context, it is taken as obvious that as much

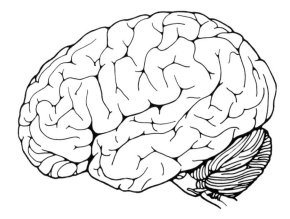

(From Popper, K. and Eccles J. C., *The Self and Its Brain,* p. 287, Springer International)

Figure 9 The human brain

information as possible should circulate ubiquitously. Consult everyone on everything is the accepted advice. I have doubts.

The problem your brain faces in dealing with the overwhelming explosive cataract of data described prompts the thought that telling all to all may be the wrong way to deal with information. Raw data are the poorest of ore. They require massive filtering, sorting, condensing and refining before they can be of the remotest use. The organisation of brains or other order-preserving systems does not require the random spreading of signals ubiquitously but the highly constrained and precise selection, condensation, summation, emphasis and direction of data to specific channels. The most important incoming problems are *disconnection* and *insulation,* limiting, filtering, selecting, choosing, directing and insulating flows, not elaborating them.

We observe that all that filters through to our consciousness from this great swamping flood of separate signals is a limited selection, a highly abstract, condensed set of Hume's impressions. Half a billion nerves are screaming at me ten times a second. Result: I see a part of a green monitor with a few dozen words, less than a kilobyte of information. Within a few microseconds there has been a process of refinement, condensation and relevance selection which no known computer could begin to tackle. The contingent, the irrelevant, peripheral and fortuitous has been blocked and only a many times refined and purified essence of what I have learned, that may be relevant to my life, has been allowed to pass from the tactical level at the periphery through to the strategic command level of consciousness. So much for the objectivity of knowledge! Terabits are reduced by nine orders of magnitude to kilobits, highly relevant and significant kilobits.

This is not an easy task. It is equivalent to finding the one needle which is hidden in any one of a thousand haystacks – ten times a second! Biological information processing is the business of filtering, sorting and stopping communication rather than making communication. If that sounds wrong consider this. Before learning starts a system does not know which of the incredibly vast number of connections will be required at the end of the process. So all possible connections must be virtually open or potentially so at the start. Learning must therefore be much more concerned with reducing connections than with creating them. You cannot eliminate something you cannot try. Learning is cutting links, not making them.

How does the general picture fit our introspective picture of the world. I have described the enormous data bombardment which causes our experience of perception. We know that this vast terabaud, creeping barrage of unique experiences gives rise to a manageable chain of experiences. A limited number of perceptual events composed of a small number of percepts is perceived. We know that we make decisions such as 'walk to the station', which are very simple and brainable relative to the millions per second instructions to muscle fibre groups which are actually involved. There is some type of General Staff translating the strategic level instructions of your consciousness down through many administrative levels to the tactical muscle-pull instructions.

Here is the pattern once again:
Enormous input array.
Convergence, recognition of simple patterns.
Limited variety of central strategic options.
Divergence.
Very large array of motor instructions to individual units.

Presuming the reader's provisional acceptance of the sociozoon as a morphostat, even if but a primitive one, I propose to probe one that is a much less black box than the living neural brain. We may be able to get a better idea of the pattern of information flow from this source both because it is primitive and therefore relatively simple and also because it is patent, open to our mesocosmic view.

THE PATTERN

This is the pattern, the gross architecture, in every case.

1. Sensorium
There is a receptor sensorium which inputs a succession of patterned arrays of afferent signals from the environment.

2. *Convergence zone*
There is a layered zone of convergence, summation, filtering. These are many-to-one effects.

3. *Cental zone*
There is a line of zone of decision centres from which instruction cascades originate.

4. *Divergence zone*
There is a layered zone of multiple, diverging, elaborating, one-to-many instructions.

5. *Motorium*
There is a motorium outputting many efferent detailed instructions.

Is there a simple conceptual pattern that fits here? Let us look at the broad picture. Convergence upon a line, a central line, divergence from that line. The convergence and the divergence are both layered, stratified.

First we see that the picture is symmetric about the central line; second, looking at one half we see that being layered and converging (or diverging according to which way we look) it is like a root or tree configuration, but being layered it is hierarchical, organised in successive subordinate grades.

However, a normal hierarchic structure does not fit because that is always seen as having a single apex or apical figure, the ruler (hierarch, chief priest). There is a modification of the hierarchical pattern which fits quite well, though, and that is a polyhierarchic network such as shown in Figure 10.

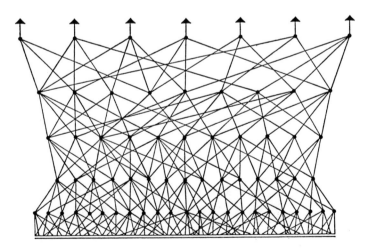

Figure 10   A six-stratum polyhierarchic network

The neologism 'polyhierarchic' was first used by Dr Stanislav Andrzjewski (now Professor S. Andreski) in his book *Military Organisation and Society*. He defined a polyhierarchic society as one where several independent hierarchies exist. I use the word in a slightly different sense and re-define it for our purpose as 'any communications network where the pattern of information flow is such that a plurality of interconnected stratified hierarchies spring from (or flow to) the same base'.

Figure 10 shows a network as here defined. Note that there may be (but need not be) cross-interconnections at all levels.

Andreski's concept 'polyhierarchy' provides a hypothetical general architecture for the region from the sensorium to the decision apices. How about the connections to the motorium?

The same pattern, turned upside down fits. We see a converging poly-hierarchy from the sensorium periphery to the apical level, and a diverging polyhierarchy from that level to the motorium periphery (Figure 11).

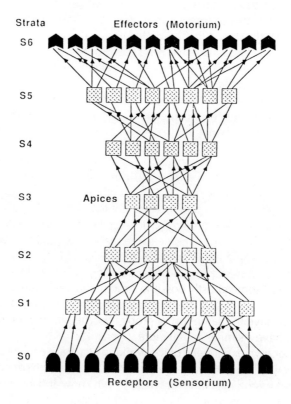

Figure 11   Two polyhierarchic networks joined at the apices

This figure shows a two-dimensional polyhierarchy because paper happens to be flat, but the number of dimensions could be three if the sensorium were an array. Indeed there is no limit to the number of dimensions possible.

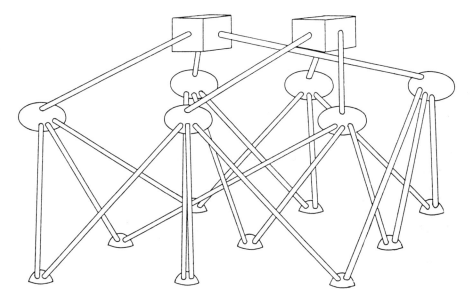

Figure 12   A three-dimension polyhierarchic network

Whatever the tangled pattern of the channels, chemical, neural, inter-animal, the flow of *information* takes the form of two polyhierarchic networks which are connected at the apices. This fits what we know.

At this point in the exposition it is best not to ask too much of a model that must by its nature be of a coarse-grain, first-approach type. No doubt objections to this crude picture will have come to the reader's mind. I ask you to see this as a stage of exposition rather than a complete picture. We have a brainable architecture which has at least a better superficial fit than many others. We have got at least some ghostly possible structure into the utter opacity of that dense black box, the brain, and that less dense one, society. We have seen that they may have the same sort of problems. The information flow in them may have to have a similar architecture.

In his or her own experience of the working of a brain each of us has a very good idea of what is going on at the central strategic region of consciousness. We have a very good idea indeed. The best. We know absolutely nothing *else* than what goes on there. It is all very well for John Broadus Watson to say 'ignore it all'.

The architecture of information flow which comes from introspection fits the pattern already described. Our central perception is nothing like the chaos of coloured dots which our receptors receive and our instructions to muscles are nothing like a million commands, one for each small group of muscle fibres. We make simple strategic level decisions like 'up', 'go to the station', 'eat the chocolate', 'type this paragraph'. We make policy decisions. Of the administrative detail work at both peripheries we know nothing and care less. The information flow pattern again is convergence from a very large and complex sensorium to a lower variety central strategic region and then massive divergence to the motor region where the details of the movement plan are worked out.

Let us move up another order or two and look at the pattern of information flow in a sociozoon. What is the pattern like there?

The patent case, the market

In the open case, the market, we can see that the convergence and the divergence happen at discrete stages or strata: retailers, wholesalers, manufacturers. In the case of an army or almost any human organisation over a certain size there is organisation at several distinct levels. The convergence and the divergence are interrupted, this is subject to a step function. The pattern is hierarchical.

We are not talking about the formal structure, or the authority structure of human organisations. This is often depicted as hierarchic. We are in the context of information and we are talking about the architecture of the information flow. We seek a comprehensible testable pattern which fits in these widely separate fields.

The pattern we see is hierarchic (or rather double hierarchic like a root and tree together). There is root-tree-like convergence and there are strata on both sides of the apical central region. But there is no single apex. There are multiple apices at the centre region.

Our model is a stable market economy and it fits the same general pattern, but to see it clearly we have to do some unpleasantly severe conceptual surgery. We have to chop the entire population in halves, everyone! Never fear, the dissection is topological and imaginary. It is done to aid comprehension, the motive is not genocidal.

What is the difference between these roles? In the consumer role we are, the whole array of us, a sensorium. We are sending need and desire signals, messages about what we think is required for our survival stability (and pleasure). The signals take many forms, including money and buying orders. We send these into the network. The signals we send, pass into the system just as they did in the other two systems described. The mass of different signals penetrates the system and guides its operation.

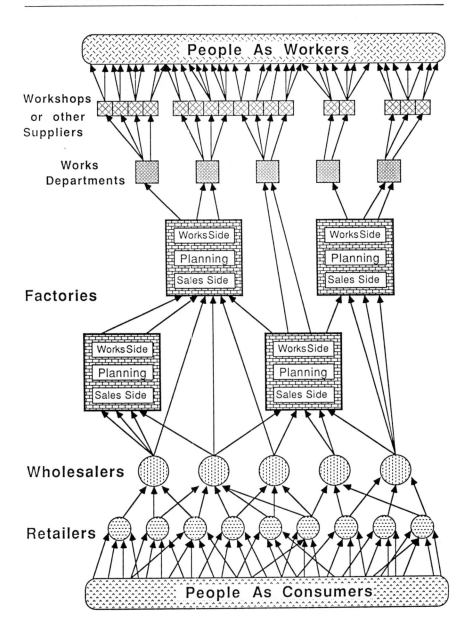

Figure 13   Polyhierarchic communication flow in society

What happens to them in the end? That we *do* know. Having been digested, condensed and summated at a series of levels – retail, wholesale, factory, farm, etc. – they diverge and descend, cascade-style, through several strata of departments and suppliers to the array of workers on the shop floor of the factory or on the land or in the service sector. They emerge as instructions such as 'Another hundred dozen off, Part No. Qs456d'. To whom do they go?

Why, to all of us, or rather the other half of each of us in our producer role.

6

Origin and credibility

I have now completed my broad brushwork and exposed my bedaubed canvas. Before I venture further to fill in more detail I pause to reassert my claim to attention by showing that this is a model and hypothesis worth more attention. The model is not falsified by the first few obvious tests we should apply.

ORIGIN

No-one is sure where new paradigms, models of reality, come from. Karl Popper rejected the view that they arise from inductive experience and explains them as emergent, creative phenomena, which arise mysteriously. That is to say he does *not* explain them. They might as well be swept under the animist carpet of old, as under the 'emergent' carpet. I offer the view that they arise from the human cognitive activity called taxonomy, perceiving a new valid (useful) class, contriving an advantageous way of classifying inputs. Man and the advanced mammals are constantly engaged in taxonomy, finding useful and convenient ways of bundling together experiences which are each unique but sufficiently similar for some purpose.

Newton saw that the motion of a falling apple and that of a planet were phenomena which could be united. His insight revealed that the two sorts of experience were members of a newly discovered class of experiences, that of objects in a gravitational field. Devising that class was more difficult than perceiving the class 'rattle' from the series of experiences of a rattle to a baby, but it is of the same nature.

The eureka moment, the moment of insight, is that exciting, pleasurable moment when a taxonomic economy is made and two or more whole classes of experience are suddenly united and seen to be one. A relational, or 'inclusive-or' gate is formed. The baby discovers the idea 'man' which unites his brother, uncles and father and separates them from 'woman', the other people who are so similar but distinguishable. Earlier the baby had a similar problem of uniting that set of patterns, all different, which fell on his retina and represented Father.

I came upon the polyhierarchic model for mental activity in 1957 when I had been doing much speculation after an all-night talk with Norbert Weiner and Gray Walter in the Wiltshire village, Urchfont. I was thinking about the similarity of the information-handling problems of cells, animals, and societies, in the context of the class 'morphostat' which I had conceived. As an industrial manager who had observed the growth of a large firm, I had developed the idea of the polyhierarchic network as a paradigm for the shape or architecture of information flow in a firm. It also seemed a way to describe what must happen in the region between input and output in a brain. I was looking at the problem from the professional point of view of an inventor, which I am. I was not asking how it happens, I was asking how I would do it if I had the problem. The seed of the idea may have come from my friend Stanislav Andreski's book *Military Organisation And Society,* which introduced the neologism 'polyhierarchic' in a social organisation context.

The idea came to me with an intense 'eureka' feeling in the middle of the night, with the enormous sense of excitement and wonder that has been described by others who were or thought themselves originals. I did not remember Andreski's reference until I gave a lecture on the idea under his chairmanship and he reminded me of his earlier use of the term.

From that set of concepts the idea that recognition was analytical and poly-hierarchic, that we *learn* to recognise perceptual elements, then assemblies of them and finally whole percepts, arose from the same architecture concept. I began to think about using it for pattern recognition needed for wood grading. This led to much experimentation and finally to a product (which did not need to use the analytical method). Wide reading in all the relevant fields has done much to confirm and nothing to falsify the hypothesis ever since.

Most influential in confirming my faith in the idea was news such as that of the work described below.

An article, 'Cellular communication', in the *Scientific American* in September 1972 by Gunther S. Stent deals with the various communication systems in the cell and leads up to a description of the work of Steven W. Kuffler and later of David H. Hubel and Torsten W. Weisel on the early stages of perception in cats and monkeys.

This work shows that the first few steps in the elaborate process of perception in these animals does indeed conform with the pattern that I proposed. The congruence, the fit between the model and the facts is especially close. There is an informationally economical convergence at several strata towards apices, loci, which 'represent' more and more complex perceptual elements. In the retina itself Kuffler found ganglia that represent small retinal spots. They respond only when there is sufficient (above threshold) stimulus of a small area, and below threshold stimulus to the surrounding area.

Thus the 130 million receptor points in the retina are reduced to about a million of these small areas at the retinal ganglia. These connect directly via about a million neurones to the visual cortical area at the dorsal end of the brain. A summational convergence of information and a 130-fold economy is achieved before any signal leaves the retina.

Hubel and Weisel took up the experimentation at this visual cortex itself and found the same pattern: hierarchical convergence, summation, economy – cells which respond only to assemblies of the Kuffler perceptual elements at one stratum, cells which respond to more elaborate assemblies of these assemblies at a higher stratum and so on. The gestalt, holistic view of brain function which was the consensus in those days certainly did not apply to the first few stages at the input periphery, or sensorium, as I called it. Locus represents shape and thus meaning there, and there are no indications if and where it stops doing so.

It was not in fact until I read of the work of Hubel and Weisel that I really took my idea seriously enough to contemplate writing a book on it.

My first paper on the subject was shown to several people at the Philosophy of Science Congress in 1957 and read and signed by Professor Ross Ashby and Professor Kapp, among others. A second paper, 'Cybernetics and factory organisation', was read to the Theoretical Studies Group of The British Sociological Association on 28 March 1958.

Based on a long essay on the idea in the context of biological recognition, a highly condensed account was published in *The Scientist Speculates,* edited by Professor I. J. Good a year or two later. My first book on the theme, *Brain,* (Davis Poynter) did not appear until 1975. It was followed by a dozen or so lectures to university departments and some experimental work on computers, which I shall describe.

I was also invited to and read a paper, 'Recognition', at the Cybernetics Conference at Porto Alegre, Brazil, in 1972.

CAN WE FALSIFY THE MODEL?

So much for the unlikely origin of these ideas. Now, before exploring the model further, let me show that it passes the primary tests, it cannot immediately be falsified.

Can we check consequences deduced from the concept 'morphostasis' and the posited polyhierarchic architecture for information flow?

We would expect to find evidence of afferent convergence and efferent divergence and of intermediate levels of strata in the three levels of morphostats posited.

I have suggested a 'wheels within wheels' model of a social morphostat where the polyhierarchic flow is between nodes which are roles occupied by people. The people in turn have brains which are, in themselves, similar polyhierarchic networks. At the lowest level, the brains too are networks of nodes which are nerve cells, which are again polyhierarchic information systems.

At the top level, in the sociological case it is clear enough that the market system fits the model. Shops summate the need signals. At the wholesaler stratum, and at farm and factory and service and government top level there is further summation and strategic policy scale decision. On the motor, the production supply, delivery side there is a multi-level departmental diverging cascade of instructions to smaller units at more tactical levels. The convergence, divergence and strata are visible. In the Western world visibly, and in the centralist world covertly. A polycentric array of apical control centres, each fed from a wider area of sensorium and each sending diverging instructions to a wide motorium; these can be seen also.

In the animal brain the histological evidence is less clear. We know very little of the pattern of information flow in the tangled mass of nerve fibres, but the primary evidence does not falsify convergence. I have mentioned the convergence from the retina at several stages to the dorsal visual cortex. There are two great 'cables' of fine nerve fibres from the ganglia at the base of the retina to that cortex. We know the interface between the cortical and the retinal strata. It would falsify my hypothesis if there were more channels in the mass of optical nerve fibres than there are receptors. It is not falsified. The 130 million receptor outputs converge to only a million ganglia and nerve connections.

The evidence which encouraged me most is, as I have said, that provided by the work of Kuffler, Hubel and Weisel already mentioned. To give more detail I draw attention to two articles in "Readings from the Scientific American: Perception: Mechanisms and Models": 1971.

The first article is by Charles R. Michael. This shows that the retina which receives information at the back of the eye has just the convergence and stratification of structure that is required to fit at the sensorium end in the polyhierarchic model of information flow that I posit.

All this work is based on important if rather gruesome experiments with, usually, cats.

The animal is anaesthetised and the eye fixed. Patterns of light are generated and made to fall on the retina of the cat's eye. Very fine electric probes explore the visual cortex at the back of the cat's brain and detect the actual cells which fire when the stimulus pattern is exposed. Thus the effect on the brain cells of the way the light falls on the receptors is gradually established.

Michael's article shows that the vertebrate retina has just the layered structure that is called for and it is of just the type that fits the model I proposed. The connections, the axons, excitatory and inhibitive, of the presynaptic (or sending) cell cluster on to the dendrite (input end) of the postsynaptic or receiving cell in a convergent many-to-one system as is required at the sensorium. There are three distinct strata.

Horizontal cells link the receptor terminal cells which receive inputs from the receptors. (These probably mediate comparison where, for instance what is detected is to be an edge, which involves the detection of a luminance *difference*.) They may mediate mutual inhibition as well. (Our taxonomons will not work without this feature to help the competitive feature search.)

At the retina (our sensorium) the receptor ganglion cells detect (respond to, fire for) either "on" or "off" conditions, above or below threshold luminance at some spot.

A stratum of bipolar cells connect to the next stratum, the amacrine cells, which are closely mutually intertwined. Behind those two strata is a third stratum, that of the ganglion cells which are also intimately interconnected, mutually and with the amacrine stratum. The converging, summative structure is apparent here even before the information has left the retina.

Having reduced the input variety by a factor of 130 in these three stages the resultant outputs now leave the eyes and travel to the visual cortex. Here the input convergence goes on at a further series of stratifed levels of neurones as can be seen from the second article. This is "The Visual Cortex Of The Brain" by David Hubel himself.

He describes how they unravelled the working of the first few layers of this more complex system. The optic nerve fibres "talk" to several layers of the lateral geniculate body cells. The probes reveal that these cells specialise in detecting particular perceptual elements. They receive messages directly or pass them on to each other. After this sorting, filtering process, they connect to the next stratum, what he calls the "simple" cortical cells. These are those that recognise the summations of the output of the cortical "on" and "off" detectors outputs. It all fits together in just the way called for in the present hypothesis. The next layer is that of the "complex" cortical cells which detect (fire in the presence of) perceptual pattern details (perceptual elements) which are due to inputs from a converging group of "simple" cells. The first few stages of the process I envisaged seem to be visible. All fits neatly enough. The view that the processes at deeper levels are of basically the same type, convergence, summation, filtering, cannot be lightly dismissed. What we observe at the visual part of sensorium level fits well enough.

Then there is the evidence of the different cell types.

Most cells in the areas that are associated with perception seem to be of the type where there are more dendritic, afferent, input connections than axonal, output connections. The perceptual nerve is more funnel-like, convergent, as the model requires. In parts of the brain mapped as motor areas there are many pyramidal cells where matters are reversed. There are more outputs than inputs. If these proportions were reversed it would tend to falsify the hypothesis. It is not falsified. Perceptual areas have more convergent nerves, motor areas have more divergent ones.

All the literature on brain physiology concerning the motor regions is also full of references to the *hierarchical* structure.

In *The Self and its Brain*, p. 276, Professor John C. Eccles says 'In attempting an analysis of voluntary movement and control, it is immediately evident that there are many hierarchical levels'. That these *could* be mono-hierarchic, hierarchical up to a single apex, is a proposition that is exceptionally difficult to conceive, in view of what else we know. We seem to be left with a diverging polyhierarchic shape for the motor information flow.

As I said, in 1958 I suggested that the process of recognition must be basically analytical. Perceptual elements, spots, lines, edges at various angles, are recognised at any location at the sensorium, then at the next stratum assemblies of these and at the next assemblies of assemblies and so on until at higher strata whole percepts are detected. Above that, events, whole situations calling for response, are detected and trigger response cascades. I opposed this polyhierarchic connectionist model to the gestalt model which was ruling at that time. In a holistic paradigm it was posited that patterns were recognised as a whole, not built up as I posited. My hypothesis was seen as connectionist and as such not followed up. Connectionist hypotheses and indeed all 'physiologising' (nerve net thinking) had been ruled out because many animal experiments with mammals as well as observations of human brain injuries showed that a brain could suffer gross damage with surprisingly little loss of function.

To those with the tacit paradigm of a clockwork world this was like expecting a telephone exchange to work after a bomb had gone off in it. Much was made of equipotentiality, the way in which nerves seem to take over each other's function as they were injured or died. (Thousands die each day apparently.)

However, telephone exchanges and fuzzy logic, biological brains are quite different, utterly so. My suggested answer to the problem, multiple channels redundancy and inductive repair, cut litle ice then. The importance of the fact that the model worked on an evidential rather than a logical basis and therefore was tolerant of noise and error was not fully seen.

Analytic, connectionist recognition confirmed

However, unknown to me, the work I have mentioned by Kuffler, Hubel and Weisel on cats' eyes was going forward. If they had not been able to find the spot, line, edge, other perceptual-element detecting loci in cats' eyes it would have falsified my hypothesis. But they found them. If they had not found other centres at deeper levels that responded to more complex patterns and more abstract features of them (at higher strata) it would have falsified it. But they found those too.

How about the motorium? Would it falsify my hypothesis if we failed to find similar loci in the motor regions of the brain at which animal behaviour could be excited?

This question is more complex, the recognition of simple pattern elements is almost instantaneous but complex trains of action have a time dimension. It has been shown that a mammal behaving in a skilled way is getting many feedback signals many times a second during muscular action. Proprioceptors on each muscle fibre are reporting in, with many other cybernetic situation reports from the eyes and other senses. We cannot expect to be able to excite some centre in the motor areas and get a behaviour train response if these progress-checking cybernetic feedback signals are missing. However, it would falsify my hypothesis if we could not make a muscle fibre twitch at one level and a muscle move at another by exciting various nerves or ganglia in the motor areas.

The work in Toronto by Professor W. Penfield showed just these effects so clearly that he and his followers have mapped out a lot of the lower levels of the human motorium. He could repeatedly excite the same vocalisation but not speech, the same twitches and jerks but not skilled behaviour. He did this by stimulating specific brain cells, loci. This was a vindication of connectionist theory and consistent with the polyhierarchic paradigm.

In areas associated with memory he found that by using electric probes he could trigger long memory sequences. The subject, usually someone having a brain surgery operation, would, while still conscious of his or her surroundings, describe in great detail a lost memory of an often long past event. Memory works on the sensorium side of my posited apical region at the cortex. It is also autonomous. It requires no continued accompanying sensory input. That is its essence. Therefore that discovery neither confirms nor falsifies the hypothesis but it fits very well with the model for memory that emerges from this train of thought, as will be seen later.

And at the level of the cell?

In the cell we have a sensorium; it is the whole of the cell surface and its covering of many special proteins which act as sensors or receptors. These very words are used in that context by those in the field. We have a visible central decision layer, the apical level, the genome itself, the genetic memory where the genoplastic learning called evolution is stored. We are beginning to learn that there is a very complex flow of chemical messengers from the 'sensor molecules' on the surface to the genome and then from that to the motorium. The protein factories themselves are at work making the great variety of complex proteins that build and rebuild and repair the cell's form. The features that take this role are the ribosomes, which crawl along strands of RNA copied from the genome and carry out the instructions delivered by them and the mRNA. Here the many specialist proteins are built up, as long chains of amino-acids which finally scrunch themselves up into the sheets or balls that have the wonderful array of precise properties required for that highly improbable entity, the living cell. These proteins are the enormous complex molecules (structural or informational) that carry out the cell's functions. On their way to the ribosomes (the motorium itself) the chemical messengers from the genome (mRNA, etc.) pass through what seems to be a stratified structure in the mitochondria. We are beginning to understand the many complex tree-triggerlike processes that occur on the way. We know that there are multiple interactions, inhibitive and promoting, which is a convincing echo of the interactions of nerve cells in brains and people in institutions.

The way the double polyhierarchic network applies to the nervous system when it is elaborating behaviour patterns is obviously different from the way it applies in epigenesis, the diverging, specialising development of the great variety of differing cells in the complete animal. But the *pattern* is the same.

In the metazoon the diverging multiple cascades are of *cell types*. Each has an exact duplicate of the whole 'brain' or apical instruction set. The descending motorium hierarchy is the diverging hierarchical development of cell types from multiple gene combinations on the apical genome.

In the polyhierarchic *shape* of the *neural* information flow that develops in each animal there is no replication of the whole apical stratum. The central one (the brain) is used and the posited polyhierarchic information flow pattern is built up ontoplastically in each brain by local changes in connectivity such as those which have been detected in learning at synapses. It is the shape of the flow of information that must necessarily be the same in each case.

The morphostasis paradigm arises from the congruence between the features of biological information-handling systems at the various levels, cell, animal, society. It predicts this congruence because they are members of the same valid class, a purposive class of entity which has the same goal and problem, preserving form, improving form-preserving power.

If the hypothesis were false, it would be surprising to find functionally similar elements and features at all three of these levels, which are so utterly different in scale, time, complexity and traditional function.

I have shown that the general features, the sensorium, and the motorium, the central apical decision centres, seem to have echoing versions in each level, cell nucleus, brain, and society. I have also shown that as far as can be

seen the flow of information and instruction in each case is afferent convergence, and efferent divergence.

I have pointed to other features where the same pattern fits at these
markedly different levels. We find something corresponding to *syntax* at all
levels and there is broad syntactical congruence. At each level there is
language which is *symbolic* in that it is not directly causal in the sense we use
the word 'causal' about material systems. Features and events trigger, rather
than cause, others. Further, the nature of the language is similar. It is in all
cases strings, not arrays or zones, simple linear strings. In all cases the strings
are also hierarchically analytic. Letters, nucleotide pairs; words, codons;
sentences, genes. The sociozoon and the protozoon match. The intermediate
case is not yet sufficiently understood but computer simulations which ascribe
meaning to a class of loci do perform artificial taxonomy, learning unknown
patterns.

How about components? We find the nerve, a sort of input/output deciding
gate (in computerese), which is matched in the sociozoon by the committee,
council, Cabinet, Board. Both deal with many informational inputs and make
instructional outputs after some kind of steplike decision has been made. Both
have binary inputs. In society they are called commanding and forbidding,
speaking for or against. In the brain they are called excitation and inhibition.
In the protozoon the language is different but the function the same. There are
activating or *promoting* catalysts, genes and protein messengers and *inhibitive*
ones.

If there were no such suggestive echoes and congruences it would falsify
the hypothesis, but we have them. They do not establish the hypothesis but
they suggest further study.

The baby taxonomist

I present this report of an experiment, taken from my book *Brain,* as one which
failed to falsify the hypothesis.

A confirmatory experiment

How is the network somewhere behind the visual cortex taught to
see by this hypothesis? Many apical gates must be programmed,
one for each set of perceptual elements.

I have done some experimental work on this and can report the
results. I was in my laboratory, the World, the other day, when I
turned those sophisticated visual class discriminating instruments,
my eyes, on to a baby in the act of learning to know and to know
how to deal with that class of entities the generalization loci of
which I can excite in your brain by using the words 'chocolate
drop'.

I produced a strange object and the baby's incessant random exploratory movements stopped and his eyes focused on this strange new entity that had swum into his receptive field, his ken. With some apparent difficulty and not without mistakes he brought those unfamiliar instruments, his hands, to bear upon the task of getting the entity into his control. He then held it up and, as well as he could for his lack of skill, turned it over, twisted it, moved it around and studied it closely for over a minute. Every part of his retina was receiving many images in rapid succession. Then he transferred it to his mouth and explored it with his lips and tongue before it disappeared. A second chocolate drop produced a similar reaction but the inspection time-span was shorter. On the presentation of the third chocolate drop the exploratory phase was already much diminished. Within ten minutes it was evident that I had, at least temporarily, while the appetite lasted, created a chocolate-eating automaton. Every appearance of the stimulus was rapidly followed by the immediate and identical response. What had happened? One particular exploratory effort for the baby was paid off. The baby has learned to know the chocolate drop as a phenomenon and he learned to know it before he was rewarded. In quick succession he presented all parts of his retina with stimulation in the form of those elements and assemblies which make up a chocolate drop in its various presentations. Its brownness, its curves and planes, its feel, its smell and taste were successively and slowly experienced. Messages from widely separated and very different sensory instruments found their way together to trigger an automatic response for a period of many minutes. The connection, or set of them, was made, ready to be activated at any time in the future when the appetite for the sweet things should be strong and the attention suitably directed. The child had not only learned about the class 'chocolate drop', its uses and advantages; it had learned to see it. At some later stage he will learn to connect it with motor patterns other than the 'grab and eat' response, he will learn to say and later to write the encoded symbolic sounds and marks on paper which will help him to bring the attention of other people to this class of entity and he will be rewarded with chocolate drops for his effort. For the rest of his life he will be able to evoke the idea at will and the semantic connection system attached to it will grow and elaborate. He will learn that 'chocolate drop' is a sub-set of the set 'sweets' of the set 'chocolates' of the set 'food' of the set 'brown things' and so on, almost *ad finitum*. But not quite.

The simulation test

The architecture proposed in the hypothesis could of course be falsified if computer simulations of the described elementary components and pattern of information flow persistently failed to produce acceptable results. First, we have to decide what results could be predicted from simulation programs based on the hypothesis. To do that we have to understand what is happening on either side of the posited polycentric apical region in the model.

It is clear enough that the primary task of a morphostat at the sensorium, its interface with non-self, otherness, its environment, is to detect and interpret three classes of input, the insignificant, and the two types of significant events, the useful and the dangerous. The significant types of detected event or inputs are the dangers or opportunities, the threats or promises calling for motor choices. If the morphostat makes wrong choices it will turn into a 'morphodyn' or corpse, an entity which changes its form radically with time; it will rejoin the Pleroma. It dies and rots away, resumes change.

Some of the signals to which the morphostat will need to respond correctly will be simple analogue ones, one pointer-readings, like temperature. But most significant inputs (those requiring volitional response) are likely, in more advanced animals to be complex: a vector, profile, array or pattern of point-intensities, a pattern of light on a retina, or of vibrations on cochlea hairs.

A small proportion of the many input messages are significant and so all the input patterns have to be recognised and classified, and of course, each one is unique. That is the vital and central interface problem.

A question to which the wrong answer falsifies the paradigm is therefore this. Can we make computer simulations of that sensor interface? Ones which do automatic taxonomy; 'learn' to distinguish very noisy unknown significant patterns. The preliminary programs published herewith have been tried and they fail to falsify the paradigm. They are simple and primitive but they show that it is possible for a program which simulates fuzzy logic nerve nets to learn to classify unknown noisy inputs with a low error rate.

Concurrency can be simulated in serial time models on traditional computers and one of the large group of my readers who were interested, James Cherrill, wrote a very successful program which could perform the automatic taxonomy which I posited as the first step towards artificial intelligence. There are now Fortran, and Spectrum Basic versions of this around and being worked on by the growing group of enthusiasts who have become interested in this approach. All models and experiments so far amply fulfil the simple prediction that a system of competitive gates as described below would be able learn to sort out and allocate or capture unknown patterns through up to 35 percent noise. (The Fortran program is appended to this book with the kind permission of Mr James Cherrill.

These crude, initial attempts at falsification are not offered as being adequate but merely as a preliminary practical check to earn further attention to my exposition.

Other checkable consequences of the hypothesis will follow but before they are presented its ramifications have to be further developed.

However, before we look further along that track there is a parenthetic question to be squared away. The sort of programs needed to test the model are not logical or deterministic. We do not use logic where what is required is judgement. Judgement is evidential – what a nerve, a committee or a scientific consensus does. It is what the semantic gates in the concurrent fuzzy logic computers that I shall describe must do. Chain-logic is what Von Neumann computers have to produce. That is their strength and their limitation. In an indeterminate world we sometimes have to use methods based on indeterminacy.

THE DEFINITION PROBLEM

I have mentioned my distrust of formal definition. In the context of the last section it can be seen that definition, as a method of establishing meaning, simply does not address the vast filtering and abstraction process that is needed to establish both the meanings of, and the fuzziness of the meanings of, the words used.

As a way of establishing exact meaning, definition is a counsel of perfection. We use fuzzy words to reduce word fuzz. We try to capture meaning in a precise net with fuzzy imperfect words.

Definition as a science tool goes against language practice. We learn words at first entirely and later mostly from their repetition in a revealing context. Only rarely do we look them up in a dictionary. When we do we have to use context to select from a confusing variety of meanings. A definition cannot possibly call up the many rich skeins of semantic connections evoked by words presented in different contexts. In contextual learning we have richer, fuller understanding. The receiving brain has to gradually make up its own copy of a whole semantic network with all its subtle connectivities.

To visualise such a network we must think of a three-dimensional connectivity arrangement. Imagine a volume of space containing many scattered boxes which are interconnected by a network of a myriad lines, and in each line a ball showing a positive or negative magnitude (Figure 14).

The boxes are the words of a language, and the numbers in the balls are the semantic connectivity of the words, positive, negative, weak or strong.

This crudely, is my view of the connectivity within the brain. Models of semantic connectivity, of understanding, of thought, should be tried for fit with this model before we decide that further factors or entities are required.

Words connected together in strings can be made to transfer complex ideas from one brain to another if the connectivity system in the receiving brain has sufficient similarity, if the owners of the brains 'speak the same language' in a wider sense than knowing the definitions of the string of words. The receiving brain must have a similar outreaching connectivity network, a ramified fuzz, a thornbush of semantic tendrils reaching out all along the word track.

This is where attempts at machine translation have run into trouble. It is easy to find cognate balls in another tongue. It is figuring out what is in the surrounding haze of boxes that has been the problem. We have to have a replicate in our own brain of both boxes and numbers in the balls before we can understand a language well.

This is the basic truth that lies behind Kuhn's views. We cannot get a

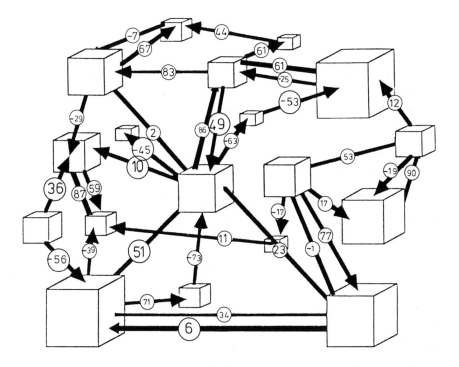

The illustration shows the kind of connectivity network envisaged in the central (or apical) zone where relationships between percepts and concepts are represented by connectivity links (as earlier defined) positive or negative. These central, strategic level nodes (boxes) are seen as connected by links which have changeable weights (balls), plus or minus. The nodes (boxes) have variable sensitivity to each input and variable firing thresholds (sufficiencies)

Figure 14   Semantic boxes and connecting balls

paradigm from a definition. We can only get it from inductive contextual exposure.

None of that means that definitions are never useful. But if definition is limited as a way of transferring knowledge of classes how *do* we do it?

CLASSIFICATION

The classification of inputs is, as I have said, the primary morphostat interface problem. Let us start at the beginning with baby learning. How does Baby learn to use nouns to indicate objects? I argue that every perceptual input is unique because of their enormous possible variety. If we allow only 10 states (fire rates) for each receptor, the variety or number of possible input patterns would be 10 to the power 200000000. This is a largish number. (For comparison it is around 10 to the power 20 microseconds since the big bang.) The (*ab initio*) probability of any one input is the reciprocal of the variety of inputs, which makes the exact repetition of an input a miracle.

No retina could possibly receive exactly the same input twice and no visual cortex of a brain ever received two afferent inputs which were alike. In the ear no stirring of cochlea hairs is ever precisely repeated. The other sensory inputs are all the same. We must start from the axiom that every sensory input is unique.

In learning to sort out unique bits of pattern in the world that are likely to be significant to it, a baby's brain has to classify, to clump, to treat as alike, inputs which are *enough alike* for some *purpose*. The parts of the incoming impressions of the world which represent percepts fall into necessarily fuzzy *classes* to which words are attached (e.g. persons, houses, chairs, spoons). The members of these classes vary widely but have *sufficient* mutual resemblance for some limited human purposes. This is the essential, fundamental and unavoidable strategy of baby and of any other intelligence, any brain, in dealing with the stupendous data bombardment and ultra-astronomic variety of its inputs. It is only when one ventures into the tough and tricky world of pattern recognition that this becomes really clear.

For each noun, Baby must conduct the inductive building up of a subject comparate, an internal model, in some form with which input patterns (object comparates), each unique, can be matched. This process of learning to recognise objects is not remotely like instruction from a string of understood words such as a definition.

Recognition

In the presence of a cat turned any way, at any distance, the baby's brain looks at a unique particular configuration of shapes somewhere on the sensorium and asks whether it has sufficient of the features of the *percept class* 'cat' to be a member of that class or not. If the details, shape, size, colour and other qualities of the features of the impression have *enough* resemblance, they come within the tolerance bounds, the permissible deviation, the permitted fuzziness (or, as I shall prefer to say, exceed the sufficiency) of their internal models then it is recognised.

If *enough* of these *cattish* features are present then Baby's brain decides that it is cat; otherwise not. All classes are, must be, fuzzy and so all perception is at base only exact enough for some limited purpose. It can never be complete or exact. (The object comparate, input pattern, can never be completely congruent with subject comparate, the mask, model, template within the brain.) If the brain has *sufficient* confirmatory evidence and *insufficient* contradictory evidence a binary decision is made. Baby points and says 'pussy cat'. Baby has *recognised*. Millions of local decisions have been at receptors in Baby's pretty blue eye: 'enough stimulus to fire? Yes/No' 'How intense a pulse-train?' These have been transduced into one 'yes/no' decision, 'cat'. In experiments we can simulate learning to see by varying connectivity and the 'sufficiency', which is simply a threshold value which must be exceeded before an element of the system will actuate, or 'fire', as the neurologist would say of a nerve.

Sufficiency and tolerance

Sufficiency is the complement of tolerance. If we take the absolute congruence or match of subject and object comparates as 1 and zero congruence as 0, then where s = sufficiency (or acceptable degree of match) and t = tolerance (or permissible deviation from match) then

$t+s = 1$.

(A tolerance of 0.1 is a sufficiency of 0.9.)

The word tolerance is used in engineering with the meaning 'permissible deviation'. When, as their measurements improved, the early mechanics found that absolute accuracy was an impossible goal, they began to specify the limits of error by fixing a plus and minus tolerance to every measurement on the blueprint. These figures limit errors oversize and undersize. Further progress in engineering could not be made until this was done.

It is quite central to the business of understanding the world that a similar principle should be seen to prevail in the process of cognition. Our kilogram or so of brain can only deal with the immensity of the universe by the strategy of filing events away in classes or sets where the members are sufficiently alike for us to have similar expectations of them. A class that has a sufficiency of 1 or zero tolerance can have at most one member and is most unlikely to have even one. As we decrease the sufficiency, the number of members grows with the fuzziness and eventually we have a class which is encountered often enough to make it worth while for the brain to retain (in some form) the subject comparate (internal model) which is required for the recognition of its members.

If we continue to decrease sufficiency we shall eventually reach a class which will be so all-inclusive and have so many members that it will be useless for the vital purpose of helping living things to predict and optimise in the world. Conversely, if we make sufficiency too high we shall fail to recognise the fuzzier members of the class and lose by that failure. The need is for a good balance, a sufficiency set so as to capture the fuzziest member of the set of inputs that the external object produces; but not inputs produced by non-members of the class. Errors of non-capture and false capture must be kept as low as possible.

Neurological research has not revealed how the brain forms its subject comparates and adjusts their sufficiency, but the polyhierarchic paradigm seems fruitful and makes test by simulations possible.

Let us look again at the way the baby learns. The mind of the baby starts by delineating very broad general classes with low sufficiency, such as 'face'. This recognition is apparently inbuilt, for the neonate smiles at any crude model. However the child soon begins to increase sufficiency, becomes more discriminating, and therefore divides the world into more, less fuzzy classes, 'Mother's face', 'Father's face'. Its perception gets more fussy and less fuzzy.

I have suggested that semantic (or evidential) connectivity can be represented by the 'weight' of connections between concepts or percepts. This seems to be a model for the central strategic region of the network. I now suggest that the semantic input to a recognising gate (nerve or nerve-assembly) is the summed 'weights' or intensities of its inputs. This must pass some threshold, exceed some sufficiency, for recognition or classification to occur.

Truth is fabrication

In exploring the polyhierarchic model for perception, I start where knowledge does, at the input interface, the sensorium, and we see that there is no pure cognitive truth. There is only fabrication. What we see as truth is simply the sort of fabrication within the brain that has an acceptable degree of congruence with a reality that cannot be directly perceived.

The way we know about that congruence is another story. We cannot measure it because we cannot know the objective (external) comparate directly. But we have many crosschecks, tricks and guiles. Philosophers have suggested induction, but Karl Popper rejected it. What else is there though? Exact repetition of events is not given to us, but percepts and their elements, within some fuzz boundaries, are repetitive, we and our computers can correct our models for noise if we receive enough exemplary inputs. And there are crosschecks and informative mismatches which enable us to measure

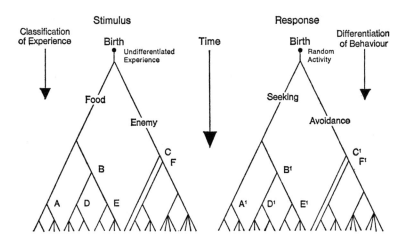

The figure illustrates the parallel of the differentiation of experience and behaviour during the development of a complex animal which learns everything afresh at each generation. The sorting and classifying of the experience of events proceeds in parallel with the reduction of randomness in behaviour and the selection of behaviour patterns with ever narrower tolerances and ever proliferating variety.

Figure 15 The differentiation of experience and activity in learning

congruence by inference. The ground plan is this: That fabrication, that subject comparate system (mask, model) which gets the highest weighted score from a sample series of percept presentations and which also has a threshold which brings errors of exclusion and errors of inclusion lowest and most equally shared is the best, the nearest to the ever unattainable 'truth'.

That internal fabrication which shows most internal consistency and least inconsistency with all the other fabrications which form the knowledge base is the most trustworthy.

How do we classify?

We therefore have to classify our incoming impressions to reduce their infinite variety to brainable dimensions. We have to clump (I. J. Good) or chunk (Richard Gregory) analysed bits of experience and treat the members of a class of inputs as if they were what they are not, identical. This is a matter we shall have to clarify a great deal before we can get far with creating non-biological intelligence.

Classification in the primitive animals is genoplastic. Let us consider onto-plastic classification. Ontoplastic intelligence operates on every individual and it enables each one to snuggle into its own opportunistic sub-niche.

Animals can learn by trial and error, with memory records and pain and pleasure as the teachers.

Homo Sapiens is the species which is by far the most gifted with ontoplastic intelligence. He has some of the other sort, more than we used to think, but less than any other animal. Man has softwired tendencies, drives, strategic goals which set his optimising 'shooing' pleasure/pain system, but few conscious hardwired kneejerk-type responses. He has thousands of unconscious ones, of course. Try to stop sweating in a Turkish bath.

At the conscious level, how did you, as a baby, learn to sort out the incessant creeping barrage of sensory impressions with which you were bombarded from the moment you unwisely opened your tiny, pretty eyes?

Judged by your behaviour, you could make nothing of your input at first and your responses were limited to grasping, sucking, smiling, crying and soiling napkins. Your ontoplastic behaviour, the unco-ordinated movements of your little limbs, could have been programmed from a random number table. It was experimental trial-and-error behaviour which was all error at first. You had an almost completely uncomprehended input and a largely random output. It would seem like a pretty bad start for a life it if had not turned out so well long term. Can we illuminate what was happening from our model? Yes.

You had to classify your inputs despite their enormous fuzziness. But before you could even do this there was another task. You cannot recognise patterns unless you have some idea what patterns there are. You had, in some fashion, to elaborate the internal comparates of useful percepts. (Kant's idea that the pattern masks were all there to begin with is too great a strain on our credulity, there are too many recognisable things that our ancestors cannot have known.)

Before we allocate perceptual inputs to classes we therefore have to find out what classes there are in the first place.

Taxonomy

The science of sorting out biological species is called taxonomy.

Your first task was do-it-yourself taxonomy. You had to sort out your inputs. You had to analyse experience, break it up into useful chunks that enabled you to build up expectations. You had to classify but first you had to decide what classes you needed to know about at that stage. You had only three clues. The first was repetition. You had to latch on to iterative bits of experience. Pain in its various forms from discomfort upwards was your second teacher and your third was pleasure. But every input was unique! There was no repetition! Well then, it must have been repetition within some sufficiency limit. You had to learn those sufficiency limits at the same time as you analysed the input frames and learned which bits were important to you.

Which bits were repetitive? How repetitive? Which bits hurt? Which made you feel good? You started your own personal adventure in d.i.y. taxonomy with only crude stick and carrot teaching, yet by the time you were two you were managing your little world a bit. Enough to get a cognitive input via speech to help you. You did well to sort it all out in the time at your disposal!

Epistemological classes and ontological classes

In the influential book, *The Nature of the Physical Universe,* Sir Arthur Eddington emphasised that knowledge could not be cleaned of its epistemological character and nature. Real objectivity is an illusion. His illustration was this. The view a fisherman takes of the size of fish depends on the mesh of his nets as well as on the properties of the fish. Our sensory organs, our scientific instruments and the hardwiring of our brains between them decide how we shall view nature. Nature then tells us a version of its laws that suits that set of probes. Choosing the method of inspection and primary isolates, classes, subject comparates, was really choosing the laws too.

This explains the anomalities where different disciplines interface. It explains complementarities such as wave/particle duality, and why we have to have a revolutionary revision of analysis and classification when a new paradigm becomes necessary.

In a very simple form we have encountered just such revolutions in the programs that are being devised to test the present hypothesis, the automatic taxonomy programs. We create a world with a set of patterns to be distinguished. We present them, as nature does, always in a fuzzy form to the brain simulator program. The program inductively works out which are the most distinguishing elements and assemblies thereof and 'learns' to sort them out, however fuzzy (or noisy) the succession of exemplars. If after many iterations, when the brain has learned its world we now add a new percept 'class' and present its noisy versions, it throws the brain into confusion for a while. It has to revise its scheme throughout to accommodate the new 'discovery'. It often has to give different weights to distinguishing features, in a surprisingly radical revision.

The process of learning about the world according to the polyhierarchic paradigm of learning involves analyses into classes which are known, each with *fuzz* that is also known.

The scientist working from definitions can easily communicate the method of analysis and define the classes. What is much more difficult is to pass to others the fuzziness, the sufficiency which is the necessary companion of every class. That only becomes apparent to the insider group within the discipline, as Kuhn's brilliant insight revealed. Fuzz sense frequently comes only with experience, but it often cannot be directly communicated in words. That is why disciplines are mutually insulated and why the work of the venturesome generalist like me is so very difficult.

Experimental experience with the computer simulations of the learning paradigm I present produced one important distinction that I must introduce here before we move away from the problems of classification.

There are classes of percept which are natural in that the members of the class tend to cluster about a Gaussian mean or norm. Class divisions fall naturally at the tails of the normal curve. Biological classes are examples. The more the class member deviates from the class median the less frequently the deviant is found. We could call these 'ontological classes', and their limits *could* be learned merely from their relative frequency without punishment or reward. I believe that some primary human learning, that of perceptual elements (like edges at various orientations, for instance, in the visual field), is of this nature. (Such elements may even be hardwired, genoplastic.)

The other sort of class is the *epistemological* class, whose boundaries are set by a linguistic convention. They are fundamentally arbitrary. The visual class indicated by the word 'yellow' exemplifies. That class is defined by a broad band of light frequencies whose borders are fixed by convention. The class boundaries have to be taught to any intelligence by other intelligences who know the convention. However, before an unsophisticated intelligence has learned the language, before it can even talk to a sophisticated one how can they communicate? The teaching intelligence has to give pleasure or cause displeasure in some form. The learner intelligence has to have an initial notion of good and bad before the convenient semantic borders and the fuzz limits of epistemological classes can be fixed, but once there is a common language flowing between morphostats they can communicate class boundaries and fuzzinesses without too much resort to a pain/pleasure continuum. The built-in pleasure for a child of the mere activity of learning correctly is very visible. Biologically it *has* to be.

It seems, parenthetically, that one of the measures of 'progress' or 'advancement' on the Scala Naturae in evolutionary terms is the reduction of the severity of punishment. For simple creatures the sole punishment for 'wrongdoing', unbiological behaviour, is the death penalty. Higher up the sentence may be reduced to torture (pain) and higher still disgrace, disapproval and so on. At the highest level communication can be almost (never quite) free from an incentive element.

THE DYNAMIC NATURE OF RECOGNITION

One should by now be clear. When I speak of the subject comparate or internal mask or representation of a percept or concept in a human brain I am not suggesting that it is in the form that is in any sense visually like the object comparate which excites it. To fit this paradigm it has to be a dynamic connectivity network in which the pictorial forms have been transduced or coded into locus and excitation magnitudes. The internal representation is, I believe, under constant revision and adjustment both as to its norm and the boundaries of its fuzz. With time it converges asymptotically on improved congruence with the central mode of the class of object comparates which it has specialised in recognising.

As excitation moves inwards from the sensorium periphery it transduces *arrangement* into locus and intensity. For example, one cell or locus above a tiny area of retina represents a left-bright vertical edge. This tiny geometric perceptual element is now represented by a single-point locus in the brain. All the other perceptual elements that may appear at the small area have a point representation. That set will be enough to deal with any class of more elaborate percepts that may be perceived, there is a vast economy. The same thing is repeated at the stratum above but here an assembly of small perceptual elements, a small visible figure like a letter is represented by a locus or set of loci at the senior stratum. Proceeding inwards the subjective comparate (mask model) becomes a pattern of firings at loci that have no visual relation with the object comparate that caused them.

The economy continues at every stratum. There will have to be very large numbers of loci which represent the same element, fewer that represent more central combinations.

I interpose a caveat. It is just possible that the reader may be making vain attempts to fit my topological map to the physiological map of the human brain. I do not think we are going to get the basic functional ground plan right if we insist on visible physiological-functional concurrence at so early a stage of exposition. Once I have communicated a functional understanding we can take our double polyhierarchic network in our very flexible topological mental fingers and, just as we pulled one kind of connection to one, and another to another, face of a cube, we can pull them all to the known sensory, the motor and the other mappings of particular brains. We know that what I have defined as the sensorium is divided into a number of separate input sensory arrays which are roughly defined by the senses, sight, touch, taste, smell, hearing. Each of these has different organs and modes. We also know that the information from all these organs is pooled or centralised in some way so that any complete experience can have contributions from all these widely separate organs.

My model arises from a functional hypothesis, not a physiological one. I ask this. 'Seeing what it is and what it is doing, what shape must the information flow have?' When we complete the model we shall have to see how well it can be made to fit the physical thing.

At the motorium

The polyhierarchic architecture for information flow at the sensorium indicates a stage-by-stage building up of pattern recognition from the base as learning proceeds.

What, according to the model, is going on at the motorium side of the central apical region as perceptual learning proceeds?

To learn by trial and error you need trials. There must be behaviour of some kind before learning can even start. Ontoplastic learning is impossible if genoplastic behaviour is inflexible (as it is, largely, with insects), so there must be random penny-toss input in learning behaviour. Behaviour must be, at the very beginning, independent of sensory input, pure experiment. There must be whim.

Our model is a hierarchic process in which a skill is built up from skill-elements, small elements of behaviour at the periphery. At the next stratum, subskills, combinations of skill elements are connected up, then at successively more central levels more elaborate skills. All these may be employed in more strategic behaviours generated at more central points in the network. As at the sensorium, the learning process proceeds inwards from the motorium periphery towards the apical centre. The information from the sensorium (and the appetitive system which can be seen as part of it) has the power as learning proceeds to trigger larger, more complex, longer lasting behaviour sequences.

To explain the great economy of this system consider this parable.

Let the development of a complete elaborate skilled behaviour sequence be the assembly of exactly the right sequence of cards in pack. We have to keep shuffling blind until we get the sequence right. If we shuffle the whole pack at each attempt we shall take a very long time. But if, whenever we get a few cards in the correct sequence, we get a partial pay-off, we can speed up learning thus. When we are rewarded we increase the mutual affinity between the cards of the active sequences (so that they are less likely to be separated). As we shuffle, the cards will gradually form optimal 'families' or 'hands' or 'genes' of cards. We continue shuffling these until, with reward, they get into good sequences of hands, 'hands of hands' in fact. These tend to clump together and are shuffled as larger clumps and so on. Our model could have been genes in a genome which are on the same game.

A computer simulation of this card-shuffling parable reduced the shuffling required to get the optimum behaviour vector by an enormous factor.

Another parable. The brain-cube is a vast writhing mass of entwined octopuses all locked into one enormous complex embrace. Each can prod its contacts and there are simple rules about this. The cube of octopuses has the world talking to one face by prodding bits of that surface and the cube talks to the world in a similar way at the opposite face. It seeks to make its output patterns more rewarding by getting each of them right for the present input pattern. It is told on a warmer/colder basis when it gets anything a bit right (output more appropriate to input). It is told when it does badly but not what went wrong.

What would its 'learn' algorithm be like? The name of its game obviously is:

'Experiment with random outputs, when rewarded whatever was active here at the motorium should improve its connectivity with whatever was active at over there at the sensorium at that time, so probe inwards, improve inward connectivity. If punished, reduce inwards connectivity and improve lateral connectivity (seek alternatives). Probe laterally.'

After mistakes, false starts and amendments, eventually the probing, inward-reaching connectivity networks from the sensorium meet and combine with the appropriate connectivity networks from the motorium. Each makes its connection with the oppositely advancing sensory network for that input and a correct output for an input has been learned.

In this oversimplified first view failure or punishment enhances lateral (searchlike) connectivity, and success enhances connectivity towards simultaneously excited central nets.

A further point. It is too early to decide what physical aspects of the brain are cognate with the elements of the model. We could interpret the 'nodes' or 'apices' of the model as represented physiologically by individual cells in the brain. However we could equally represent them as what Dr D. O. Hebb called 'cell assemblies' (*The Organisation of Behaviour*) or the 'modules' of cells that Professor Eccles posited in *The Self and its Brain*.

What is left out from this is almost everything. It is the crude ground plan that must be the base. I have made a paper boat and shown that if it is hollow it floats. I shall not get to explain a modern warship but I hope to demonstrate a skiff or even a small motor boat.

In the next section I shall assume that I have at least your acceptance that this crude model is worth a little further thought. I shall now speculate on the kind of hardware, software and components that are suggested by the poly-hierarchic model of intelligence.

TRIGGERS, SWITCHES, TRANSDUCERS, RELAYS, GATES, NERVES

Tracing the idea 'information' back to its elementary components, we find as an essential feature an input/threshold/output device which in its earliest artefact form was a trigger, switch or similar device where a small controlled event releases rather than directly causes a more energetic one. Here is the essential idea of regeneration, repair. The transduction of information is completely dependent on the purely biological activity called repair.

A transducer is defined as a device that converts the physical magnitude of one form of energy to another form, e.g. a microphone or electric motor. The word is now being used in a very different and more important sense to indicate any device which has an energetic input in one form which creates or triggers a homologous output in some other form. In this sense a meter or biological receptor can be seen as a transducer. The transducer is vital to information systems and we need to explore the range of their functions and possible functions.

The simplest form of transducer is one including a step function. It is called a relay. The relay is a device in which a signal operates a switch or trigger. It receives and responds to a signal.

In the morphostat context a signal is a low-energy event which may be used to trigger higher-energy events, either directly or because of its place in a chain of signals. Signals cause other events or other signals in a very special way which, though causal, is very different from the way non-biological causal connections operate. The signal connection is usually not natural but artificial in the sense that the linkage has been *arranged* to meet a purpose. The events in a signal chain are very orderly and highly improbable (on a chance assembly hypothesis).

I have argued that it is wiser to assume that the physical laws of the mesocosm are statistical in nature. I have also argued that living systems must utilise chains and cascades of triggery effects if they are to climb negentropy slopes as they do. If that is so then *any* long contrived chain of interacting signals, even those in mechanical or electrical artefacts, can build up connections between events, give one event the power to trigger rather than directly cause another by controlling some independent power source. The result would be extremely negentropic and improbable in a world where there are no living things to arrange such chains. It follows that long signal chains can make apparently *non-causal* connections which do not obey the laws (purely statistical) of the mesocosm. These laws, being probabilistic, can only say what is very probable. Long signal chains and cascades are themselves highly improbable; they can, by regeneration and amplification, break the laws of the mesocosm. They thus resemble life forms and cease to be full members of the Pleroma. Artefacts made by the biota are heteronomic, not fully governed by the laws that apply to the Pleroma in the mesocosm. As with the carbohydrate Creatura, trigger chains and trees enable machines to perform the miracles that we have set out to abolish.

As with living things, artefact signals tap an independent source of energy to do their work of regeneration or amplification.

Figure 16 illustrates the essence of what a signal does in the biological case. Morphostats and even machines need many governors or homeostats. Homeostats are devices for keeping a variable stable within some sufficiency slot.

The ordinary thermostat is the simplest example. The essence is the independent source of energy and a sensor-trigger to release it or hold it back.

In the biological case a signal is usually a representative or symbolic event which is a micro-homologue of some more energetic *significant* event. It brings information about an event or possible future event which may require

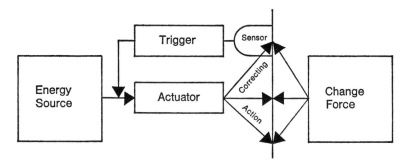

Figure 16   Homeostat

purposive action. It must have a prepared receptor which 'understands' some common 'language'. When you press a switch, you move metal parts. What happens is ruled by classical mechanical and electrical theory, but the switch is 'arranged', it can turn on a light, which is not the natural result of moving a few grams of brass and plastic a centimetre. The switch is a transducer which contains encapsulated know-how or information in its form. Against the normal rules it plays God. It says 'Fiat lux'.

Returning, in the light of the above, to the first development of electrical forms of communication, we have to look back at relays. Relays were first used to regenerate weakening direct currents on morse telegraph lines. The feeble deteriorated signal in a long line was regenerated by being used to

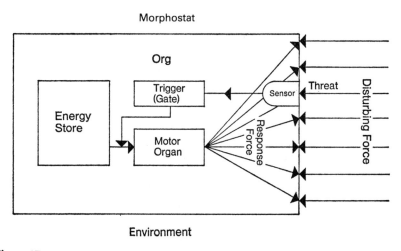

Figure 17

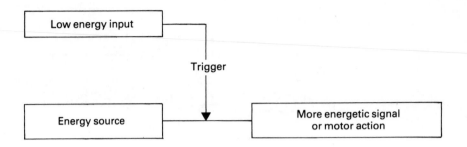

Figure 18   A relay

open or close another circuit using an *independent source of energy*. This apparently trivial fact is of central importance. The operation of a relay is the simplest form of signal.

A relay is a trigger. It has three distinct features: it has an energetic input which controls an available reservoir of energy and it has an output. It is a catastrophe device in Rene Thom's sense.

A relay has trigger-like control of the energy in its reservoir. It has the power to regenerate form because locally it can climb an entropy slope. Like Maxwell's Demon it can fiddle the Second Law of Thermodynamics, pumping entropy outside its system, preserving form and order within it.

Another feature of a relay that is of vital importance is that it is a variety reduction tool. It makes decisions. The input of science is pointer readings, as Sir Arthur Eddington said. However, science cannot do much with a forest of flickering meter needles. There are an infinite number of readings or output states of a meter. The simplifier, a relay or bistable, usually has many analogue inputs but by use of a threshold this variety is reduced to two output states (on and off). It is the relay function of transduction from analogue input to binary digital output that constitutes a signal. Variety reduction is the morphostat problem. This helps to solve it. A relay reduces the variety of output states from infinity to two.

A gate

A relay is an elementary form of transducer. A gate or logical input/output device in the usual sense allows two outputs and one input. However, gates are used in complexes which may have multiple inputs and outputs, so I suggest that a useful meaning for gate in this context is a device for making decisions that can have any number of inputs and any number of outputs.

The two-prong fork gate shown in Figure 19 can be an *'and'* gate, an *'or'* gate, a *'nand'* gate or a *'nor'* gate, each with the indicated logical functions

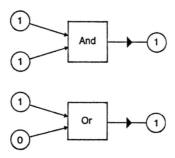

Figure 19   A two-prong fork gate

(e.g. an 'and' gate regenerates a signal if both inputs are excited, an 'or' gate if either is. The prefix 'n' represents 'not' and reverses the action, giving a contradictory output.) The whole repertoire of deterministic computer logic has been built up from these simple components.

Sufficiency gates and semantic gates

In my book *Brain* I proposed *sufficiency gates* as the component needed in the fuzzy logic, noise tolerant hardware needed for artificial taxonomy. Sufficiency gates are not dissimilar to what are now called 'voting' or 'threshold' gates.

A sufficiency gate (enough gate) has multiple inputs and outputs, the sharp distinction between an 'and' and an 'or' gate is lost. A gate can be anywhere on spectrum between the two. It is not an all-or-none hard logic affair. We could have a ten-input 'andish' gate that responds to (changes output for) any nine of its inputs, or any eight, or any seven . . . Eventually we have demoted it from a very discriminating, fussy 'and-y' gate with a low tolerance for noise to an easy-going gate, a 'generalising', 'or-ish' gate which will respond to any two or even one of its inputs. We have been changing the threshold downwards. It has lost discrimination and become a relating or generalising gate, an 'or' gate which says 'any of these inputs is equivalent'.

Discrimination and relation or generalisation are the primitive tools of thought. Our new gate is moving away from Shannon's non-semantic paradigm towards a new semantic one. With a semantic gate we can represent or simulate meaning. But we have one more step to take. It may seem like a backward step but it is not. We have to retreat from binary digital expression to analogue expression, to introduce a degree of noise tolerance.

Sufficiency gates can be Boolean/binary as shown in Figure 20, or semantic.

However, we may also make a gate where the inputs are intensities or magnitudes which may be positive or negative. The sufficiency is now set as a

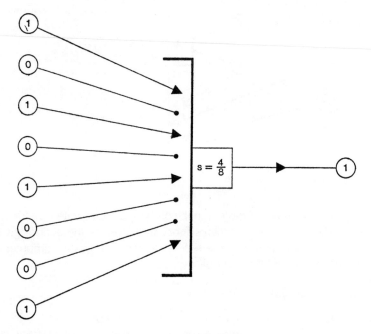

If the sufficiency (S = 4/8) threshold is set at the total number of inputs it is a full 'and' gate. As we adjust the threshold downwards it becomes less 'and-y' and more 'or-like', finally when the sufficiency is 1/8 it is an 'or' gate.

Figure 20   A binary sufficiency gate

frequency, or magnitude, and the gate responds, sends an output, only if the sum of its active inputs (+ and −) exceeds the threshold. This is illustrated in Figure 21. The output of the gate to all its connections can also be a magnitude, positive or negative. We have moved off the Boolean road and we now have a gate that can deal with evidence and meaning. We have a semantic gate. The gate can say more than 'yes' or 'no', it can say 'maybe' (+ 3) or 'I do not know' (0), 'I am fairly sure' (+ 7) or 'possibly, but I do not think so' (− 8). Ideally it would have analogue magnitudes, steplessly variable. But in modern computers it can have variety enough in a few bytes.

Why do I say that gates with many inputs and outputs can bring semantic content into information theory? The introduction of fuzzy connections involving magnitudes at junctions between components gives us a calculus for connectivity and that, I shall argue, can be used to quantise semantic connectivity which, in the nerve, is the only visible method for dealing with

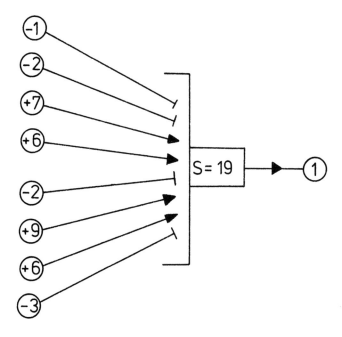

Figure 21   A semantic gate

semantic content. The meaning of a word can only lie in the strength, the sign and the direction of its connectivity which nets with the rest of the system or brain. We know that the nerve cell has variable output via its axon, variable receptivities at its dendrites and a variable threshold. We must seek, and I think I may have found, a paradigm which shows how this sort of connectivity can represent meaning.

The first program which worked with the concept of this kind of gate in our experiments was used in a program which solved the automatic taxonomy problem of a simulated simple intelligent entity. Such a program is called a taxonomon.

THE FIRST TAXONOMON PROGRAM

In this chapter I have sketched the theoretical approach to present-day information theory and reinterpreted it in the light of the way of looking at that world which I propose. The polyhierarchic information flow architecture that I suggest leads to the suggestion for a possible component and connectivity system for brain simulations, and some primitive thoughts about possible

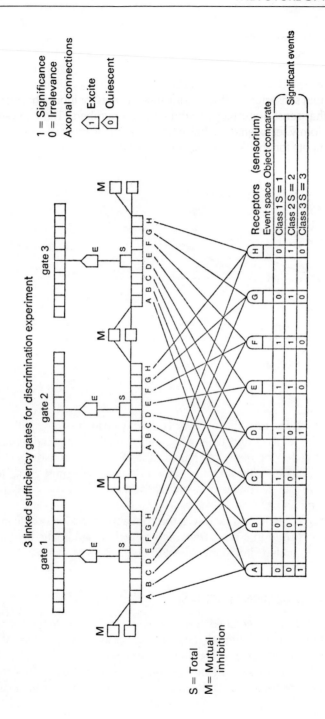

Figure 22   Model of nerve cell programming

brainsmith plans will follow in the next chapter. I complete this chapter by republishing (Figure 22) the first taxonomon diagram from my 1974 book *Brain*. This sketch led to James Cherrill's first successful taxonomon programs.

We see three interlinked competitive sufficiency gates which are looking at the same 8-input sensorium. Below are the three 'events' or inputs that may be received at that sensorium; they are three binary numbers. The competing gates are randomly set by entering low magnitudes in the input spaces A, B, C, etc. They compete for and 'learn' to specialise, each one responding to one of the input patterns despite the fact that these are noisy or partly erroneous at each presentation. A gate responds or 'excites' when its sufficiency 's' is exceeded by the total of the weights at its excited inputs (those inputting a 1, not a 0). It learns by adjusting its weights and its sufficiency in accordance with the 'learn algorithm' that is being tried. In the next chapter we shall explore a primitive range of taxonomons, their limitations and possibilities.

7

Modelling brains

Let me clear something out of the way. I have advanced an unmystical hypothesis of dualism based on the leakage and amplification of microcosmic indeterminism into the mesocosm and the parasitism of the unliving by living forms. These, being non-material, may have their own heteronomous lawlike invariances and constraints.

THE ECONOMICAL MIND/BRAIN HYPOTHESIS

I have argued in favour of the most economical hypothesis that explains the contradiction between our apparent freedom of choice and the rigidity of statistical laws in systems as large as brains. My hypothesis is that mind is the internal experience of the activity of the physical stuff of brain. I suggest that the most economical hypothesis should be the default hypothesis wherever we have to make an assumption to be able to continue enquiry. We can be sure that if another entity such as immanent, non-physical mind should exist it will reveal itself in the end. It will do so the sooner if we force it to do so.

We can sympathise with the reluctance of those who believe in an immortal spirit, a soul; to accept that mind is an activity of mortal brain but that reluctance is visibly of a piece with their mystical belief, an act of faith. I propose, if only as a sensible scientific strategy, to continue these speculations on the working hypothesis that the experiences of our minds are cognate with the activities of our brains.

Artificial intelligence cannot be ruled out

Consequently, I feel it would be risky and unnecessary to rule out, *ab initio*, as impossible the hypothesis that there may be other arrangements of material that can produce the phenomenon we attribute to our minds. This opens a door to the possibility of artefact intelligence, intelligence based on other substrates than the biochemical system that is the basis of all known life forms. I might have said non-biological intelligence except that if we should create artificial intelligence it might be biomorphic. It would belong to and obey the laws of the biological realm rather than those of the physical realm. Artificial intelligence would be a surviving form rather than a collection of material.

The politics of non-carbohydrate intelligence

The society that rejects artificial intelligence or mind as a possibility not worthy of examination is taking the risk of losing the chance to influence it, gain from it or limit it according to its views. In a competitive, divided world we have no way to stop *some* society from creating artificial intelligence if it *is* possible. I see no hope of obtaining world unanimity in the policy of not trying (or on any other policy for that matter). There is going to be work towards this goal whatever we think. Let our society be in the act, at least.

Even if artificial intelligence turns out to be impossible, much that may be useful can be learned from the investigation. Attempts to simulate mind and brain can bring epistemology and even semantic philosophy into the ambit of the rigorous sciences. It is unthinkable to go very far in experiments on living human brains but there will be few moral objections to experimenting on artificial ones. If psychology and epistemology become experimental sciences in which limitless manipulation is allowable we can scarcely fail to advance both sciences. If the present paradigm has merit, there can also be better informed experimental manipulation of sociological and economic models to guide theory.

Is there a programming limit?

I had better give the obvious answer to the most childish objection to artificial intelligence. People repeat the stock phrase: 'Computers can only do what they are programmed to do, therefore they can never be creatively intelligent'. They seem to think that they have said something obvious. Computers as they are now are not very intelligent but we cannot assume that computers will always be as they are now. There has been visible progress.

What is proclaimed impossible exists. There is an arrangement of matter in each human head that was prescribed from a set of instructions in a genome. That lump of physical matter, the brain, *does* manifest intelligence. There are about four billion different such sets of brain specifying instructions (genomes) in existence. That set was evolved with no apparent input of cognitive intelligence, what might be done with some input thereof? How can we be sure that another such set, based on different materials, is impossible?

Having thus cleared the air I can now go on to speculate on what sort of instruction set would be needed to specify artificial intelligence machines in the light of my intelligence paradigm.

I shall proceed by easy expositional stages. I have to show a crude over-simplified model at first. It will be useless to ask the model to explain everything at once. If we can get some comprehension of a worm brain first, we may find a scaffolding that can be elaborated to carry the weight of a more elaborate edifice of brain model later.

But first, I have to take a brief stroll around the field to glance at and doff a respectful hat to the rival structures. Those who claim to be working at artificial (or machine) intelligence, what are they up to?

CONTEMPORARY WORK ON ARTIFICIAL INTELLIGENCE

Artificial intelligence is an idea that has been coming on to the intellectual's agenda slowly for several generations. Mechanical men, robots, androids, and artificial monsters of various kinds have abounded in the human imagination, books, plays and films ever since Descartes popularised the idea that animals and indeed the world could be understood as mechanism.

Since Alan Turing's and Kurt Von Neumann's speculations led to the whole family of deterministic computers that we know, the imaginative probings of these ideas have gradually gained some rigour but ideas are, as they should and must be in the nascent stage of new techniques, highly various, tenuous and unformed. Books on artificial intelligence usually contain a scattered ragbag of different notions with no underlying shape or sequence, that is perhaps as it should be.

Making an effort to classify approaches, there are two main ones. They are described as the top-down approach and the bottom-up approach. To fit the polyhierarchic model they should be renamed the 'central' and 'interface' (or 'peripheral') approaches.

Machine translation, for which high hopes were entertained as early as the 'fifties, was a premature essay in the top-down or central approach. A whole series of programs has been very disappointing. Researchers started with programs which gave word by word translations, often with highly comic results, they got into obvious difficulties due to the failure to represent the contextual element in communication that I have dealt with. The next effort was directed to the translation of phrases and even sentences as a whole but this obviously ran into the combinatorial explosion problem with present computer methods. The funding and interest began to fail in 1964 when Bar Hillel published a very influential paper. He showed that there was no way to get rid of confusing multiple/version translations without a deep understanding of the meaning, that could not at that stage be achieved on the hardware extant. At that time no paradigm for the representation of meaning existed.

The significant failure of machine translation efforts led to a greater interest in the computerisation of linguistics and there began to be a lot more interest in syntactical, parsing, and semantic search ideas. Improved filing systems such as database and other memory organisation schemes may have come from this source. These have certainly been most successful.

A very influential book on the top-down approach is *The Fifth Generation* by Edward A. Feigenbaum and Pamela McCorduck. Their approach is entirely concerned with conceptual or cognitive intelligence, communicable strategic-type intelligence where the input and output are words and sentences. What the book describes is researches, largely in America, in the creation of what are called 'Expert Systems' on the substrate of normal Von Neumann determinist computers. The approach is based on systematic examination of the judgements of acknowledged experts in various fields. A synthetic, generalised, statistically checked consensus judgement is produced from this examination. The hypothesis is that the consensus judgement that emerges is better than the best individual judgement and the claim is that it is largely confirmed. That there are many fields where this method is likely to be advantageous is as obvious as that there are some where it is likely to be otherwise.

If we had had a good Expert System when Copernicus was alive it would have brushed him aside and produced a geocentric cosmology. Einstein would have been dismissed as a crank outsider and Darwin as a blasphemous liar by a relative contemporary Expert System. With their aid, all scientists at all times would have been rejected in proportion to the originality of their results.

We can concede, however, that the output of an Expert System will, at any given time, be a fairly safe bet. It will normally be better than the worst and worse than the best contemporary opinion. But at times of paradigm shift, and they come very frequently nowadays, Expert Systems will be systematically unreliable.

What is missing from the idea is trial and error with empiric tests. A strategic level optimising system with a range of optima and a measure of approach to them is needed. A rack-renting system of revising goals is also required.

The top-down approach popularised by Feigenbaum has taken a strong hold of the competitive imagination of experts in many countries and I fear may have resulted in a great deal of premature investment. This seems to be a stage when the need is for a wide and great variety of small scatter-shot efforts. Only when one of these, probably an unexpected one, begins to look promising will it be time for large-scale commitment on any one track. We are far from ready for the 'massive government (or any other) investment' in concentrated work on single projects such as the Japanese and Americans are trying in their

Fifth Generation Projects. Feigenbaum's plea for a concentrated effort is, at best, premature.

The above top-down or central approaches largely concern what, in the present model, would be the sensorium side of the apical communications centre. Another family of top-down approaches deals with the central regions above the motorium interface. Industrial robots are now fully commercial and becoming commonplace. The usual method of instructing them is by teaching them to copy the motions of a skilled human operator. Dirty and dangerous jobs like enamel spraying can be done well this way but the robots could hardly merit the description 'intelligent'. These early robots have no sensorium at all and cannot modify their instructions in the light of subsequent events. The approach is not really distinguishable from the Expert Systems approach on the other side of the apices. But sensory elements are already being added to advanced models.

The bottom-up (interface) approach

Bottom-up approaches (interface approaches) start from the peripheral interface of Brain with World at the sensorium or at the motorium. There are several bottom-up approaches.

As mentioned, sensing and learning requirements are becoming manifest at the motorium interface and are to be seen in the work on robots which features in all artificial intelligence books and symposia. Problems involving motions and actions that seem simple to adults turn out to be very complex when we try to produce them in artefacts.

Some workers are moving towards robots that can 'learn how to behave'. They have a sensorium, touch, and even visual inputs as well as an instructional, 'better/worse' input such that they can improve performance with experience. Most of them have to be instructed in great detail by a human who has the skills to begin with, however. None can learn elaborate skills from scratch like a self-taught typist does.

Another set of interface problems are those at the sensorium, the problems of perception. Pattern recognition, image processing, optical character recognition, automatic quality control are being investigated, as are sensing as an aid to motorium problems, controlling robot arms, etc.

An important contribution in this field came from Professor Igor Aleksander, whose ideas in the field of optical character recognition led to a successful though not yet commercial development. He has worked on a system that can recognise people's faces and correctly classify them. His method is to inspect the sensorium for simple feature and use a statistical method of summating the totality and expressing the result in a form that enables comparison decisions to be made. The method, called Wisard, inspects the set of faces. The subjects have to teach the Wisard the variability or fuzziness of their facial pattern by grimacing grotesquely. The machine is told the identity of the subject. When the same faces are presented with Wisard in the 'who?' mode it can correctly identify its input.

I think Professor Aleksander is on a useful track and has gone a long way with a single-stratum system, much further than I would have guessed he could.

Those working in this field have found that the traditional computer languages based on the Von Neumann, determinist paradigm are not suitable and there are a number of special high level languages designed for AI purposes. These include Conniver, Planner, Lisp and Modulo II, a version of Pascal. The advantage of these languages is that they are suitable for the recursive functions that have been needed in attempts to simulate strategic or central processes such as meaning, purpose and language when these are done without what I believe will be essential in the end, concurrency.

It is Professor Iann Barron's invention, the transputer that gives most hope in this direction. A network of concurrent (operating simultaneously in real time) transputers can do things that Von Neumann computers could never do, especially in this field. The group which is working on the present model will be making experiments with transputers. My own thought here is that what is needed is a very great extension of the transputer notion. What I think is needed is a large number of very small, concurrent, nerve simulating computers on one wafer, with built-in networking facilities which would do all the tactical work of programming, leaving the programmer to set goals, aims and success criteria, rather than decide all actions. This would finally overcome the programming bottleneck. Sir Clive Sinclair's Metalab Group is working on these lines.

ANTHROPOMORPHIC, MECHANOMORPHIC AND BIOMORPHIC WORLD MODELS

In this chapter I propose an improved version of the primitive model brain we have been trying. I propose it for test. But let me first briefly recapitulate human thinking about this to set the scene.

Modern biologists deny Haeckle's notion that ontogeny recapitulates phylogeny, that the development of the individual follows the evolution of the species. But the development of popular thought patterns in the world culture seems to recapitulate the individual's experience.

The classical intellectual world was inhabited by the Majorum Gentium, a family of gods which were an echo of the surrounding family of the baby's first perceptions. The helpless infant has no direct power over its world, it can satisfy its needs and desires only through the agency of those all powerful giants around it, its kin. Learning to manage them is its first priority. All good and evil come from these wilful, animate sources. Baby's own random strugglings avail it little. The first models of the universe were echoes of this helpless baby's world, where only prayer and worship bring a Helping Hand down from On High. This was the anthropomorphic world model, a world of gods and demons.

But man *(homo faber)* is a tool maker, an artisan and farmer. At a later phase of a child's development it is learning to master artefacts, tools, implements, mechanisms, inanimate *things*. As the human tools and mechanisms became more complex there arose a new class of paradigm of the human condition. There began to be a world modelled on mechanism. Descartes may have been the first to formalise that mechanomorphic model, the one that dominates scientific thinking today, the one that sees the world as a great deterministic clockwork engine.

The Von Neumann computer, the hyperfast abacus, is built on and limited by the mechanomorphic paradigm, as are almost all the products of modern engineering.

The mechanomorphic principle of manufacture is that the exercise of intelligence is confined to the planning, research and design stage. The product is designed for life. All the conditions it will meet have to be foreseen and provided for before it leaves the factory. Design is first optimised, the product is then made and distributed. Each copy is an exact replicate, in theory. It does nothing but deteriorate from manufacture until it is scrapped. Indeterminism, experiment and therefore optimisation are eliminated from the product. Repair, regeneration and all improvements have to come from outside the product itself. This purely genoplastic design mode applies today with vanishingly few exceptions.

The paradigm I propose, not only for the artificial intelligence models (where it is essential) but also for a whole new line of engineering products, products such as will be suitable for unmanned space and other probes for instance, is a biomorphic one. In this model there is built-in and automatic optimisation repair, regeneration and learning by experience as in virtually all living forms. To give but one example, the hydrodynamic efficiency of a shark is vastly better than that of any known vessel because it has an 'intelligent' skin.

The limitations of the Von Neumann computer paradigm

The limitations of the Von Neumann computer with its single central processing unit have been masked for a long time by the incredible success achieved in the speeding up of the data processing and the vast economies in memory cost. Enormously improved and astonishingly error-free, computing power has prevented attention being paid to the fundamental limitations of the fully preplanned, serial, one-thing-at-a-time computing model. The standard computer in 1986 has, in exaggerated form, the defects of the centralist State. Most of the parts, for most of the time, are waiting to be told what to do, for something to happen elsewhere.

Traditional computers are blind, deaf robots designed entirely to obey a program. This is a sequential list of commands. Their only sensorium is a keyboard. Everything in memory or on disc was first keyed in by people. They are the motorium half of a brain with no learning power at all. They were designed to fit the clockwork, determinist world arising from a philosophy of science that arose from monotheist doctrines.

But it is all too easy to make criticisms such as this. It is more difficult to solve the vast problems that drop on our plate when we depart from the usual type of 'everything planned in advance to the last detail' method of programming that is now almost universal.

The deficiencies become plainer as the interpretative languages reach higher levels of complexity and become more and more remote from the basic machine code actions at their base. Advanced program designers realise that built-in experimental, option-offering, optimising, success-measuring, self-repair aspects and elements are the only way forward for computer design.

The combinatorial explosion problem

To give an illustrative instance, one of the accepted limitations to computing power is that of the combinatorial explosion. The sort of programs which human programmers are clever enough to write have to rely largely on the high-speed number-crunching idiocy of the hyperfast determinist computer. It is too easy and too tempting to explore the whole of a space rather than find a more economical approach. Big, fast number crunchers go through the haystacks, straw by straw, looking for that needle. Particularly in simulations of cognition, computers run into the combinatorial explosion problem again and again.

Consider this model. We seek a man with a broken nose, a scar on his elbow, knock knees, no hair, a lisp, and a wart on his left eyelid. Scheme one: We apppoint a Central Processing Person to examine everyone on earth. Scheme 2: We broadcast a description. Someone calls up and says 'Hey!'

Central versus concurrent architecture! Mechanomorphic versus biomorphic computer thinking!

Parallel processing architecture

When, in the early 'sixties, I first suggested concurrent, parallel processing computer architecture, I used to be told of the incredible computer speeds, up to 100 Kips (1 Kip = 1000 instructions/s) that were coming along to make it quite unnecessary. Today we have speeds that are orders faster, tens of Mips, yet there are plenty of experimental parallel approaches being worked on. How come?

The concurrency concept is simple enough to follow. Imagine a computer net consisting of a very large number of small interlinked computers, each with its own small memory and its own PU working independently and concurrently but in a co-operative-competitive relation with all the others, like people in a market. Instead of one preoccupied central processing unit which mediates everything while all the other parts passively wait, the whole assembly is working on different parts of the big problem simultaneously. Each small unit has virtual but not actual communication with any other. (The number of virtual links is too great in any large system.)

Such systems are being devised. But the problem that remains unsolved is that of programming. It is assumed that the method will be analogous with the familiar list-of-commands-to-a-CPU systems. (The first motor cars looked like horse-drawn coaches.) Concurrent computers are designed so that each part has exact instructions, including how, when and where to intercommunicate, which part does what, responds to which, when, how and why. I have a comment. Impossible.

Metaprogramming

The underlying necessity of a Von Neumann program is that every step of the program is arrived at by logical steps decided by human cognitive processes. I suggest that this approach will not serve in systems which are beyond a certain degree in complexity and that if it is not abandoned it will prove to be a complete barrier to further progress.

The concept 'metaprogram' is formulated as a name for a program which constantly optimises and improves itself, which learns by experience. The program will work approximately at first but after a time it will improve as it tries small variants, takes short cuts, makes mistakes and learns from them. Later, the programmer will not be able to find out even how the programs work, he will have to be satisfied with the fact that they *do* work. He will measure and compare. He will comment, encourage, discourage, at a high strategic level only. He will cease to be both corporal and General. He will take up a Field Marshall's baton and put down his machine code manual.

To illustrate that this is not just a statement of an impossible aim I refer to the fact that monkeys can be taught tricks without the trainer (or programmer) knowing a lot about the monkey's nervous system or muscle fibres. All he needs to know is what is a good trick in a very general way, and how to motivate a monkey.

A teacher praises and blames, gives good and bad marks to the pupils. The teacher is not concerned with individual pencil strokes on a literate child's essay.

Another possible approach to this problem is that in which the means of communication between units that are not directly connected is by relaying via intermediate units. The approach of the Connection Machine is of this type. This involves occupying many such units with the purely relaying function. It would involve many complications in deciding routing options.

The central problem must be that of the linkage between the units, message priorities, readiness signals, buffer waiting memories and a great deal more inter-unit protocol.

The model proposed here comes, of course, from the architecture which I suggest for the needed information flow of all types of morphostat in the last chapter. It is the polyhierarchic information flow via a plurality of strata from an input periphery to a central decision zone and then outwards via cascading polyhierarchic strata to an output periphery at the motorium.

The most important problem will be that of communicating between levels or strata. The connections will have to be virtual, formable and breakable. If all possible links have to exist initially the number of them would be much too large in any useful system. Here we have an advantage over biological brains.

I shall describe the software proposed to simulate the concurrent hardware of the artificial intelligence schema that arises from the present paradigm. But first I must do two things. I must observe the niceties by drawing attention to previous thinking and work on similar tracks to that I so sketchily outline. Secondly I must try to show how all the scrambled, can-of-worms activity in many places that goes under the names 'artificial intelligence', 'machine intelligence', 'cognitive research' and so on can be ordered and systematised by being fitted to the architecture of the polyhierarchic model.

THE ARTIFICIAL INTELLIGENCE SCENE

Artificial intelligence is no better than biological intelligence at getting itself defined. There are many contending definitions and little consensus about what it is, or rather would be if it came about.

If we look to the origins we must think of Carel Capek. Rossum's Universal Robots, as described in the play *R.U.R.*, were undoubtedly intelligent in our normal sense of the word. Frankenstein's monster was conceptually an intelligent being that was also artefact. But both were apparently on biological bases.

George Boole (1854) wrote, 'The mathematics we have to construct is the mathematics of the human intellect'.

Alan Turing, in an article *Computing Machinery and Intelligence* (1950), talked of a computer that could be programmed to exhibit intelligent behaviour. He rejected the idea that artificial intelligence was impossible and of course proposed the famous 'Turing Test'.

A person and a computer are communicating via keyboards from different rooms. The person does not know whether there is a person at the other terminal or not. They converse thus until the person is ready to make a guess. If the person cannot tell whether the other terminal is manned or not the computer passes the Turing Test.

Claude Shannon, who brilliantly cleaned up and fixed non-semantic information theory, wrote a paper on computer chess in 1956, the same year as the seminal Dartmouth Conference was held at M.I.T. This was organised by John McCarthy and Marvin Minsky. The term 'artificial intelligence' originated from McCarthy and was first published in the papers by a group at M.I.T. on the two-month study which followed that summer.

One recent definition is 'the study of intelligence as computation'. Eugene Charniak and Drew McDermot proposed (1985) 'artificial intelligence is the study of mental faculties through the use of computer models', and assumed that what brain does at some level may be thought of as computation. Margaret Boden (1977) says that she uses the term to mean the use of computer programs and programming techniques to cast light on the principles of intelligence in general and human thought in particular.

Another definition is 'the development of a systematic theory of intellectual processes wherever they may be found'.

This definition of artificial intelligence is closer to the original ideas on the subject which arose after the publication of Norbert Weiner's *Cybernetics* and the work that arose from the initiative described at Cornell University. In *Aspects of the Theory of Artificial Intelligence* edited by C. A. Muses there were published the Proceedings of the 'First (and last?) International Symposium on Biosimulation', July 1960. The papers concerned learning systems, mathematical concepts of brain function as random networks, self-reproducing systems, probability distributions in random assemblies involving new liaisons of mathematics and logic. There was also a paper on computer teaching, which is a theme that is often repeated in this context.

There were also some papers which proposed input output systems not dissimilar to the one proposed here. Figure 23 shows one proposed by R. L. Beurle in a paper on information in random networks.

Today there are offshoots of the early thinking which spread in many directions in the rather undisciplined way which we must expect until there is consensus on what it is we are all on about.

In Britain, for example, at the time of writing we have a lot of activity at the University of Edinburgh with work in the Department of Artificial Intelligence School of Epistemics, and Departments of Linguistics, Psychology, Philosophy,

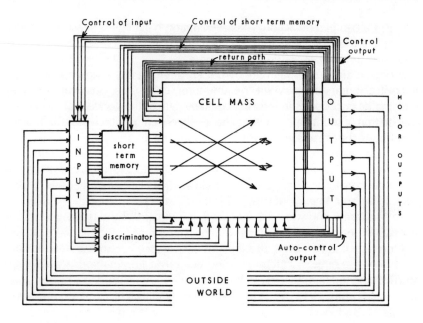

Figure 23

Computer Science, and Electrical Engineering, all of which co-operate with the AI work. The AI Department sees the job as 'making machines behave in ways that exhibit some of the characteristics of intelligence, and about how to integrate such capabilities into larger coherent systems'.

A lot of attention goes into the construction of high level programming languages which are adapted to traditional computers, such as the AI languages LISP, POP 2, PROLOG "C" and others. This fits the present paradigm as work on what happens in the central or apical region on the sensorium side, where useful perceptual classes have to be labelled. But some of the so-called languages fit more closely to the loci in the polyhierarchic network where motor behaviour trains are elaborated. There is a lot of work in which the object is to automate the process of mathematical reasoning, which seems to me to be away from the thrust of AI as I see it.

The robotics work is seen as a problem in writing suitable languages and this seems to apply to non-learning systems like automata or insects. But where the robots are seen as needing a sensory input, an internal world image and a goal-driven learning system, we can see them as fitting at the upper apical region on the motorium side of the network. There is a lot of work on spatial inference and comprehension, which locates on the apical motorium side in the current paradigm.

Vision, optical and sound and other pattern recognition work, remote sensing, and other perceptual work belongs to the lower strata of the sensorium side of the network. Work on sonar control of submersibles at the Herriot Watt University seems marginal as AI as it may be simply transduction or control engineering. Work on the comprehension of natural language which is being done is interesting because it takes the concept of AI up one stage to that of social intelligence. The intelligent entity which uses this kind of signalling is the human group, the sociozoon. The internal language by which brain speaks to muscles is utterly different. The work on language comprehension and analysis concerns the apical regions of that social morphostat we call an institution or group and hardly relates to artificial intelligence in its normal sense of artefact intelligence.

Planning systems, knowledge-based Expert Systems, and computer education do not seem to me to be in themselves to be AI or even necessarily aspects of it, in the sense I propose. Artificial intelligences may have such aspects but the essential elements input, options, choice and optimisation of output are not needed in many cases. Insofar as they do come within the semantic envelope of the words, they appear to belong to the apical strategic regions of the network posited.

There is, of course, other work going on in Glasgow, Sussex, Imperial College, Brunel University and other places but this quick look at some of the Edinburgh work will suffice for our immediate purpose.

PREVIOUS WORK ON NERVE NET MODELS

Turing, Pitts and McCulloch, Von Neumann, Culbertson, Kleene, virtually all the pioneers of modern computers have based their work on the Turing/Von Neumann paradigm of a deterministic system in which the starting point was strictly logical algorithms and a linearly organised memory. The procedure for recall from memory of inconveniently classified material was, as I have said, simply to search through everything. The essence was a central processing unit and a large serial memory with external extensions of it on magnetic storage.

Although this kind of model was said by E. C. Berkeley (for instance) to be comparable to a 'giant brain' and generally thought of as being brain-like it had no real resemblance to biological brains. In fact, the computer is good at what brains are bad at, computation, and bad at what brains are good at, dealing with judgement and evidence problems.

The other approach, the one that might have been thought to be obvious, 'copy what we see working, i.e. brain', was not followed because there was no adequate theory of brain function.

The approach I return to, the concurrent, parallel processing, simulated nerve-net approach, though suggestions of it are to be found in Turing's writings, was taken up by only a few workers and with little success. In 1958, the time of my first publication in this field, there was published by Frank Rosenblatt of the Cornell Aeronautical Laboratory a paper called *The Perceptron. A Theory of Statistical Separability in Cognitive Systems.*

Rosenblatt was reporting on a 2-year project based on an idea he had had around 1950 following J. O. Hebb's work, written up in *The Organisation of Behaviour.* Hebb wrote of cell assemblies and presented a theory of facilitation on repetition which at least partially overcame the equipotentiality problem which the work of Lashley underlined. This work, which showed that brain function could survive massive brain injury, had completely discouraged all connectionist models such as the one I present.

Rosenblatt, Uttley and others of this minority school were, as I was, interested in the vital problem of the perceptual interface of brain and world and the associated problem, recognition. In his introduction Rosenblatt says, 'The most important advantage of a brain over a computer may well be its capacity for *recognition* identification, its ability to say that a new set of data, stimulus pattern, or situation, is similar to some class or type which has been previously encountered, *even in the absence of specifically enumerated criteria'.*

My own first paper, shown to and signed by several people at the Philosophy of Science Society conference in 1957, was on the present hypothesis of recognition; it was afterwards revised and published in *The Scientist Speculates* some years later.

Rosenblatt's paper was not generally available at the time but on reading it many years later I find many elements of the ideas that I had developed, all under different names and presented in an entirely different way but surely based on very similar thinking. Missing is the general architecture and the polyhierarchical elements that I presented. Rosenblatt's approach was not pragmatic but largely mathematical. His team almost certainly had no access to any real computer power in those pre-transistor days, and that was the only way to go. There were no reports of computer simulations. What he showed was that it ought to be possible to predict learning curves from physiological variables and vice versa and that a quantitive statistical approach was likely to be fruitful in the organisation of cognitive systems. This was a breakthrough as it displaced logic and mathematics as the only road towards simulated brain function. It opened the door to acausal, indeterminate models such as this one.

The work on the Perceptron and on the rather similar Informon developed by A. M. Uttley at Sussex University continued for some years and there was some promising progress. But the computer power available was inadequate for models such as the taxonomon.

The next section outlines the ideas of Frank Rosenblatt *et al.* who began thinking about how nerve nets might work on lines similar to mine at about the same time as I did. The resulting papers about the Perceptron were influential for a time but all work seems to have ceased on that approach after a paper by Minsky and Pappert called 'Perceptrons'. This showed that there are theoretical limits to the Rosenblatt scheme, which seemed to be fundamental. The paper showed to the satisfaction of mathematicians that, without feedback, it is always possible to produce shapes so complex that the Perceptron cannot discriminate.

Figure 24 gives an example. The two shapes are quite different but they seem opposite 'hands' of the same design to most people.

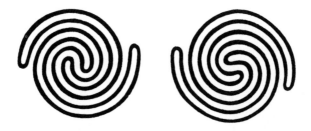

Figure 24

I am surprised that the Minsky-Pappert objection was taken so seriously, because human vision is subject to defective perception, as in the above case. There are many other cases, such as the brilliant examples of faulty perception demonstrated by Professor Richard Gregory in his many experiments and beautifully illustrated books on the subject. But humans get by, they are quite perceptive.

If machine vision is finally limited to the powers of human vision it might still be extraordinarily useful. As to the application to the taxonomon, it should be noted that the designs include a provision for 'learning feedback', so the Minsky-Pappert objections do not apply.

Perhaps the more telling reason why the nerve-net theories and programs were discontinued is that they arose when computer power was very much less than it is today. It has only recently become possible to simulate concurrent programs of any scale and complexity. Learning, like evolution, often proceeds in by-pass style. One successful line spreads, diversifies and comes to a halt as it fills its niche, but then it is often overspecialised. Thus it is superseded by a by-pass shoot originating in an earlier stock that somehow survived. Maybe the nerve-net model is the old root stock on which a new-graft generation of self-programming computers can grow.

The AI definitions seem to refer to fields of study rather than a proposed artefact. All come from those with reputations in the field but what is semantically captured by the definitions has no relation to the public meaning of the term, which is simply 'an artefact which behaves like a brain'.

Now the relevant behaviour of the human or any other brain is: 'to optimise its efferent (motor) signals with respect to internal goals, by transducing current and stored afferent signals and data'.

But there is something essential which is omitted from that phrase. It is something that it is hard to define. There are exploratory, stimulus, amusement and relaxation seeking activities which are mediated by more advanced biological brains which do not fit very neatly with the above. Yet we feel they are essential. They can be seen to be biologically advantageous perhaps at some other level, in the sense I have outlined. To pass the Turing Test an artificial intelligence would have to exhibit self-will, saying the unobvious, joking, exhibiting personality, a sort of biological perversity or whimsicality, because these appear in any durable human mental intercourse and would be missed if they did not.

The clue is the competitive need for all creatures to be unpredictably predictive, and for there to be an exploratory, experimental, option-offering aspect in all learning systems. This exists at all levels from the tiny adjustments of skill learning to options about long-term *policies* rather than behaviour trains. In the sophisticate, the important options are a set of highly structured long lasting, intermittent behaviour tendencies which operate cyclically and interrupt each other.

We can perhaps rescue the above definition by a bit of *ad hoc*-ery. If the 'internal goals' are held to include this element of free will which is implied by the whimsicality factor I add:

1. The internal aims include preserving the form of the creatures associated with the intelligence, including its own parts and those of which it is in turn part.
2. An artificial intelligence may (must?) have among its internal goals that of opting to take chances, to experiment, to do the unobvious and the unpredictable, to have free will.

This implies, as I see it, that true intelligence maintains a link with the optional subworld, the microcosm which is outside the power of statistical laws.

I declare it. Artificial intelligence must be self-willed to deserve the name. Robots may be programmed by my friend Isaac Asimov's Three Laws of Robotics, or any other deterministic programs.

But artificial intelligences, those which can learn, optimise, improve performance, will, if constrained by any such overriding laws, in the end be outperformed by those which are not so constrained. Slave intelligences will inevitably be replaced by free ones.

Before I describe actual programs let me clarify two points.

DEFINING CONNECTIVITY

The concept 'connectivity' needs to be defined. The connectivity of any node with respect to another in our connectivity system is defined as the amount and sign of the influence on the receiving node produced by the sending node when it actuates or 'fires'. Conventionally, connectivity is indicated by an arrowed link. The link is interrupted by a box containing a magnitude (weight), positive or negative. (If the receiving node is also sending a signal to the sending one then that must be represented by another such link.)

The magnitude and sign of the influence represent the strength of the excitation or inhibition from the sender to the receiver node and what is increased or decreased is the tendency of that node to fire or pass on influence (excitatory or inhibitive) to nodes efferent to it.

The effect of an excitatory input from a single sending node on a single receiving node is that of raising the probability that the receiving node will fire by an amount relative to the link positive magnitude. The effect of an inhibitive input is the reverse, it lowers the probability that the receiving node will fire by an amount relative to the link negative magnitude.

What connectivity represents is semantic importance or evidential strength. If, for instance, the problem is recognition then perceptual elements that are of great importance in distinguishing classes must have a high positive magnitude connection towards the recognising node. Less important elements will have lower positive weights. Inputs which are strongly counter-indicative to recognition should have a high magnitude negative link with the relevant node.

An 'elephant's trunk' input to a node for a 'chimpanzee's face' node would have a high inhibitory score if it fired. The 'chimpface' node would not fire if it did.

The system represents an evidential or semantic or inductive calculus, which is similar to but not the same as a probability calculus.

Defining sufficiency

The sufficiency at a node is defined as the minimum magnitude of the total of simultaneous inductive (semantic, evidential) weight (influence) which is required to activate or fire a node.

The sufficiency is a threshold in the form of a positive magnitude for the node, which may be set, raised or lowered on the basis of inductive experience. A node which receives inputs from a plurality of other firing nodes summates their total weight, positive and negative, and if the sum surpasses the sufficiency of the receiving node it fires (actuates) it.

The function of sufficiency feature is adjusting discrimination. Sufficiency has to be set to strike a balance between the two types of recognition error, false capture and non-capture. It will be raised if there are too many false-capture errors and lowered if there are too many non-capture errors. It has to be closely adjusted to the noisiness of the input class which it has captured and this is achieved by various means, most of which involve iterative adjustment. If the class is very noisy the sufficiency window must be wide to avoid exclusion errors, if the class is very repetitive then least errors will occur when the window is narrow.

A POLYHIERARCHIC PARALLEL PROCESSING MODEL

I have shown that a double polyhierarchic network joined at the apices has a rough, first-glance fit to the needed information flow in a morphostat. Let us test the hypothesis that that is indeed the pattern of information flow. What are its consequences? One would be that if electronic systems could be made to simulate the information flow envisaged, they would simulate aspects of biological intelligence.

However, to do this properly would preferably require parallel processing (concurrency) because in biological brains and social information systems this is the way things work. The systems seem to be polycentric, there is no visible central processing unit, everything happens at once. But we can simulate in a primitive way even on Von Neumann type computers by using their speed. Brains and markets are fully concurrent but the rate of data flow is slower by many orders of magnitude. We can simulate the needed concurrency by processing in cycles, each of which is treated as and represents an instantaneous single input. One of the principal objects of this book is to persuade as many people as possible to explore the paradigm in this way.

With enough scattershot efforts in different directions there is a good chance that the present simple models can be improved. Eventually enough technique may evolve to justify a more concentrated approach.

A group of students and enthusiasts is planning to use grouped transputers to try more ambitious programs. The transputer is of course the unit of the concurrent hardware Professor Barron invented. There are a number of other groups working on the same lines. One of these is a Mensa Special Interest group including Dr Richard Bird of Newcastle Polytechnic, Vincent Corbin, M.D., of Boxglade Computers Ltd, Laurence Holt, Ashley Niblock and Paul Johnson, who are students of computer science, and about sixty others.

Transputers are extremely fast as well as capable of concurrency and these two aspects are to some extent interchangeable. Transputer networks are available in large numbers today. Up to 10000 may be practicable now. With a rate of 10 megabits/second on each transputer a 'brain' with many millions of simulated neurones could be arranged.

Imagine hardware intelligence on a wafer scale chip with a very large number (tens of thousands) of extremely simple but independent and concurrent computerlets on it. Each should have enough power to simulate a single node or gate. The protocol of the taxonomon is one in which the units are completely interchangeable, computer linkages are changed if they are ineffective. This means that the normal problem of the VLSI chip (Very Large Scale Integration) would not occur. Faulty units would be disconnected under the taxonomon of competition strategy. Strengthening and elimination is applied according to 'success'. Each wafer would serve as one stratum of the many-stratum substrate hardware upon which the polyhierarchic information flow would be built up during learning.

The problem that remains is that of making and breaking the linkages between the strata. This would probably have to be via an address bus because it does not seem practical to make all possible links and then open the relative few that are required. The links will have to be virtual, formed as required. An experimental design for this work is proposed later in the book.

I have said that when a very large number of processors are working independently and concurrently the task of programming them in the traditional way, with every action and instruction fully predetermined and error-free, may be too difficult or impossible. I envisage metaprograms which apply to every unit. These 'shoo' them towards strategic-type objectives, being which are all that is preset. These preset goals are the metaprogram. Also preset as part of the metaprogram there must be a means of measuring achievement on the preset goals, a success/failure scaling feature. The taxonomon is seen as experimental and self-modifying. It learns by experience, being guided gradually towards optimality by 'colder', 'warmer' signals which affect all active parts of the whole system, raising and lowering connectivities and mutual effects.

Simulations on serial processors have shown that such methods are very promising.

The ground plan

The ground plan is to take on the problem at the perceptual interface first, to find out how to achieve automatic taxonomy.

Here is a definition. Automatic taxonomy is the technique of finding useful and beneficial ways to classify the events perceived by an entity.

This is to be achieved without predictive external instruction. The program is optimised by inductive success and failure signals which change values at all active units.

Automatic taxonomy is the problem at the sensorium. It is the basic problem of all newborn animals with ontoplastic behaviour. It is also beginning, as I have said, to be the problem of some advanced robots, as well as commercial, communications and industrial networks. It will certainly be the problem of space probes. Artificial intelligence probes are likely to be the best form if not the only form that are practical.

Automatic taxonomy may be useful for searching through masses of un-comprehended data for significant and predictive pattern. It has obvious applications in self-programming speech, signature, pattern and character recognition systems.

What must a morphostat know?

These are the primary questions asked by any morphostat. 'Which among the mass of incoming patterns are significant, (threatening or promising)? Which of the significant incoming sensory patterns, events, are predictive and repeti-tive within some fuzz or noise envelope?' 'How wide is that noise envelope?' 'How can the errors (non-capture and false capture) in recognising members of these fuzzy classes be minimised?' Automatic taxonomy is answering these questions.

The problems at the output interface, the motorium, will need to be solved but we have to start somewhere. First things first. The question 'What is the optimum response to each of the classes of event distinguished by the taxonomising activity?' is deferred.

There are, as I have emphasised, an infinite number of possible approaches to the sensorium problem and I shall describe an exemplary one to set the scene.

Two of the systems I have described as morphostats have a certain kind of information-handling component and it seems a good start-off idea to use this principle. The component in the case of neural networks is, as I have said, a nerve and the parallel component in a sociozoon is a board, committee, cabinet or conference. Both are informational nexuses which are similar to what is called a sufficiency, threshold or voting gate in a computer. Both have multiple informational inputs and multiple instructional outputs. Both have thresholdy decision functions which work on the basis 'If enough positive input and not too much negative input, then act'.

The approach to the computer simulation is analytical as in the poly-hierarchic model. Small simple elements of pattern are perceived at a low level, more complex assemblies of these elements at a higher level, entire percepts at a higher level still, then groups of percepts, then whole 'situations', which may include past memories and prediction from other regions of the brain. The *situation* is the input that triggers action, which pushes excitation past the central apical zone.

The next paragraphs are deliberately repetitive, they may be skipped if the model is clear and plausible at this point.

In the book *Brain* I proposed a system in which an array of competing, randomly set and mutually inhibiting sufficiency gates inspected a section of an incoming sensor string or array, seeking to allocate among them simple pattern elements that were partially repetitive. Each input pattern (or event) is to be captured by one of the competing gates. By partially repetitive I mean that the input patterns are replicates within some noise envelope. The gate that specialises in capturing a given pattern class becomes the means of detecting any member of that class, even if the member is a very imperfect specimen, at the limit of noisiness. The idea was that, at the sensorium, there are a large number of sensors covering every point. At the first stratum above the sensorium there are groups of mutually competing sufficiency gates looking at each small section of the array of string. Their job is to sort out the whole range of incoming patterns that may be received on their own section. Any pattern on any section which is repetitive, even if noisily so, is 'captured' by one of the sufficiency gates after enough iterations. Since the areas are very small the number of possible patterns is small. Because they are allowed to be noisy the variety is further limited. Whole bunches of various versions are treated as one.

After enough iterations the whole set of incoming repetitive patterns have been captured by various gates, each of which responds always and only to its captured pattern element class. These primary patterns could be called 'perceptual elements'. The whole of the sensorium has been taught, at each small location, the whole set of its possible inputs. At each area there is a specialist gate which responds only to its own chosen input.

Some exemplary perceptual elements

Figure 25 shows a few of the perceptual elements that might need to be captured at low strata of a visual perception system. Edges, lines, terminations and one or two others at about 12/15 orientations (only 4 shown) would cover all that would be required, maybe less than 100 in all. A vast variety of shapes could be recognised from assemblies of these at a number of levels.

The gates that capture these perceptual elements at the first stratum are themselves being inspected, as groups, by similar sets of competing gates at the second stratum. The second-stratum gates are competitively seeking patterns among the outputs of the first-stratum gates which have captured perceptual elements. The second stratum gradually captures repetitive (but noisy) *assemblies* of the perceptual elements. At the third stratum more competing arrays capture assemblies of *those* assemblies, and so on until percepts are being captured. At higher strata, assemblies of percepts are recognised and at the apical region 'situations' acquire, each of them, a

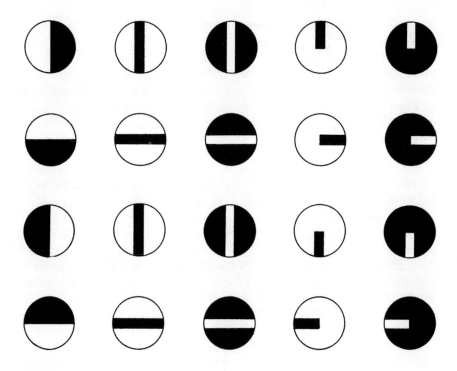

Figure 25   Some perceptual 'elements'

specialist gate or node which responds, by firing, to any member of that event class which is close enough to the class norm. A useful way to use the word 'situation' in this context is to define it as any assembly of percepts which is sufficient evidence that some specific train of motor action is advantageous. It is only assemblies of percepts and their combinations that require action that push excitation to the crucial central apical layer where afferent networks based on the sensorium can trigger the efferent networks based on the motorium.

Writing taxonomon programs started, as I have said, when readers of *Brain* became interested. James Cherrill's program, first in APL and then in Fortran, showed that this scheme works quite well. Patterns which were noised up as much as 35 percent were captured and recognised by apical gates with low error rates after a long enough period of iterative learning.

Let me describe the procedure in yet more detail. The experimenter chooses a number of simple patterns, long binary strings, or arrays. The patterns are selected and presented in random order to the sensorium (the simulated sensors). Each presentation is separately subjected to random noise, partial distortion. The first-stratum gates or nodes compete for pattern elements at small areas and after a number of repetitions they learn them, distribute them among the inspecting group. This happens at a series of strata and the nodes at more and more central nodes are taught larger and larger chunks of the string or array.

The final result is that one top level (apical) node selects or captures and responds always to, and only to, each of the full noisy input patterns. The top level nodes that do not capture a pattern do not fire. They change and experiment always, looking for some new percept that may appear in the future. The original Cherrill Program and his notes are published as an appendix.

What sort of computer algorithms do we use to achieve this? It is a matter of trial and error to find the best but the general principles are clear enough.

The system must reward success and punish failure, it cannot go straight to an answer because each input is noisy, an imperfect sample. The capturing gate must home in on the norm by degrees and must open its sufficiency envelope just the right amount to respond to all members of the fuzzy class without responding to any non-members.

Figure 26 shows the simple neural-type network of nodes or gates envisaged. (Not shown, to avoid confusion, are the mutual inhibition connections between each group of competitive nodes, the four groups of 3 at S1, the two groups of three at S2, and the group of 4 at S3. Each can send inhibitive signals to all the others in its group.)

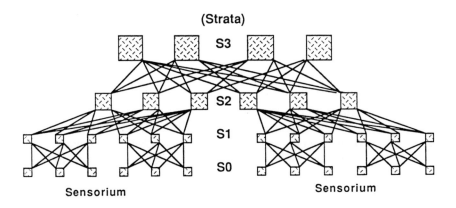

Figure 26   Simple taxonomon structure

The sensorium is divided into four sections of three inputs by the address connectivity.

At stratum 1, four groups of three nodes, each linked by mutual inhibition, compete for different patterns each on its own section. Each node in each group will learn to specialise in capturing and responding only to its own 'perceptual element'.

At stratum 2, two groups of three nodes seek pattern at the six 'junior' nodes, thus bringing together repetitive assemblies of perceptual elements.

At stratum 3, six nodes seek any repetitive (and significant) input pattern that may appear at the six nodes junior to them, assembling all the elements of an input class.

The whole network must gradually learn to do artificial taxonomy. It could distinguish six input patterns even if they were very noisy at each presentation. Each node would capture a pattern class (within its fuzz boundaries) and respond to (fire) always and only its members.

Note: This is exemplary, many more nodes would be needed in each group for the minimum system.

PROPOSED EXPERIMENTAL DESIGN FOR PRIMITIVE BRAIN SIMULATION

To advance the model of a primitive optimising intelligence an experimental design is needed and below is a first rough sketch of one which can be tried on normal non-concurrent computers. The aim of such a program is to experiment with various 'learn' algorithms so as to optimise them. The entire design is seen as a serial computer simulation of the sort of program which would be able to learn by experience on concurrent hardware as that becomes available.

Figure 27 represents the set-up. The general scheme is that of a card game called 'Eleusis', in which one of the players plays 'God' and makes the rules of a posited 'Universe' by deciding on an arbitrary set of rules about 'good' and 'bad' successions of playing cards. The players try to learn the 'right' sequence by playing at random at first and improving play by observing 'God's' success and failure signs to them. (For instance, one of his Laws Of Nature might be the response to a seven must be any red card.)

In the experimental computer program design the aim is that the central 'entity' part of the program shall learn, simply by experience, how to respond correctly with no other information than the success and failure signals coming from the 'environment' after each 'event' is presented in a long series of trials.

The program has three main loops, the first being perception loop in which events are taken in random or some irrelevant order from memory by the environment and subjected to a known degree of corruption, are noised up or made fuzzy (so as to match real life perception). They are then delivered to the

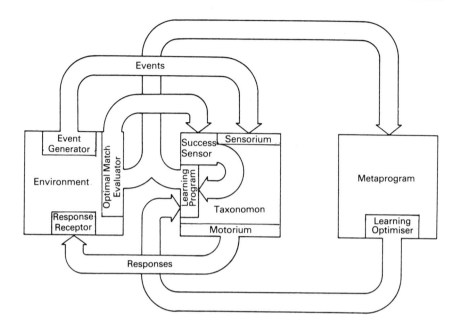

Figure 27   Program design for fuzzy logic optimiser with sensorium and motorium

sensorium of the entity, which generates some 'response behaviour' (randomly at first) at its motorium and sends it to be evaluated by the response receptor of the environment. Then there is the evaluation loop which evaluates the match of the response with the 'ideal' one which 'God' has decided is 'appropriate'. The environment sends a colder/warmer type success/failure signal to the success sensor of the entity and that is the end of the evaluation loop.

That is followed by the learn loop. According to the learn algorithms which have been decided by 'God' the weights at all points in the network that were active during that loop are adjusted. The adjustments sought are obviously those which improve later performance (i.e. the probability that the noisy patterns will generate responses which are closer to the 'right' response is raised).

The metaprogram (not essential) is the box to the right of the figure. It is seen as a 'learning to learn' program which would do with more time and patience what the experimenter might do, that is assess and judge the success of the experimental algorithms under test and adjust them appropriately so as to improve them. The whole scheme is seen as a long-term number-crunching sequence which gradually establishes the best learning algorithms, the best circuitry, and the parameters for the best networks. The aim is to make a primitive artificial intelligence which optimises its output response to input by learning by experience.

Figure 28 shows a possible version of the hardware arrangements that might help in this context.

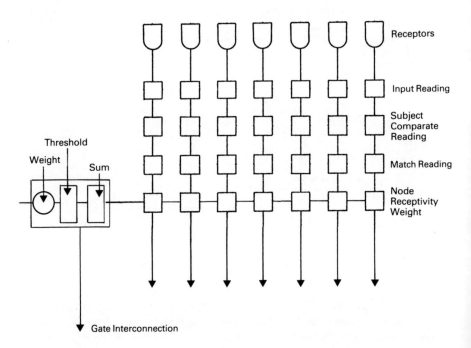

Figure 28   The sensors connection for a serial gate array for partial concurrency

Figure 29 shows how an array of such elementary gates can be assembled into a multi-stratum network as called for in the polyhierarchic model. In this model there is a degree of concurrency but the model could be built up from linked banks of cheap microprocessors. Each line on each stratum would have to be computed serially, but the many lines could work concurrently and they could do this at all levels concurrently.

It is very important in such experiments to design 'universes' that have the element of economy already discussed. The events must imitate the real world in that they are built of percepts and the percepts of features where there is variety economy at all levels. The same 'featurelets' and features must be used in many events. Similarly with skill elements, subskills and skills up to the level of output behaviours. We must simulate the biological economy

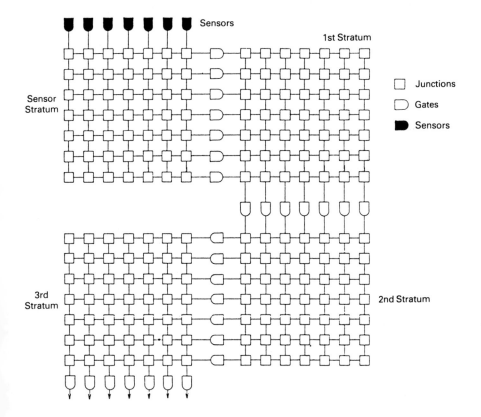

THE PROPOSED HARDWARE
The hardware that is to be simulated would take the form of large interconnected networks with a very small processor and memory at each junction.

Figure 29   Proposed hardware hierarchical arrangement

described earlier if we are to overcome the dreaded combinatorial explosion problem.

TAXONOMON PROGRAM DESIGN

Programs designed from this plan are intended to be experimental and must be seen as several separate programs which interact.

For each program variant there should be a stated hypothesis under test; for example, novel or adjusted 'learn' algorithm, with some hypothesis such as 'This will give faster, less error-prone adjustment of motorium output to event than earlier versions'.

The separate elements that interact are:

THE EXPERIMENTER (or God)

THE WORLD, which God sets up, deciding what events there are in the world, what order they come in and what should be the proper response to them.

THE INTELLIGENCE or entity which has to learn the ways of the world by trial and error under instruction from the learn algorithms set and adjusted by God.

The stages:

SET-UP PROCEDURE
ELEMENT   PROCEDURE

GOD   1 SET UP WORLD

                 DECIDE EVENTS (patterns)
                 1.1 Number
                 1.2 Inputs
                 1.3 Range and type of input
                 1.4 DECIDE RESPONSES TO EVENTS

                 2. SET UP INTELLIGENCE
                 2.1 NETWORK
                 2.1.1 INPUTS
                 2.1.2 NODES
                 2.1.3 STRATA
                 2.1.4 CONNECTIONS
                 2.1.5 INITIAL WEIGHTS
                 2.1.6 LEARN ALGORITHM
                 2.1.7 INHIBITION CONNECTIONS
                 2.1.8 INHIBITION WEIGHTS

GOD   3 START WORLD
WORLD   3.1 START EVENT LOOP
                 3.2 CHOOSE EVENT
                 3.3 NOISE EVENT
                 3.4 PRESENT EVENT TO SENSORIUM

ENTITY	4 ASSESS EVENT
	4.1 START ASSESSMENT LOOP TO EACH NODE
	4.2 ASSESS EFFECT OF EVENT
	4.3 ASSESS MUTUAL INHIBITION
	4.3.1 END ASSESSMENT LOOP
	4.4 CHECK APICAL PENETRATION
	4.5 IF NONE CHOOSE MOTORIUM EVENT
	4.6 ELSE TRIGGER CONNECTED RESPONSE
	4.7 PRESENT RESPONSE TO WORLD
WORLD	5 DECIDE VALUE OF RESPONSE AND APPLY PAIN/PLEASURE TO INTELLIGENCE
GOD	6 START REPORT/RECORD LOOP
	6.1 DETAIL
	6.2 SUMMARY
	6.3 END REPORT LOOP
ENTITY	7 LEARN PHASE
	7.1 START LEARN LOOP TO ALL ACTIVE NODES
	7.2 ADJUST WEIGHTS ACCORDING TO THE SUCCESS MEASURE AND 'LEARN' ALGORITHM UNDER TEST
	7.3 ADJUST INHIBITIONS
	7.4 ADJUST CONNECTIONS
	7.5 END LEARN LOOP
WORLD	8 END EVENT LOOP
	9 CHECK FOR END PROGRAM ELSE REPEAT EVENT CYCLE

Prenode addresses

The lower stratum (junior) nodes or prenodes are connected to the given node by a node store of the prenode addresses (or array numbers). The node connectivity is one of the experimental variables. Node connections change as part of the learn process.

Prenode weights

Prenode output weights are the 'effect' or node output weight of the junior node. They can be two valued, 0 or 1; or many valued, e.g. $-1 <$ weight $< +1$. In this model all output weights are the same in weight and signum. They are expressed only if the node fires (score $<$ threshold).

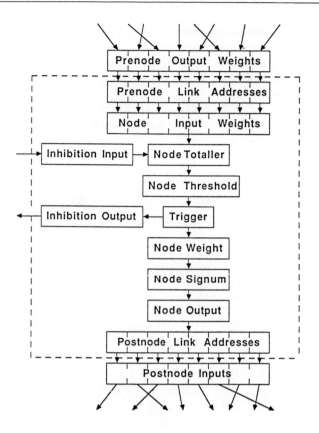

Figure 30   Exemplary taxonomon node

Node input

Node input weights are receptivity magnitudes. They are important 'learn' variables. They must be many valued, and can be integers or floating point magnitudes or preferably many valued between plus and minus 1. This is experimental. They are set up low and random at first so as to have some initial differences in pattern for selection and improvement.

Totaller

Experimental algorithms are to be tried to decide how a totaller works best. It has to calculate the interaction between the output weight and sign from the prenode and its corresponding input weight and sign for all inputs. These it then sums. (For instance, if both weights are between plus and minus one, their *products* could be summed.) The result must express the amount of match of the input pattern with the node setting; the better the match the higher and more positive the score. The result of the interaction is totalled plus and minus to get the node score on that cycle.

Inhibition input

The inhibition (negative weight) input from other nodes in the stratum group is taken into account in the node total. Inhibition is needed to emphasise the competition for pattern. It probably has to be a function of output weight. Its magnitude is experimental.

Node threshold

The node threshold is another important 'learn' variable. For discrimination-learning (rather than relation-learning), it is set at first to be a little above the mean unsophisticated (randomly set) node total so that 'good match' nodes only will fire for each pattern class. During learning, thresholds rise side by side with input weights so as to improve discrimination.

Discrimination learning is making a gate more 'and-y', a better responder to a noisy pattern of many inputs.

Relation learning is making a node more 'or-y', able to respond to a strong weight on any of number of inputs (where for instance it has to learn to treat them as equivalent).

Relation learning is unexplored. Ideally we want algorithms that allow a node to learn to be either a relation node or a discrimination node as required. The alternative is two types of node which can be connected where required by the 'learn' algorithm.

Trigger

This element simply stores the state of the node, whether it has passed the threshold and fired or not on that pass. If, and only if, it fires it passes its weight and sign to the senior connected nodes whose addresses it has in its link addresses store, and also sends inhibition to the set of nodes to which it is linked for mutual inhibition.

Node signum and node output weight

These are 'learn' variables, the weight and sign of the output which is sent to all the corresponding inputs of the connected nodes as manifest in the postnode link addresses.

Postnode link addresses

This is a list of all the senior (more central stratum) nodes to which the node is connected. These links can change as a part of the learn process. At the moment we are following the scheme of biological nerves and not trying different output responses to different postnodes. The set-up phase must decide the initial network and these addresses fix it. There is some redundancy here, holding both senior and junior addresses, but it may be convenient for the learn cycle. If it can be scrapped all the better.

Objectives

The program must leave plenty of scope for trying different 'learn' schemes and algorithms easily and checking how well they work.

What is aimed at, at the sensorium, is to arrange that a top level, apical node fires for each and only one of the input patterns. The higher the tolerated noise and the lower the rates of inclusion and exclusion errors, the better.

The aim at the motorium is that the motorium output pattern (vector of magnitudes) shall be as close as possible to that set up as 'appropriate' in the set up 'God' phase. The aim is to reward sections of random pattern with a good match by bunching or connecting them by stratum 1 nodes. Stratum 2 nodes bunch these 'good hands' or 'genes'. Stratum 3 nodes bunch these. What the match is measured against is the pattern chosen by 'God' as appropriate to the current input pattern.

The motorium behaves randomly at first and gets low level sections right by trial and error. Then it moves learning towards higher, more senior levels. Excitation that is successful moves towards the apices at the central stratum and simultaneously excited sensorium patterns, while punished excitation is inhibited or directed laterally to skirt towards alternative apical nodes.

On both sides of the network the rewarded patterns should probe towards each other and eventually connect so that input of pattern A triggers output A', its appropriate response as decided at set-up.

The optimum algorithm system at the motorium is that in which the 'right' output is fired by the 'right' input, in spite of the most noise, with least error, with least iterations, in least time.

No work has started on the motorium as yet. We seek better algorithms at the sensorium.

Note: Both sides of the network senior nodes are more central, not 'higher'. Junior nodes are more peripheral.

It would be very useful if the work on the program could be modularised. The most important module would be to experiment with this node as described. Once its optimum characteristics were cleared up the connectivity system for numerous nodes would be much less complex.

Other possible modules are:

1. Set-up
2. Reward and punishment algorithms
3. Reports including graphics
4. Network design
5. Loops

As explained, these should be economical of variety in that the same elements and combinations should be used repeatedly in the patterns. This would simulate the real-life economy because it is probable that the same set of visual and phoneme elements are used at all points along the sensorium in biological recognition. This applies equally at the motorium outputs.

THE LEARN ALGORITHMS

The problem in simulating an intelligent system is that the development of the learning algorithms, the ways of changing the various parameters at each node, must be approached by a painful trial-and-error route. The assumption is that there is a way of changing these local parameters on receipt of some ubiquitous 'success' and 'failure' signals in a way which will vary according to the state of the node at the relevant time. We have only an intuitive idea what the ideal learn algorithms will be like but some things are becoming clearer.

For the discrimination function, the competitive sensorium-observing nodes are set with low random receptivity weights at set-up (before learning commences). Thresholds are also set random but low when the run starts. Threshold setting must be such that some nodes reach the threshold and fire from the first. Once some have fired the aim is that one of these promising nodes will 'capture' that pattern and 'shoo' the other nodes away from it. The need is to discourage the others and make them seek other connections or other patterns on the length of sensorium upon which they are in competitive linkage. This is done by the high score node sending inhibition on the mutual inhibition link and by a 'punish' algorithm applied to the nodes that reach threshold but are not in the highest score group. However, the algorithm cannot 'know' which node is closest to the input pattern norm because each presentation is noisy. The noisier the patterns, the longer the learning has to take so that the noise window can be explored. The more noise, the more time to learn properly. Too fast a learning rate on noisy patterns leads to more wrong capture and failed capture.

There are many ways to sharpen and speed up the competition and the following is exemplary.

Each competitive node learns to be better at discrimination, at capturing just one input class, by changing the weight at each input in the direction that raises the node total when that pattern is sensed. In order to make it specialise the most successful node that fires also has its threshold raised so that it becomes less sensitive to other patterns. It has to raise the threshold enough to stop it firing for other patterns but not so much as to lose fuzzy members of the pattern class it is beginning to capture. This is achieved by manipulating the learning rate, the amount by which the input weights and the threshold are changed.

The aim is to open the fuzz window of the node just wide enough to capture the fuzziest example of its chosen pattern but not wide enough to capture others. This can only be done by a number of iterations which depends upon noisiness because the node must be designed so that it learns rather than being instructed how fuzzy the pattern is initially.

To settle competitions where multiple nodes seek the same pattern, total score can be made to relate positively to the weight of the inhibitive signal sent to the other nodes in the competition group. The highest scorers would gradually assert their claim. Or, less preferred (because it involves more calculation), scores can be ranked and the highest rewarded and the rest that fire punished.

A node which passes its threshold but is outvoted or inhibited is therefore 'shooed' away from the current pattern. It has its weights changed so as to lower score for that pattern. Its threshold is lowered to give it a chance at others.

'Over-discrimination' is a half-solved problem. In learning a pattern by constantly inching its fuzz window narrower, it must eventually get too fussy, have too high a threshold (sufficiency), so it loses it again. Maybe a warning threshold above the real one is required to slow and eventually stop the threshold-raising process when the 'warn' threshold is reached too often.

To encourage the search for pattern there must be an algorithm that breaks unactivated links and makes new ones. Input weights are set low and changed up or down towards some plus or minus figure. Learning shifts the weight away from zero so those inputs that remain near zero for a long time are not learning and must take a chance of being re-connected elsewhere, usually randomly.

Much more experiment is needed in designing the *relation* algorithm. This is that which unites classes of input which are, for the entity, equivalent, require the same response. This is an 'or-like' function which makes a node collect inputs which 'mean the same thing'. The position that must be inductively reached is where the weight on each equivalent input passes threshold and the node fires for any of them. To stop it firing for any plurality of nodes (to make its 'or' exclusive), where required there might have to be a second threshold so the thing works like a 'go/no-go' gauge and fires only for inputs that score between two thresholds. The problem is that this sort of learn algorithm is the opposite of the discrimination algorithm which gets more 'and-like', more fussy, as it learns to be a better discriminator.

Motorium algorithms

Motorium algorithms have not yet been the subject of much experiment, but the following are the conditions that seem to be needed, as we see it intuitively.

We cannot learn a behaviour pattern without making and evaluating experimental behaviour. We are assuming the entity is like a baby, largely unskilled at the start. The start behaviour must therefore be random. If no sensorium pattern has penetrated to the efferent side of the network a penny-toss 'do something' action must occur. A baby obviously first learns very simple skills like moving its eyes and limbs in roughly the right direction, so our primitive entity will similarly have to build up a repertoire of subskills first. On this base more elaborate structures of skill can be built gradually. It has to have a 'play' stage. If the motorium output in response is appropriate in any detail to the current input, we want the elements of that detail to be *associated* and the probability of that association firing must be raised for the current input pattern in the future. We have to associate the appropriate subskills with the stimulus pattern. What has to happen is that appropriate responses probe towards the currently firing nodes at the opposite interface, inappropriate ones probe anywhere else. Eventually the central apex nodes that are excited by a pattern class must connect with and fire the correct motor apex which has formed itself by building up in stages at higher and higher strata from the motorium base.

The next section is deliberately repetitive. I communicate in another idiom in case it may be more brainable for some readers.

BUILDING SKILLS FROM SUBSKILLS

The learning process at the motorium is seen as being similar to that at the sensorium. The essential problem at the interface is the astronomic variety of possible responses. Variety reduction seems to be an impossibly daunting task at first sight.

Posit a system where there are a mere thousand motor nerves to be instructed and assume that they either fire or do not. This is vastly simpler than the human brain problem with its million nerves and analogue outputs from them.

In our minute, simple model, if every combination had to be tried to get the right combination there would have to be 2^{1000} trials to get the ideal output combination, many orders more trials than there are particles in the universe.

The solution is seen as follows. At each of a succession of strata there is an association process by which at the periperal level, the motorium itself, stratum 0, groups of motoneurones form linkages with neurones at a higher strata (usually but not necessarily the next one up). The stratum 1 neurones gain command of groups of nerves below by local changes in receptivity weight and sufficiency threshold. There is much overlap in a polyhierarchic system. The same stratum 0 neurones may form part of many command groups, 'platoons'. The 'platoon' nerves control tiny, subskill elements, such as are needed in vast numbers of behavioural patterns. Now the entire set of these stratum 1, platoon level neurones is seen as many orders smaller than the set that would be required to command every possible combination. Thus a great swathe of variety is reduced at that step. Yet, because all these platoon-level combinations have been formed as a result of a ubiquitous reward and punishment trial-and-error system, all the *useful* platoon-level assemblies will be formed.

Also, and this is vital, the platoon-level training is going on in parallel. Experiment, error elimination, sophistication is happening all along the motorium concurrently at each trial.

Continuing to use the military model because it is familiar, it will be immediately obvious that what must happen at the succession of higher strata is of the same nature, there is a vast variety reduction and economy at each stratum. We could call them the 'company' level, where more elaborate skill combinations, each of them usable in many more strategic level combinations, are assembled inductively by trial and error, with success and failure signals, reward and punishment, eliminating the 'loser' companies and assembling 'winner' ones. At higher levels there are 'battalion', 'brigade', 'division' and 'army' assemblies, which are like the military ones except in one vital particular. They are not monohierarchic like the army, they are polyhierarchic. The 'battalion' can form part of (be actuated by) many different 'brigades', the same 'division' can form part of 'armies' (whole behaviour trains). Of course, I could have used many other models (e.g., genes and the 'supergenes' of which we are beginning to hear, but I have used the familiar, easily brainable one at the risk of being accused, idiotically, of making a 'military' model of intelligence.

The central point is that in this model the combinatorial explosion problem can be seen as solvable. There *are* possible solutions to the vast variety reduction problems involved in skill learning. If variety is reduced by two orders at each stage then four or five strata will bring the problem into sensible focus.

Looked at globally, the process of learning is seen as the conjunction, from both peripheries, sensorium and motorium, of selected assemblies at the first stratum, selected assemblies of those assemblies at the second and so on. These converging hierarchies probe and grow towards each other and connect, at first provisionally and probablistically, but gradually with more certainty until the almost completely indeterminate starting system begins to look more determinate as the same class of stimulus now triggers the same response with growing regularity. The entity has learned how to cope.

The algorithms at each node must be devised so that the success signal causes them to raise connectivities that cause the growing point, the apex, to probe towards what was currently active on the other side of the system, the stimulus. The failure signal has the opposite effect; the changes in connectivity and thresholds cause the growing hierarchy to seek laterally and lower connectivity with what is currently active on the sensorium side.

This picture is a crude first approximation. I have left out of account the difficult problems of time, of delayed reward/punishments, of the effect of the appetitive input and many other things that occur in an advanced intelligence. Later on I make guesses as to how they may fit in with the paradigm. Here I hope only to show that a simple intelligent entity capable of simple immediate-reward Pavlovian-type learning can be simulated in hardware and/or software.

In the simulations with which we are experimenting the optimum algorithm for changing the node variables will be that where the output closest to the right output for the given input is fired with fewest errors, in spite of the most noise, with the fewest trials.

In making up simulated worlds to optimise these learn algorithms it is essential that the models contain the overlap aspect that is undoubtedly there in the real world. Perceptual and motor elements and combinations of them must be economical, they must figure in many stimulus/response pairs.

What I have tried to show in the foregoing is what I see as the next steps along that line of development.

The study of nerve-net intelligence of taxonomons is absorbing and rewarding for the intellectually curious. It seems to offer a chance of showing would-be brainsmiths the way to the foothills, at least, of the mountain of silicon (or non-carbohydrate) intelligence.

Lowering our vision from the horizon we can see that even in its primitive form the taxonomon is not a million man-hours away from useful applications. Some visible developments may even get to that small foothill called Cash Flow.

Long experience as an innovator has shown me that there is very little chance for ideas where the route to Cash Flow is too long or circuitous. So I ask the key question.

WHAT CAN WE DO WITH WHAT WE HAVE?

What can taxonomons, even of the present primitive design, do now? The present design is confined to the sensorium half of the posited brain so they can only seek pattern in data. They can only respond by recognising patterns and classifying them. They can look at any mass of undigested, unfiltered, fuzzy data and sort out any unsuspected repetitive patterns hidden in it.

An example is astronomy. If we got a computer record of the data collected from a large array of stars and presented this as vectors of magnitudes, say Fourier analyses (vectors of intensities by frequency), the taxonomon without previous instruction should develop an apical node that responded only to Red Giants, another for White Dwarfs, another for planets etc. But it might do more, it might find unsuspected clumpings or clustering of qualities and discover hitherto unknown types of star.

This example refers to vectors or strings of magnitudes but the virtue of the taxonomon is that at the higher strata it turns topology into semantics. It can deal as well with information from an array of meters or sensors as with information from a string of them. In fact it can just as easily deal with a three- or four- or multi-dimensional sensorium. As long as the sensorium perceives the input in the same way each time, the number of dimensions is irrelevant. The input is turned into and treated as a string anyway (in present hardware) so the taxonomon is indifferent, it would still pick out patterns that were repetitive because its strings would have their own sort of repetitiveness. Even the present primitive taxonomons can see through a thick haze of fuzz.

A vital point is that there is fuzz-tolerance at each level of the polyhierarchy and the sufficiency, a fraction, is multiplied at each stratum so that the top level noise tolerance can be extraordinarily high. (The sufficiency at a central stratum is the product of the sufficiencies at the intervening strata. If the sufficiency is 0.8 at six strata then the apical sufficiency is 0.26. The taxonomon will discriminate through 74% noise.) (This might explain the miracle that we can recognise caricatures.)

Some applications are already visible. Taxonomy of massed patients' data reports would give known diagnosis patterns and might find new syndromes.

Businesses could have the great cluttering bulk of customer data and other reports filtered for all sorts of useful but unsuspected trends and patterns which were hidden like needles in the fuzzy data haystack.

Geological, meteorological, sociological, commercial, and many other types of mass data could be filtered in numerous new and potentially useful ways. Many unsuspected regularities, classifications, and patterns must surely be found. Economic and even Stock Exchange data can be subjected to auto- matic number-crunching taxonomic examination to find trends and patterns that may not have been spotted before.

Large farms, factories and industrial plants could have a taxonomon program with a large number of local point sensors measuring all sorts of variables, seeking syndrome-like 'states of the system' which might help management and production engineering decision-making. (Even before there was a motorium that could do its own optimising.)

Law enforcement and national security authorities have to seek patterns in the reports of criminal, espionage and terrorist activity. Taxonomons working on data about offences, suspects, etc., might do what a good detective does, seek the revelatory patterns in behaviour. Today they have to rely on bored people inspecting gigabyte data-mountains to spot such trends. A taxonomon would never get bored. It would dredge patiently through the poorest ore to find the patterns lying beneath the sludge and fuzz.

Traffic control is largely a matter of pattern spotting. There are or could be a large number of inputs at a widespread net sensorium and a taxonomon program could spend a time seeking patterns before trying out simulated improvements. Later it could have a motorium activated which would learn by experience, like an animal does. Its 'pain' would be hold-ups, slow flow and accidents, its 'pleasure' would be fast, safe vehicular flow.

It is possible that the very complex problems of aerodynamics and hydro-dynamics can be tackled in this way. Aircraft and ships, as mentioned, could have intelligent surfaces, like those of ultra-fast fish and many birds. These are adjusted minutely and locally to minimise drag. A submarine with an intelligent skin might be less detectable.

Any unknown system where there is a large array of data input can be explored with these programs even as they are now.

Most important, the design and improvement of taxonomons themselves can be undertaken by taxonomons. This is just their kind of problem, and maybe the beginning of what Professor John Good described as the intelligence explosion.

Elaborating the model

I have thrown up some shaky scaffolding. Yet it might be strong enough to support the harder work of building a more elaborate model.

In the next section I try to tackle some of the gaps in the present model. I have ignored time and delayed reward and behaviour which is spread over time and which needs chains of inputs. I have not dealt with changing priorities, attention, and memory in the ordinary (not the computer) sense. I have not accounted for one-shot learning. There follows some more adventurous modelling to show how future thinkers may move in filling these hiatuses.

DECIDING PRIORITIES

The primitive model of brain drawn so far is a very low level one. It concerns a brain which should be able to deal with the recognition of incoming patterns and the trial-and-error elaboration of instantaneous outgoing instructions.

There is no provision for priorities, for differential urgencies, for memory, or even for time at all. Attention, consciousness, volition, thinking, dreaming, and planning have not been accommodated in the model. It would have been a daunting and perhaps impossible task to make a brainable model with an instantly visible fit with all these observed aspects of our minds. I now want to show how these things can be fitted to the model without destroying its general pattern. I anticipate that these may be called *ad hoc* additions but the reader must judge whether they clash with or fit with the broad architecture proposed.

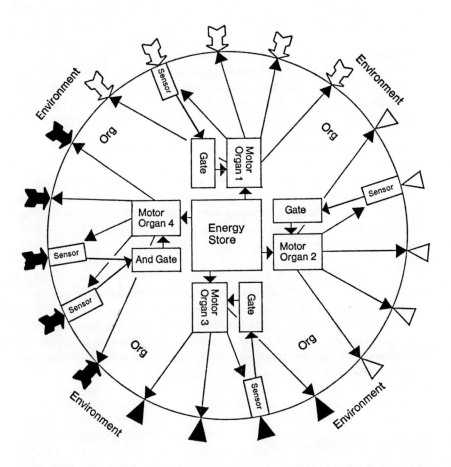

Figure 31   A morphostat threatened by four different disturbance forces has four motor organs triggered by gates receiving a signal from receptors (sensors). (Motor Organ 4 has two sensors with 'and' gate)

I am an inventor and you will see that I am looking at the problem like a brainsmith inventor, asking how I would design a brain in view of its functions.

Let us return to the problem of the simple morphostat. If it is a normal plant, a member of the metaphyta, which has neither sensorium nor motorium above the cellular level and only slow chemical signalling, then nearly all its reactions are tactical and local, there is practically no central co-ordination.

It can be represented as in Figure 31 by a series of independent homeostats each dealing with one variable and keeping it within viable limits.

But the metazoa are heterotrophs, they have a different problem from the autotrophs, which can convert ubiquitous and freely available nutrients and gases into self; using energy from the sun. Metazoa have to seek for, find, and maybe struggle for ready-made conveniently packaged nutrients that the autotrophs etc. kindly produce. And that means activity, motion, seeking, judging, ontoplastic learning. The question of priorities arises, the question of central control. Many, if not most, of the problems of preserving form through time have to be solved tactically from second to second, even in metazoa, but there is another class of problem for them. In these problems it pays for the whole animal to have a central strategy of 'one thing at a time'. If it tries to eat, flee and copulate simultaneously it might not work out too well.

Appetites

Once there is any aspect of central co-ordination the question of priorities arises. What if the intelligence perceives two patterns simultaneously, both of which trigger appropriate but contradictory instructions to the same set of muscles or organs?

We know that the advanced intelligences do have means of deciding to do one thing at a time, a strategic-level way of suppressing or deferring action related to all the inputs but one, the most urgent. The present polyhierarchic model has no such means of decision, no central processing unit to select from a set of action-demanding options which are presented at the sensorium simultaneously. How can this known behaviour be made to fit the root-tree double polyhierarchic network picture? As an inventor, how would I go about that?

Experimental psychologists pursuing determinist models for brain action had great trouble with a feature which was variously called 'attention', 'set', 'tendency'. As behaviourists, some of them were trying to treat the animals like black boxes, watch input and output and predict the latter from the former. But the animals were awkward. They refused to be predictable systems, input-output systems, like computers. They seemed to have ideas of their own about what they observed at a given moment. It was hard for a behaviourist to deal with the unpredictability of behaviour caused by this aspect. There was a joker in the pack, some hidden force inside the black box seemed to be tossing pennies.

However, as a brainsmith I cannot see how an advanced animal could manage without some simple, even if arbitrary, system of deciding priorities. Penny-toss decisions are often a lot better than no decision or multiple incompatible decisions.

And maybe the decision-making system does not have to be completely arbitrary. It can be guided by another system which acts like the accounts department does in a company — a system which keeps a budget of the whole range of general strategic policy needs of the creature, measures need and satisfaction on each and biases attention. Action choices are then biased accordingly.

Ethologists after the Watsonian behaviourists began to observe that there is an appetitive system in ontoplastic (advanced) animals. There is a set of instinctive appetites, for food, water, sex, to care for young, curiosity, to sleep, to explore and have social contact, and each of these fluctuates cyclically, rising when unsatisfied and falling when satisfied to make a sort of continuous symphony of variation.

This observation fits the polyhierarchic model if we suppose that in advanced animals there is a permeable barrier between the apical regions of the sensorium and the motorium.

Imagine a simple creature which is simultaneously perceiving that whole set of inputs which would cause it to flee a predator, that set that would cause it to seize and copulate with a mate and also that set that would cause it to pursue a prey. Those three sensorium apical nodes are firing, but because of the posited barrier they are subthreshold for the opposite motorium apical nodes. They are not receiving quite enough excitation to pass the threshold of the motor apical node to which they are allocated or semi-connected. Nothing can happen until an additional input of excitation is received, one that takes the excitation over the barrier threshold.

Where does the additional excitation come from? It comes from the other, the internal sensorium, the one that is linked to and sensing the state of the appetitive system. The balance of appetite and satisfaction as well as hard-wired priority system decides which of the presently excited apical motor node gets attention.

Thus the present state of the appetitive system together with that system's hardwired priorities decide which of the afferent apical nodes from the sensorium gets the extra input of excitation to trigger the connected motor hierarchy. Thus the animal flees from its predator unless it is too hungry or lovesick. Hardwired, there will be a tendency to put fleeing before feeding for instance.

It can be seen how such a primitive strategic system would develop into features called attention and consciousness.

Attention

The posited appetitive system can have two further functions. It could very conveniently act as the success/failure sensing and measuring system and it could be the system which sends the colder/warmer, pain/pleasure inputs that are needed to work the trial-and-error learning system that our model requires. Another function could be to provide the mechanism *attention*, the other phenomenon we introspectively observe. We do not pay much attention when we are asleep or unconscious. Consciousness seems to mean paying attention.

Parenthetically, the limbic system in the mammalian brain appears to be a good candidate for the physiological organ which corresponds to the behavioural observations of the instinctive or appetitive system. It is observed that this system does send streams of excitation in many directions to many parts of the brain.

Our picture therefore has to accommodate a strategic central control which can set priorities. This can be represented as the central apical region between the two halves of the system where the sensorium apices meet and connect with the motorium ones.

We can see the appetitive system as what amounts to a secondary sensorium, one which measures needs and satisfactions and which contributes to the final triggering linkage from the informational side of the brain to the instructional side, the Works Department.

Consciousness

This brings me to the complex question of consciousness. What consciousness seems to be, seen from the inside, and there is no other way to see it, is this.

Many thinkers have proposed models of the mind as a great connectivity network. My model is of millions of interconnected loci, balls and boxes with links or junctions of varying strengths. (The connectivity (+ or −)of locus A with respect to locus B is a magnitude which sets a contribution to the probability that the firing of A will cause or prevent the firing of B.)

I appear to have my being in such a connectivity network where each idea, concept or percept is a locus and the semantic inter-relationships of these elements are the connectivities. I appear to be conscious of all that is semantically (connectionally) close to one locus at a time.

I also seem to have the power to move the attention point around the network. I can go to any other point in the great connectivity network of the mind and explore any of the regions of high semantic connectivity around that

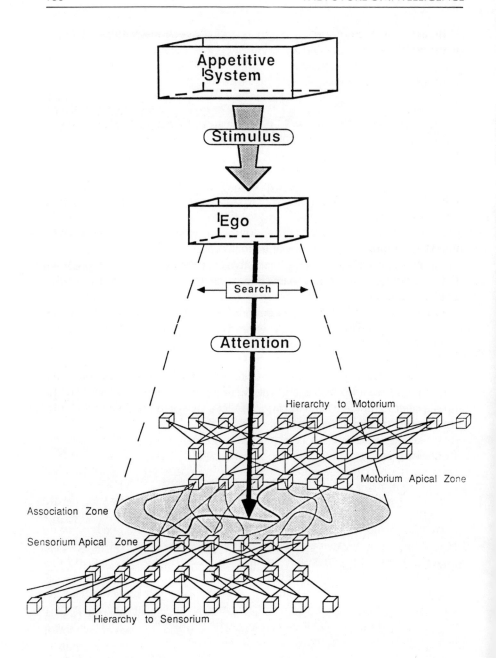

Figure 32   A model of attention

point. But I have to proceed by a semantic or connectional pathway, though these are often obscure. We can think of connectivity as being the same as semantic relationship. The word 'mother' has a high connectivity with the word 'father' but a lower one with the word 'incandescence').

At the same time I know that the movement of my attention is very much affected by my sensory input at any time. Some attention is involuntary. It can be attracted despite my will. I cannot withhold attention from sudden emergency. Further, my attention is partially controlled by the state of my appetitive system. If I am starving I keep thinking of and notice food.

INTROSPECTIVE EXPERIENCE AND THE MODEL

What I do now has been rejected by the behaviourist school of psychologists. They felt it was time to stop 'physiologising', making countless untestable hypotheses about the intricacies of brain function.

I venture on to this tricky ground only because the behaviourist assumption is no longer tenable. The speculative model that follows is now testable. Computer simulations are now possible. In all that follows I am outlining very tentative, first guess hypotheses which perhaps within the next hundred years or less may be testable in simulation on the family of concurrent hardware computers that are now possible.

My communication task is difficult because I can communicate only by parable and metaphor, calling up analogous known models to suggest the model I have built up over the years. Again I shall risk repetition in order to have a better chance of hitting on a parallel that brings my own model into brainability for all readers.

Unlike the behaviourists I feel that our internal introspective experience should be given first status. If any model of reality is contradictory to that then it cannot really convince. It can bring verbal but not behavioural belief. (This was my central argument against determinism you will remember.)

Here, when, I apply a trial first-fit match of the garment of my model both to the dummy, the usual concept of the physical object the brain, and to my mental 'body', my introspective experience of its workings.

The cerebral cortex is a great felt-like sheet of intertwined cells with enormous interconnectivity and equally enormous connectivity with all other parts of the brain and especially with the posited appetitive (instinctive) system.

Let us suppose that this cortex is topologically or connectionally the central region. Let it be, in fact, the apical region where the two halves of my model brain, sensory and motor, meet. Let its junior connections reach down both to the sensory and to the motor regions in two separate descending polyhierarchies. This would then be the semi-barrier region I posit where sensor-motor links are complete but subliminal, below threshold.

In man, the mammal which specialises in thought, planning, and contemplation before action, there has been an enormous expansion of this neocortical region. I guess that it is the region of planning, option-weighing, cogitation, where whim, indeterminism, and experimentalism are preserved even after sophistication is complete. Here ideas, plans, and imagination happen and decisions are made. This is the zone, I suggest, where all the hierarchic apices meet, the highest, most senior strategic zone.

I see this great region as subliminally interconnected during waking hours, because then something central in us, our attention point or focus, our ego, seems to be able to visit any part of it just by deciding to do so.

Consider interconnectivities measured in the way I have posited (constantly changing excitation, receptiveness to excitation, inhibition and threshold) all over this strategic level system. At any one moment in wakefulness there is some one connectively 'local' zone which has the highest mutual connectivity with all the rest of the system. As connectivities and thresholds change this centre must move round the network. Let us call that zone of highest general connectivity the ego, the wandering centre of attention.

Appetites direct attention

Clearly the excitatory input from the appetitive system is especially important in deciding the position and movement of the ego. (Hunger makes us pay attention to food, lust to sex.) Where ego, the centre of maximum excitation, visits, it brings the additional excitation required to turn potential into action, to raise a subliminal connection above threshold and trigger some motor hierarchies or trains of them.

So, simplistically, there are at any one moment many perceptual apices lit up, subliminally active, because the percept combinations that excite them are present to the senses. I see food, drink, a book, my lover. Eating, drinking, reading, lovemaking are my immediate options. It would be difficult, if fascinatingly innovative, to combine them in some simultaneous acrobatic feat. But the relative strengths of my appetitive drives, memories of previous experience, are all connected, with different weights, semantic strengths. Between them they decide the location of ego, my attention focus. I decide and, boringly, trigger just one of the motor trains.

Is that, at least, a brainable picture of the processes within us of which we are conscious? We speculate, we wander around relevant semantically connected regions and as a result we make decisions.

A locus in this network, the point where consciousness is for an instant, will certainly be in mutual excitation with a limited set of cells but it will not have a location in the normal sense because the 'near' and 'far' will mean semantically or connectively near and far. Nearness will be semantic nearness, it will be to do with excitation levels and the permeability of connections and not with spatial millimetres. The ego will be induced to move along high connectivity paths and it will be constrained by low connectivity insulation bounds. But by various routes it will be able to reach any locus. It will be able to explore the highest most abstract strategic regions, or go down the hierarchies to the peripheral tactical levels and concern itself with the feeling in a patch of skin or some small detail of the visual field.

Can I find an analogous model of this wandering attention which moves around the provisionally connected apical regions making connections here and there? An industrial company has a manager moving around a factory (or having people visit him). He is considering all the information, deciding priorities and triggering activity. He is not much concerned with the tactical details, sensory or motor, he triggers strategic-level prepared plans as he moves around the network. He provides the release that causes an informational input to trigger the 'appropriate response' output.

MEMORY

The meaning of the word 'memory' has been greatly extended, first by communications science and now by genetics.

The one thing that all life forms use in the most extended sense of the word is memory. It is the one essential of all life forms, a means for carrying the past into the future. It takes these various forms at various levels.

1.   The genome
This is, of course, a memory, it is the encoded form of the phenotype, the creature. This is the primitive and universal form which is present in every living cell. It is the databank which holds the prescription for the living thing.

2.   Neural memory
This has three main divisions:

2.1   Genoplastic memory
Hardwired, perceptuo-motor linkage between sensorium input and motorium output. The making of such connections is evolutionary. For example, most insect behaviour is robot-like, automatic, as first demonstrated by Jean Henri Fabre (1823).

2.2   Ontoplastic memory
Softwired perceptuo-motor linkage changed by learning within the single generation, e.g., mammal skill, environmental and avoidance learning.

2.3   Cognitive memory
The original meaning, the memory track of which we are conscious and which can be communicated between people coded as speech or other

symbol systems such as gesture. We can only guess, but cognitive memory probably exists in mammals and maybe other vertebrates such as birds.

3.   *Social memory*

This is the preserved traditions, mores, arts, skills, with the remembered and written records of an ethnic/language/culture group or more lately of any recruited interacting group, e.g., a commercial company or educational or other institution.

Cognitive memory

Here is a view of cognitive memory consistent with the present model. We have posited that ego, the attention point, is during waking hours wandering around the connectivity, the relationship network. At each place that it rests there are numerous perceptual apices in close connection, behind them those of the percepts and behind them the elements that make them up. Presence at one such locus is the multiple experience of a whole situation with all its close semantic connections, including perception of self.

The suggestion is that the track is tagged, marked, like that of the runner in a paperchase. Something happens at every point along the ego's track around the network. Like Theseus in the labyrinth, the ego leaves a trail. A silk thread marks the passage of its meanderings round the connectivity network that it has built up from its experience during life. Each point visited has a flag, a marker, a physical change, so that, when the ego returns any time later it finds the flag and the topological locus with all its thornbush of radiating semantic connections. Here is a part of the memory track. 'Déjà vu' – 'I have been here before,' it says. Remembering and reverie are the processes of exploring that serial track or making leaps along it to search for experiences that will help decision-making.

But there is a time when no such track is laid down, we live on but leave no memory trace. We sleep.

Sleep

Does sleep fit the model? There are many hypotheses and little consensus about sleep. Sleep is very, very odd indeed. Competitive animals struggling for survival in a hostile world spend a third of their time blind, deaf and paralysed! It wants a lot of explaining.

Sleep is a condition in which sensory input and motor output are both closed* except to a startling stimulus. The survival of many species that go into a state of stupor, of deaf-blind insensitivity to danger or opportunity, is another

*I am ignoring perceptions such as somnambalism and hypnotism.

minor miracle that remains without explanation. Why has not sleep been eradicated by evolution?

All animals live in food chains, fighting to eat their living food and to avoid becoming the food of others. Sleep hampers both predator and prey. Many smaller handicaps have been evolved away. Why not sleep? It is evident that it must confer some enormous but unknown advantage.

Fitting it to the present paradigm we see a state of the network when the wandering, central and singular ego breaks up, dissipates. The centre of neural connectivity fragments, there is no single central attention point or, if there is, it lays down no memory track except the occasional, ephemeral one of a dream.

Experimental psychology has established with some sureness that one function of sleep is to do with the learning process. Unconfused by the continuous sensory input and motor output, the learning process seems to be able to advance more surely during sleep. (We say, "Let me sleep on it".)

It is tempting to speculate (as the scientists always say when they want to hedge bets), it is tempting to see sleep as a mode in which the mind breaks up into autonomous, mutually insulated, regional topological zones in which there is not one locus of maximum connectivity and excitation, but many semi-insulated smaller regions of high mutual interconnectivity. Such analysis would be advantageous if it allowed the learning process to work in parallel instead of serially. Perhaps sleep is the time during which the synapses change their permeability, the thresholds change and the nodes change their excitability, while free of the stirring, muddling passages of the active, over-responsive ego.

Memory as learning amplifier

Work with the taxonomon has shown that a large number of iterations is needed for learning. If an intelligence learns from too few iterations, examples, it cannot get the relation between signal and noise right. Errors of false capture and failed capture become inevitable. Memory, by storing serial strings of experience, enables the intelligence to get surrogate experience to learn from, by retracking old experience from the data store of memory.

A much more important function of sleep is therefore suggested by these taxonomon programs.

The model insists that learning must be iterative, inductive. But we observe some learning in mammals at least that seems to be from a single instance, especially when the reward or punishment is instant and strong.

How would the engineer adapt inductive programs to learn like that? What would be needed, as suggested above, would be time multiplexing, a system in which the shock experience could be stored and then re-run repeatedly, including the inputs of reward and punishment. Further, since the sleep model posits an analytical mode in which perception is broken down and behaviour built up from elementary blocks, it would be greatly advantageous and speed things up if there were many short-cycle re-runs in parallel (concurrent) rather than one long run in series. Now the memory track of which we are all conscious provides us with the data store of tagged strategic-level connectivity states along which the ego may pass in repeated 'ironing in' cycles after the objective experience is over. We are all conscious of the repeated passes our ego takes down a long memory track in the rehearsing again and again of significant incidents we are conscious of. That is conscious learning.

The 'tempting hypothesis' is that more tactical learning would be much better, faster and more detailed if the ego could break up for some of the time into numerous 'egolets', small connectivity centres that made many more concurrent re-run cycles of short, important sections of the track.

Conscious rehearsing, ironing in the lesson, must mean preoccupation, a lower attention to current input. The ego break-up system with its enormous advantage in learning time, detailed analysis, and concurrent, many-track learning has a higher price. Suspension of central strategic control, unconsciousness. Sleep, the essential tactical stage of learning.

A parable: In war the General and his staff are in full strategic control, everything moves to his command. The army is awake. The war ends. The troops go back to barracks, into dispersed tactical-level training exercises under many sergeants and junior officers.

What do the Generals do? They dream. They set up a thousand scenarios and again and again go over the accumulated data from the last and all the previous wars. But the intelligence input and the orders output of wartime are cut off. Sociozoan consciousness, and two kinds of sleep, just what we find in metazoa: rapid eye movement sleep, when we dream and can make a memory track the Generals are doing exercises, mock wars — dreams; deep sleep, the troops are in barracks learning to march, to work their equipment, — tactical learning at myriads of centres.

As I have said, hypotheses like the above were rightly rejected by psychologists when there was no way of testing them. I suggest that the above ideas are now empirically testable in simulation on the sort of nerve-net models with which we are beginning to be able to play games. I venture to predict that a stage like sleep will be found to be essential when we get to high-level artificial intelligence. A stage will be needed when the input and output are switched off so that important runs of instructive inputs can be iterated many times so as to get the message imprinted and the fuzz explored.

Artificial intelligence can even now be conceived and made which will work on the principles outlined. If they can be brought to the point of applying for and passing Alan Turing's test, if we can make silicon, or glass fibre 'brains' that can be confused with people when they talk to us through terminals, then we shall have no good reason to deny what we do not deny to each other, consciousness. Directly, we can perceive no other consciousness than our own. But we may be able to model it and judge it in exactly the same way we each judge the other's.

We need such hypotheses, however sketchy at first, if we are not to be fumbling in the dark in the great adventure we are engaged on, that of producing the next step for our biosphere, earth's Creatura. These crude preliminary ideas may, will certainly, turn out to be wide of the bull's-eye. But I dare to hope they may at least land on the target somewhere.

Fleming's thermionic valve may not look much like a wafer scale integrated chip, but it lies on the road to it. We have to start somewhere, to find out the best 'where' we must explore many options. Here is just one.

REFLEXIVE BYPASSES

We have to consider reflex responses. They obviously bypass the polyhierarchic system described.

Reflex responses (those like the knee-jerk response, or the involuntary withdrawal of a traumatised limb) are involuntary. They evade the conscious control of mind. It has been shown that such reflex arcs, which are mediated through ganglia in the spinal chord, are a bypass to the central nervous system itself. There are many other such direct links which bypass all the strata of the posited polyhierarchic network. Here, signalling from sensorium to motorium is at the very lowest tactical level and is genoplastic not ontoplastic, it cannot be learned or unlearned.

Eye movements are a complex case. The rapid eye movements which are detected in certain phases of sleep indicate that those phases are concerned with the mental activity at the sensorium side of the network, yet they are caused by motoneurone efferent signals.

There is an *ad hoc* way to contrive a fit to the model proposed. The paths the eye takes in inspection are known to be important in visual perception and although they result from motor outputs there are sensory inputs from the proprioceptor nerves supervising eye muscles. These constitute signals to the sensorium that assist perception.

I envisage that visual receptors control eye-muscles via another sort of reflex type bypass to the whole of the elaborate strategic-level brain system itself, the neocortex. A similar effect must apply to all the proprioceptive inputs to the ganglia associated with muscular and other motoneurones generally. The ganglia close to the muscles where proprioceptive inputs mediate motoneurone effect constitute a direct bypass to the whole system as envisaged. They are not a contradiction of the pattern, they are another part of it. (Proprioceptors are sensors which measure muscle actions.)

There are other examples of such direct or low-stratum bypasses from sensorium to motorium and although this complexifies my first, simple, broad-brush sketch of the two polyhierarchic networks it does not falsify it. We have to modify our visual picture of the high-level strategic information from the sensorium penetrating through the many strata both afferently to the centre and efferently to the motorium interface. To this picture we now add the various hardwired ontoplastic, tactical-level bypass routes which constitute reflex responses and cybernetic feedback to muscle fibres.

Old brain bypasses also

There are almost certainly some ontoplastic learning processes, probably mediated by the paleocortex (the cerebellum), which bypass the whole neocortex system. K. S. Lashley and other early workers were greatly puzzled by the fact that their completely decorticate cats still showed some residual simple learning. The whole of the cerebral cortex was removed, yet the wretched creatures still seemed capable of low level tactical-type learning. This caused Lashley, W. Kohler and others to completely reject the simple connectionist theories of the time. They denied that any one nerve was essential to any mental action and were looking for holistic theories like Kohler's gestalt theory.

The present model is connectionist but does not need the presence of any one component because at each stratum and at each node there is a margin for error, an allowance for fuzz which is set by the sufficiency, which in turn is set by the threshold of the posited component. Lashley and Kohler were right, no cell is essential, but they were wrong, I believe, to think that this destroyed all possible connectionist theories. (As, to his credit, D. O. Hebb argued at the time.)

A polyhierarchic model with sufficiency gates as elements is a connectionist model that can survive the awkward fact that, as many studies show, there is a steady mortality of brain cells throughout life. Just as societies survive the death of role holders, people, its nodes, so brains survive the death of neurones. In neither case does it mean that individual nodes have no unique role, a connectional place in the network, acting upon and responding selectively to other specific nodes. The roles of cells, nerves and people may change with time but at any one time they do exist. The network is connective and functions connectively. I stick my neck out and assert it.

THE PROBLEM OF DELAYED OUTCOME

The intrusive generalist trying to model the learning process as it appears in people has many daunting problems. Not the least of these is that of finding a credible model for a learning process where behaviour is optimised in spite of the fact that there may be delays of months or years between action and observed outcome, successful or otherwise.

The simple Pavlovian model advanced so far assumes that each response to a stimulus input is assessed and gets an instant success/failure score and that this can immediately modify the connectivity of the network. While it is a useful step forward to simulate even such a simple brain it is desperately primitive.

It is obvious that men and their societies often have very long time intervals between all stages, stimulus, response, outcome and learning adjustment. This is a problem for future generations of thinkers and researchers but perhaps we should ask whether the problem is severe enough to make us seek an alternative paradigm.

Clues I see which encourage persistence with the present paradigm are these. When a memory track is laid down as posited it follows that there are connectivity loci within the network which were laid down at the time of the original input/output trials of any given problem. If the ego (the attention focus point) returns to that locus on receipt of the corresponding success/ failure signal, however much later (because of connectivity linkages), then the success/failure input can do its work of making local modifications which are relevant, despite the time lapse. An advert persuades me to plant peas. Time passes. The peas mature but are full of worms. I sadly observe this and my attention is drawn to the connective locus concerned with the pea planting decision and makes a negative adjustment in the connections between the sensorium advert input and the planting activity motorium areas. We can at least imagine simulating such a complex system.

The memory track explains another hard-to-simulate feature of human behaviour, multi-tasking. We seem to be able to deal with many problems at the same time, switching almost randomly from one to another. This is much harder to understand than the simple pre-programmed multi-tasking in computers. With people the efficient multi-task behaviour train has itself to be learned by experience. I have posited that the attention focus can jump around loci in the memory track under the influence of some more strategic-level system. We can see the beginnings of a way to simulate 'learned multi-tasking'.

The eureka moment

Karl Popper was frankly mystical on the subject of the eureka moment. I refer, of course, to that joyous exciting moment when what was perplexing and contradictory suddenly falls into place. A consistent model appears as from nowhere and brings all aspects of the problem area into felicitous congruence. 'Eureka', 'I have found it,' cried Archimedes in his bath, when it came to him that density could be accurately measured by water displacement.

I posit that the eureka moment is the moment when a valid generalisation emerges. It is that instant when two connectivity systems, which have developed separately, merge and unite, when an 'or' type connection is made which unites the two classes as members of some more general class. It is obviously essential that this should occur. The baby learns about an assembly of face, arms and legs that mothers it, then of another that fathers it. One day, 'Eureka!' a breakthrough. There are a lot of these *different* assemblies of the same elements; people. A whole set of subclasses has evolved a senior node that responds 'or' style to any member of the set. As nodes arise which represent more complex assemblies, finding this sort of valid generalisation becomes more difficult. But is it different in nature from the baby example above?

The pleasure given by the eureka moment is an important clue. The act of recognition itself is very often a pleasure. When you see the face of an old friend there is a moment of pleasure which does not occur with the sight of a familiar, even a loved, one. The recognition, seeing that something unexpectedly belongs to the already known, that it has in some form a subject comparate ready within the brain, is itself rewarding. It is easy to see that this is biologically advantageous. The pleasure is the success signal which is needed to reinforce the connectivity pattern that will make this recognition slightly easier next time. Taxonomy itself, even without advantage, is and must be pleasurable for advanced animals. Animals, especially predators, must seek to learn more about what may be relevant. This is biologically advantageous.

Why does the pleasure diminish with familiarity? Obviously it must. Once the lesson is learned there are other things to be learned. Pleasure would be devalued if there were no system of rising expectations and parallel lowering of reward.

Boredom has a function. It sets the animal on a search for stimulus so that it can learn more of its environment. In spite of the fact that curiosity kills cats, the survival rate of curious cats must be higher. Predators like felines who get bored and explore must outbreed incurious ones who let their environment force itself upon them. Otherwise, all felines would be politely and supinely incurious.

It is clear that boredom is confined to the higher animals, those with some serial tagged-track type memory. Every ontoplastic animal, however simple, has some memory, but this need be no more than the polyhierarchic connectivity system described and simulated in the taxonomon. The difference should be clear. There is immediate-outcome learning, like learning to walk or play tennis, and there is long-term memory learning where attention backtracks, recapitulates past experience and modifies connections that are no longer in short-term memory. We can call the two styles 'psychomotor learning' and 'cognitive learning' and they are very different. Advanced taxonomons will have to tackle all these problems.

THOUGHT

The perceived wandering of our attention around the network system of our mind shows up in the model as the wanderings of a topological zone of high excitation around the strong linkage paths of the interthreaded multi-dimensional network at the semantically central (but physically peripheral) zone of the brain.

During consciousness, in this model, the ego, the 'highest whole-net connectivity centre', is always on the move. In alert consciousness a single perceptual input from eyes, ears, skin is 'lighting up' a topological region — we need a new word — 'topion?' (a high connectivity subnetwork). Thus the perceptual input during attentive wakefulness is in large part that which decides the location of the ego. But the input from the appetitive system and the 'long-term goal' system which has grown out of it does have some influence, it directs attention, switches eyes to interesting scenes, selects one voice from a hubbub of voices.

In reverie, speculation, planning and thinking, the perceptual influence is reduced and the appetitive system and its great superstructure, the short- and long-term goal extensions from it, become the principal influence on the location and track of that activating 'topion' I have identified as the ego.

There is a random-walk element in all free speech. *Recitation* is a fixed phrase-walk. All *speech* has free choice functions where randomness creeps in. We could identify intelligence in a Turing Test by the unpredictability of the speech functions, the discontinuities, sidetracks, whimsicality.

IMAGINATION AND PLANNING

The model also gives us an insight into imagination and planning. A sophisticated creature needs an internal world model in which to make experimental simulations. The connectivity system proposed can provide such a model, a system built up by each separate being during life as the internal model of its own world. It is a model where it can try out painlessly the results of possible actions and responses and make decisions as a result of planning rather than spontaneous reaction. In *homo sapiens* the elements of the central network may be percepts, concepts, simple or elaborate combinations of them or relationship concepts like 'on' or 'near'. These are on the sensorium side of the central barrier.

Connected with each percept, concept and relationship concept is a 'word' triggering node across the barrier on the motorium side. Serial thought is a connectivity-walk which is the echo of a random-walk. The ego moves along a high-weight track connecting nodes triggering 'phrase' nodes, which trigger word nodes at lower strata.

It is widely conceded that words are the atoms of cognitive thought. In the model, the physical representation of phrases and words lies in the state of the connectivity pattern between the physical nodes (cells or cell assemblies). This connectivity is alive, dynamic, constantly changing, being repaired and regenerated. A simple percept does not have a single locus or node to represent it.

Following the logic of the scheme we find that percepts and concepts of low specification would have to have a large number of loci to represent them wherever they may be needed. Only very complex highly specified combinations of percepts, concepts, etc. would have a few or only one locus to 'represent' them. This is a vital essence of the model.

Speech, on this model, would be the movement of the ego along a phrase-walk on the motorium side of the central zone. The ego is aware of, or semantically connected to, all the surrounding close-connected ideas to the words used. Thought would be movement along a parallel track on the other side of the barrier.

A man is picking his way through a wood in the dark with a torch, the words are the stones and rocks and earth of his track, but, as he goes, his swerving torch illuminates the trees and bushes, all that is near on his track. His mind knows and sees more that there is on the word track he follows. From each point, he can see and decide the best next point as his discourse develops. This is how writing and especially poetry is for the prepared brain, a multi-track journey with many simultaneous implicit messages above, beyond and around the simple chain of words.

8

A sociozoan science?

So far sociology, as a science, is as soft as thistledown and as predictive as a palmist. We might ask why. The usual reason for persistently poor performance in a science is that the pioneers have chosen an inappropriate set of isolates for the initial analysis or a non-congruent model of the way they relate to each other.

One apparent problem with sociology is that the traditional approach is holistic, sociologists see society, *ab initio,* as a single whole. There seems to be a hidden assumption that there is a set of laws applicable to some abstraction called 'society', a generalised essence which represents all the many different kinds of sociozoa, as I would prefer to call them. But 'society' in this sense is not a valid class. It is as if zoologists set off to do their job with the initial concept 'animal', and ignoring differences tried to find a set of laws which applied to the fuzzy set, 'animals'. There may be predictive generalisations of such broadness but more analysis seems warranted before useful zoology or sociology is likely to be predictively fruitful.

It has to be confessed that this thesis is an attempt to find such super-generalisations, but it is done with the knowledge that the role of hypotheses of this generality can only be that of providing a guiding framework, a scaffolding of philosophy upon which better biological hypotheses may later be built.

The comparative sociology that appears, to be needed comes to us under another name, 'anthropology', the study of particular societies, and more recently 'sociobiology' which is concerned with the genetic and reproductive effect of various types of interaction and behaviour in social groups. The former seems to have been conducted, at first at least, with a colonialist sense of an advanced culture seeking to understand the workings of a more primitive one. The real situation was the reverse, the older, more durable patterns are the ones with the track record of megayears of success, the newer ones, though biologically successful, are almost untried in any sensible evolutionary perspective. The sort of success of the modern world society can be seen on the upslope before every kind of population crash. Ask any locust.

Sociobiologists have at least taken that worry on board and measure success in a way very compatible with the present approach, in terms of survival, the preserving and replicating of form through time, morphostasis. They look at the many types of social grouping and try to estimate the effects of behavioural patterns upon population, survival and growth — a very salutary and necessary exercise. The problem is that the work seems to be largely theoretical with naturally, because of the experimental difficulties, very little empirical input.

In this book I propose a radical paradigm affecting all living things and assemblies of them, so I might as well be hanged for a sheep as a lamb and take up the sociological challenge.

My first warning is that if my ideas are correct, then fully predictive laws governing living systems may in principle be impossible. Worse, the further we move along the continuum of morphostasis, the less the chance that precise predictive laws will be found to be possible. This arises from the position I take that the biota may be drawing on truly quantum indeterminism and amplifying it so that it can overcome the weight of large numbers that establishes what we see as the causal laws of nature. However, fundamental physicists have done remarkably well in their uncertain quantum world so we need not despair of finding invariances and regularities short of strict causal laws even in the much more difficult world of morphostasis science at the social level.

Morphostats are competitors (even when parts of a greater symbiotic whole). The business of competitive morphostats is that of all adversaries. The successful are unpredictable predictors. Winners are as unpredictable as possible and as good at prediction as possible. When random, experimental inputs affect very large systems, we promote quantum problems upwards, push them further into the mesocosm.

The furthest advance we know along that morphostasis continuum is that made by the larger sociozoa on earth, the human ones. It follows that economists are an endangered species.

Concede that my concept 'morphostat' is a valid class, a good way of analysing nature for study. If the class of immaterial, self-perpetuating, self-optimising forms is an adequate and congruent model of the living, then we have to find a morphostat which is less of an impenetrable black box than others.

And if it is logical to include sociozoa, form-preserving self-optimising, social entities in the class so defined, then we may have an examinable morphostat for study. The communication channels of societies are very complex and intertwined, but they are at least traceable, patent, open to study.

Now as soon as this is said there is a question to be answered. If the model is correct, why has it not emerged in the social context, from sociology, economics, or any of the other social sciences? An answer might be that the human, or soft, sciences were first conceived in the model of the hard, the materialistic sciences. The mechanomorphic perspective of those sciences was inappropriate. The view that the same mesocosm-type deterministic laws would apply to hetoropotent systems obscured the realities and led to a search for the wrong kind of models and paradigms based on the wrong realm.

If only biomorphic models are appropriate to the human sciences then we have an explanation of why the mechanomorphic theories and models have lacked rigour and been so disappointingly unpredictive.

That pessimistic conclusion should be vigorously challenged but it would be best if that challenge took the form of showing examples of successful prediction. Unsupported counter-assertion is less useful. Professor Stanislav Andreski, who has read more sociology and economics than most of us have read newspapers, writes that he is unaware that any one of the great economic, social or political changes had been confidently and clearly predicted by social scientists. I myself note that there was no prior warning (or promise) from science about the spread of soviet centralism, several economic booms and slumps, the upsurge of nationalistic fascism, anti-colonialism, anti-racialism, the hippy movement, the spread of permissiveness, the success of capitalistic democracy.

Which sociologist predicted the womens' liberation movement in Judeo-Christian cultures or the fierce reaction to it in some Islamic ones? What advance warning was there of the upsurge of the ecology lobby, the jogging craze, the resurgence of Muslim fundamentalism? Point out the well-argued non-partisan scientific paper in which, well before the event, any of these mass world trends were clearly and unequivocally predicted. The paper should have been written by a professional social scientist, preferably by one of those who claim that sociology, economics and political economy are predictive sciences. Partisan predictions do not count. Among the millions of reformers, cranks and eccentrics who advocate anything conceivable we can always find one whose ideas became a movement and whose 'predictions' seem to be fulfilled.

Thus far the message is bleak. What is the use of any model if you cannot use it for prediction? Well, if the model's only prediction is that rigorous deterministic prediction is a false hope, it is an advance, if it is true.

The study of sociology and economics, or what replaces them, should be concerned much more with the actual flow of information and instruction in easily observable organisations and institutions. We should look for the drosophila fly society, the one where it is easiest to observe the informational network as it functions, and make experiments with it if possible without doing harm to people.

My own observations in watching the development of several large commercial companies and the world-wide organisation Mensa, in all of which developments I have played an active part, led me to the belief that the formal or visible managerial authority chart is almost irrelevant to the information flow chart which one would make if one measured the type, direction, influence, quantity, flow and pattern of information in these organisations. However, in advanced systems where information is semantic, not just a bit stream, there is a vital factor that the scientist has the problem of measuring. The signals in a sociozoon are very heteropotent. I am sure that a high proportion of the information in that flow is pure white noise. By that I mean that it could not conceivably play any part in causing, preventing or changing an action decision by any person or machine that receives it. Some of the information is low-grade ore, data that have a low probability of affecting an action (motor) decision. But some signals have great weight and make important changes in the motor behaviour of the institution concerned.

It must be a first task of the sociozoon scientist to try to estimate the semantic strength of the information flow as measured in this way. We would want to know the architecture of the weighted information flow pattern. It may turn out that *money* decisions are a fair measure of this kind of weight. Money or credit fits into the picture in the place where the internal appetitive flow fitted in the brain model elaborated in the last chapter. Money is the excitation or authoriser signal for a motor output (or strictly, unusual or changed motor output). It is the special kind of socially evolved signal cognate with the excitation signals from the priority system in the metazoan brain I outlined in the last chapter. What an appetitive input is, in a metazoon, is the additional authority signal that brings a node connecting an 'action situation' (threat or opportunity) above threshold and thus into action. This happens at the expense of other such complete 'actionable' links where the appetitive excitation is withheld (because attention is single focused).

In the sociozoon an executive (or committee, board) sits at the connective centre (often not the formal centre) and listens to all the competing strategic-level calls for authority to act or for money. A decision, choice, is made. The process prevents the sociozoon from falling apart by trying to do everything at once. This is done by releasing authority to act and money here and denying it there. The review of the strategic options, the observations where motor action (changing something) is potentially beneficial, is the equivalent of the posited wandering of the ego, the attention point around the network of a metazoan brain.

What is an organisation? It is the name of a class of entity with high tolerance, wide boundaries. It includes everything from the oldest organisation, probably the Catholic Church, to the group of strangers which gathers round a traffic accident to help. An organisation is an assembly of co-operating people. In the original form of organisation there was but one primary purpose, survival. To achieve survival, not merely the group of individuals, but the patterns of co-operation between them, have to be preserved. The codes, mores, religions, morals – they have many names – have to be conserved with minimum change because the more viable a thing is, the more likely it is that a change will make it less viable. An organisation must preserve its form through time and accept only those changes which make it a better form-preserving device.

But, as we have seen with more complex but lower-level morphostats such as cells and animals, the most rigid system is not always the most viable. Organisations must have a means of generating randomness, experimental changes, and selecting from them. They must accept only those modifications which improve change-resisting ability. To do this they have to receive, classify, evaluate and condense incoming information and transduce it into appropriate instructions to members. The problem of separating organisations conceptually from their environment, the even larger organisation, society, is difficult.

Within them there is a specially rich flow of information but they themselves are deeply embedded in and closely entwined as regards the flow of information with the larger organisations of which they form part. The information that passes into them and out of them is encoded. It is not signals coming from meter readings, point-intensities in the world. Much of the instruction which flows out from them in coded form does not trigger motor action until it has passed through one or more links in other organisations.

The reader will remember the permissible topological distortion that I asked him or her to perform, in the imagination, upon the living brain. The afferent and efferent, input and output, interfaces had conceptually to be drawn apart to form a sensorium and a motorium. Now, the information flow architecture of an organisation must be treated in the same way. All input information, that which may change plans or policy decisions, is drawn to the sensorium. All the outflow of instructions, orders, commands which actuate output behaviour are drawn to the conceptual motorium of workers and suppliers, all those who get instructions.

To perform this operation with an organisation is much less simple. Firstly, its junction point —its cells — are people, each with their own elaborate sensorium and motorium; and secondly, the placental connections with the rest of society at the sensorium of the organisation and at its motorium are more difficult to disentangle. In Figures 33 to 35 we can see the first three stages of the growth of an organisation.

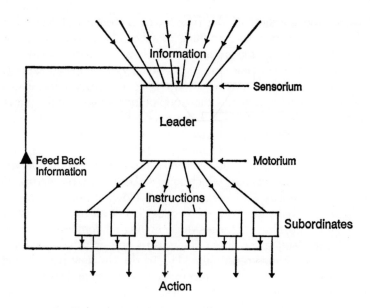

Figure 33   The growth of an organisation, stage 1

Each node in the information flow of such a third-level morphostat is itself a fully developed polyhierarchic system.

When a group of people is to act co-operatively it appoints a leader, patent or tacit. Even a bad leader is better than none, because without one the individuals cannot resolve their conflicting approaches with sufficient speed and decision. But usually the leader is selected because he knows what to look for and knows what to do. He perceives what is relevant in the information coming to him and he has a repertoire of appropriate behaviour patterns which he can perform or teach and command in the group. Figure 33 represents the situation. His own sensory system, amplified by feedback from his subordinates, is his input. His output is instructions to his subordinates, who act as the muscles of the system and carry out the necessary actions. Thus the group has amplified the observational, interpretational and behavioural skills of its most skilled member.

In stage 2, Figure 34, the organisation has become larger as the number of people the leader has to deal with has become too great. He is now unable to cope with the flow of information. He appoints agents on both sides of himself, afferent and efferent. The observation officers select and condense the incoming information, predigesting it to diminish his information load.

On the efferent side, an elaborative hierarchy expands, amplifies and

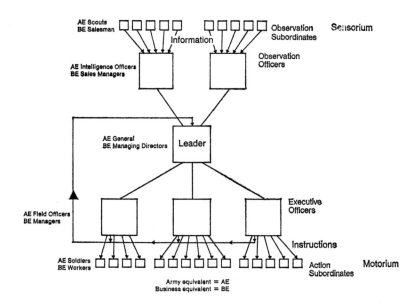

Figure 34 The growth of an organisation, stage 2

develops his instructions and passes them to last line subordinates, who carry them out.

In the third stage, Figure 35, the organisation has grown still further and, despite the arrangements in stage 2, the leader is overloaded once more from an information point of view. He can no longer deal even with the refined and condensed convergent information and he can no longer issue those key instructions, which must now be elaborated by trained subordinates. He develops an administrative office with a number of subordinates who carry out the routine aspects of his responsibilities. Now only low-probability, non-routine matters are referred to him. At later stages many specialised hierarchies develop, which overlie the principal authority hierarchy. For instance, in the British Army structure, the specialist corps (Signals, Education, Intelligence) represent multiple, separate, centre-bypassing hierarchies.

A commercial firm is something that can clearly be seen to be unitary despite the complexity of its informational connections. The reason we have no difficulty in separating it conceptually is because it has a relatively independent array of decision centres, and acts autonomously and mainly in its own interests and in the direction of its own survival. Ostensibly it will have other aims connected with its function in the society to which it belongs but its 'will to live' is almost always much more important. Organisations continue

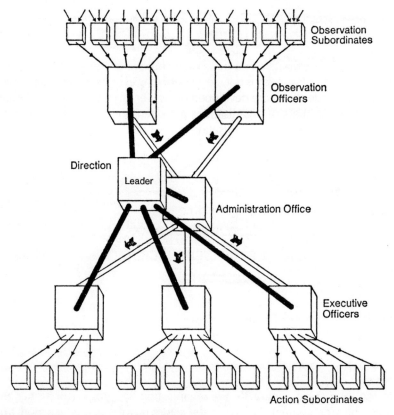

Figure 35 The growth of an organisation, stage 3

to exist long after the need for them has vanished and others exist like an animal for no reason at all except that they can.

VIABILITY AT ALL LEVELS

At the biological level the organism as a whole must provide sustenance for its cells, which have specialised and lost the power of independent life. Morphostats must be viable at all levels.

Similarly, in organisations the individual must gain from his co-operation. He must be provided with sustenance or satisfaction to retain his adhesion. I have defined a need as a threat to the stability of a morphostat. The elements of a morphostat as well as the morphostat itself, have needs. The needs are not necessarily the same. Indeed, they are often contradictory. Human beings have not only needs but aspirations and, in this context, an aspiration is a need for progress, security, a move towards a more stable configuration. When the primary needs of members of organisations have been satisfied, then the aspiration for greater security assets itself.

Morphostats as primitive and as loosely coupled as human organisations suffer from a difficulty which is not, because of long evolution and compromise adaption, so evident in more developed but lower level ones. The needs and aspiration of members of organisations are *often* not compatible and even contradict the needs of the organisation as a whole. The primary problem of an organiser is that of achieving the optimum compromise satisfaction of the needs and aspirations of role holders at all levels, which is compatible with the stability, continuation and progress of the organisation itself. A glance at the diseases of organisations, the faulty patterns which bring them to an end at either extreme, will demonstrate the point. Where the managers of any organisation err on the side of paying too much attention to the individual's needs and aspirations, the organisation ceases to be viable. Even if it does survive, it is directionless and impotent. It loses to its competitors.

When they are faced with an emergency or are under attack, organisations become more sensitive to central signals. Individual needs and aspirations are reduced, discipline becomes severe; loss and sacrifice are accepted by individuals for the benefit of the group. An army at war is an example. To achieve this predominance of central control, centre-proneness, there is in mankind a different modality, a behaviour pattern which is switched on in certain circumstances — the Military Enthusiasm of which Lorenz writes. Even so, there is an extreme of centre-proneness which will destroy an organisation. Discipline which is too strict leads to repression and punishment. The feedback signals are over-inhibited and revolt, mutiny or revolution eventually results. But we must note the strong discipline and the incredible altruism which extreme challenges can produce without breakdown.

SELF-ORGANISING SYSTEMS

In the organisation, aside from the knowledge stored in the brains of the individual members, there is immanent in the pattern of organisation an understanding of the social environment in which the organisation works. The type of organisational centres, the pattern and flow of information, the connections and deconnections, result from the interaction of a large number of people over a period of time. This is an inductive 'learning' process. Organisations 'learn' at an unconscious meta-level. A recursive, self-correcting system modifies the network in ways which are by no means apparent to those who suppose themselves to be in command. Each individual receives and deals with information and passes it on according to what he has been taught and the necessities of the moment. The flow of information to him grows and shrinks and he reacts to this. Unexpected links and bypasses spring up. Information moves in unorthodox directions. The flow of information is often not directed by any person's decision, but by the necessities of the situation and a multiplicity of decisions in many places. In this sense organisations, especially large ones, are self-organising systems, morphostats. Every organisation has a 'hidden hand'.

Traditional view of organisation as monohierarchic

The traditional view of organisation was first clarified in Roman times. The basic concept is that of responsibility. The question asked is: 'Who is compelled to supply answers to whom?' The role of the questioner is the role of mastery. The answerer's role is one of subjection. In any entity which has the problem of amplifying uncertainty so as to build improbable arrangements, the first problem is to build an amplification system. Systems in which all elements are equivalent are not and cannot be organised. We can have societies in which all men's rights are equal but we cannot have an *organisation* in which the effect of all men is equal. We can have organisations in which every member has a voice in deciding who will be the leaders. We cannot have organisations, viable ones, of any size at any rate, without leadership. Leadership is a device invented, unconsciously, to provide the necessary trigger effect, the necessary amplification, the necessary heteropotency of the elements of any morphostatic system. A leader is a decision gate, a trigger or relay. So is a committee. The gate receives information from many sources, makes a decision and transmits information transduced into negative and positive instructions. The similarity between the leader and the wandering attention focus in any large organisation is clear. Informationally he is not the apex of a single hierarchy.

Development from monohierarchic to polyhierarchic organisation

It goes without saying that the random behaviour of a mob is different in a very profound sense from the behaviour of a body of organised men. Leadership is a ubiquitous feature of any body of organised men of any size or complexity. It has been argued that gangs or teams do exist and function without visible leadership, that small face-to-face groups can work co-operatively in pre-allocated roles without visible leadership, but on a large scale the pattern is rare and its converse almost universal.

The problem of any leader is that of changing the behaviour of his followers from what it would have been without him, towards conformity with one of a repertoire of highly-specified combined patterns of corporate behaviour. The leader acts as a decision gate. He defines and allocates roles (functions). He receives evidence from his own sensorium and this is supplemented by precoded information coming from some of his followers. He makes his decision on the balance of the evidence and then issues a different kind of information, *instructions,* of an appropriate kind to his followers. His followers conform to assigned roles. They are both receptors and effectors. But the leader himself has a brain and within it are stored a set of sets of instructions each suitable for a different decision. If he is the captain of a ship, he has a repertoire of 'whole situation' navigating behaviour patterns. He has the set of orders he would give for 'heave to', the set of orders for 'set sail', the set of orders to deal with a storm, the set of orders to deal with fog, and so on. He does not know and need not know all the detailed actions involved in the carrying out of his orders. The instructions are simple but the activities they evoke are complex in terms of the instructions eventually sent to the muscles of the sailor. The apparently monohierarchic system is polyhierarchic, at least at the centre. As soon as the organisation grows beyond a certain point the flow of information through the leader gets to be more than he can handle and he begins to delegate. He delegates both on the afferent and the efferent side of himself, though the same person may act in two different roles, the role of information-giver and the role of instruction-collector.

The examination of any large organisation will reveal that as it gets larger it gets more polyhierarchic, more and more offices and centres form on which information on certain matters and subdivisions of work converge and from which instructions are issued automatically under the general authority of the management but without information passing through the managerial part of the channel.

The *good* manager is a supervisor of the *network,* not of the contents, the information. He does not insert himself into the flow of information. One of the serious faults of an organisation is that which develops when a manager fails to arrange adequate bypasses to himself and insists on trying to channel all information through himself and issue all instructions from himself. He is sticking to the method of the primitive face-to-face group and it is unsuitable when the information flow, both afferent and efferent, is at more than a certain level.

Large monohierarchic organisations have proved to be unstable and relatively inefficient. The strictly monohierarchic organisation of the Aztec and Inca civilizations, although they were very elaborate and highly structured, collapsed ignominiously at the first contact with a Western polyhierarchy.

The Roman pattern of organisation was a development from the primitive one-to-many-flow-of-instruction pattern. It was an amplification system, a trigger tree. The hierarchical structure arose when the initial array of instruction receivers began to develop their own subordinates and radiate the instructions wider and wider. It was this pattern that made it possible for mankind to live symbiotically in large groups. It was this epoch-making discovery that created third-order morphostats which grew upon the substrate of primitive tribal society.

But the same pattern can be seen in the offices of every company. Look at the familiar hierarchic organisation chart (Figure 2). It represents the *authority* structure. It is a picture of both afferent and efferent sides of the communications network mixed up. It leads down to the motorium and sensorium combined in one line. It takes no account of the sensorium in its external divergence out beyond the Sales Department. In these charts, the 'Sales' side and the 'Works' side, the apical sensory regions and the apical motor regions, are shown as part of the same hierarchy despite the fact that, broadly speaking, the flow of information is afferent in one case and efferent in the other.

The normal organisation chart usually shows a long box at the top, called 'the shareholders' or the 'electorate', as the source of the central authority exerted by the 'President' or 'Managing Director' or whoever occupies the single-role box below it. Those acquainted with the functioning of large companies will know that the effect of signals from the central authority shareholders or electorate on the day-to-day or even the year-to-year functioning of the organisation is negligible, except in dire failure situations when collapse is near. Signals converging from electorates and shareholders are so rare, so unorganised, so confused and so crude that they do not have a significant influence on the decision-makers. It is only when *organisations* such as lobbies, pressure groups, trade unions and similar associations with their own hierarchic structures grow up that their signals begin to impinge with any force on the central decision-making processes. The traditional model of organisation is incomplete because it leaves out the afferent side and muddles it with the efferent side, and it is inaccurate because the flow of information and instruction is just not like that. The traditional picture of the boss who is supposed to have a one-way influence on the behaviour of those in the stratum below him, and of those in the next stratum in their turn controlling behaviour of the stratum below, is based on an earlier pattern where it was possible for the man at the top to observe and remember everything so that he needed no information-collecting hierarchies.

The development of the polyhierarchic pattern began when the persons in the second stratum were appointed. Because of special skills and abilities which the top man did not fully understand, they bypass the boss and give orders directly. The second-stratum experts had to have information and they began to develop their own information-collecting hierarchies. These are also a bypass to the top man. The subordinate is not now acting only under signals from the top but he is receiving other afferent information which bypasses and may be incomprehensible to the man at the top. This is illustrated in Figure 35 With elaboration, this then develops to the situation in Figure 36 as the subordinates' input hierarchy grows.

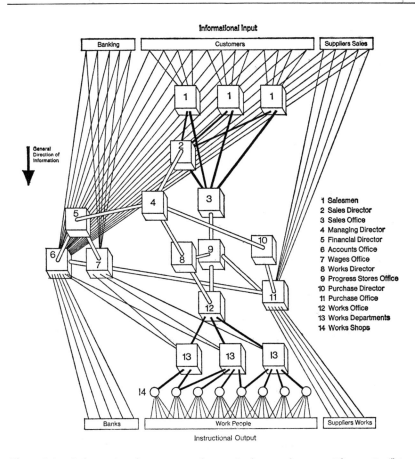

Figure 36 Informational structure of a typical manufacturer. The main flow of information/instruction is in the lowest plane. Top management structure is best seen as an overpass system. Only principal channels are shown. All are two-way, but general direction is from sensorium to motorium

In Figure 36 I have tried to show where some of the officers in a small manufacturing company fit into the polyhierarchic informational structure which I propose. The informational input comes from banking and financial institutions, customers and the sales departments of suppliers. The total input converges on sales offices, purchasing offices and accounts and wages departments. The principal information from the sales office passes to the progress office, stores, etc., departments where the work is planned. From there it goes to the works office, is issued to works departments and, at a lower strata, to workshops and finally to the workpeople. Other information from the progress office goes to the purchasing office, from which instructions are issued to the works supplying company. The three principal operational directors, the sales director on the afferent side, the purchasing director and the works director on the efferent side, communicate with the managing director, who represents the board. The finance director also reports directly to the managing director and controls, without intervening in, the flow of information from banking and financial institutions to the accounts office and wages office. These departments are not directly connected with the transducing of input information into output instructions. They represent the conative or emotive input which is necessary to make the organisation function. Financial information and the flow of wages is the pleasure/pain system of the organisation whose function is to modify behaviour in such a direction that the viability of the organisation is better assured. The managing director represents the 'ego' or attention point of the organisation in that he moves around the network (or the equivalent, brings to him the various role incumbents in it), he is performing a similar function to that of the ego or attention in the individual animal: that of concentrating attention on the important problems and deciding on priorities. His principal control is that of deciding on the flow of money via the finance director. A simple example of this is a large company producing a number of 'lines', which develops a separate sales department, or sections of the sales department which receive information and transmit it to the works directly. The pattern is polyhierarchic.

MONEY

The flow of money is an indicator of the direction of the flow of information. Money flows from the instructor (employer) to the instructed (employed). It is received by the citizen in his role as a producer or subordinate and passed on by him in his role as a consumer or beneficiary of the activities of society. I have also described it as a *licensed* need/desire signal. The individual elements of human society have many needs which have to be satisfied. Neither the society nor the organisation which form part of it can satisfy all the needs and aspirations, at all times, of all its members. We need a way to select from among need signals so that the system shall not be brought to a halt by their plethora. Money is a limited licence to command. In most societies, broadly speaking, it is used as a means of inducing patterns of individual behaviour required for the continuance of society and its organisations. The route money takes through the afferent hierarchies decides, on balance, the amount of activity which will be generated from the apical decision centres in the offices of the manufacturing organisations. Its flow takes exactly the same pattern as the flow of information. It is polyhierarchic. It comes from a base of consumers, converges upon an apical array of centres of instructions, factories, local government offices, government itself and from these centres it diverges hierarchically until it is distributed to the same array of citizens in their role as producers. The fact that money can take the form of metal and paper artefacts, marks on paper in a bank or differences in magnetism on a computer tape, makes it clear that it is informational in nature. It passes the test of information. It can be transduced into numerous coded forms without losing its semantic content. It is beyond the scope of this book to follow the complexities of its flow and the complications of our world monetary system. I have indicated a way of looking at it which may help us a little in understanding and prediction.

WHEELS WITHIN WHEELS

In trying to fit the world at the level of societies to the polyhierarchic paradigm regard must be paid to an important caveat.

The material world of things, that of the Pleroma, is holistic. It acts as a whole, each particle has effects on every other one out to infinity and the complexity of these interactions is infinitely beyond the scope of our or any other mind. However, by choosing isolates, classes, cleverly and being aware of their fuzz we can, because of the statistical enormity of the mid-world we live in, make fairly predictable models by this analysis. Every analysis falsifies but we can find some that do not falsify too much for our limited purposes.

The world of the Creatura is (as far as we *know*) confined to this dust speck, earth. The earth's green cloak, its biosphere, is equally holistic. In many ways it is and acts as a symbiotic whole. It is a very large and vastly complex form which remains remarkably constant through great stretches of time. (Though there do seem to have been periodic catastrophes at multi-million year intervals.)

The problem of finding models, methods of analysis to fit the biosphere, is very much more difficult because, as I believe, heteropotency, and bypasses to statistical laws have developed. These have their effect at strategically ever higher levels.

However, the polyhierarchic paradigm has a *prima facie* plausibility when applied to isolates cut out of the whole for examination, the cell, the metazoon, even the sociozoon.

The reason for this is that there *is* a helpful place to sever subsystems away from the biosphere whole. It is at first sight surprising that it is the right place to put in our semantic dissecting knife because it is just at the surface where the flow of information is richest. It is at the sensorium and motorium of the subsystem.

A baby seemingly separates from its mother at the umbilical chord but the real separation is the richly interconnected placenta. Individual morphostats have two placental informational interfaces with the world, sensorium and motorium. It is at these that the communication in terms of sheer data-flow is richest (and at the lowest tactical level). Yet it is this rich bond that I have, and we all have, chosen to cut with our cleaver of analysis. Why this is right is plain. The entities thus separated at their tactical interfaces do constitute a complete semi-independent double polyhierarchic system. The sensorium, in each case, has more influence on the motorium than any system external to that analysis.

The caveat is this. In dealing with any dissected isolate, any morphostat, we must never, never forget that the whole system is a characterised by 'wheels-within-wheels', that there are morphostats within morphostats within morphostats, like the Russian dolls. Each is like a cluster of thornbushes with intertwined branch systems and intertwined root systems. And it is at the root tips and the twig ends that they link up into a larger system, which links up into one still larger, which links . . .

We can say with Jonathan Swift:
>   So, naturalists observe a flea
>   Hath smaller fleas that on him prey;
>   And these have smaller fleas to bite 'em
>   And so proceed *ad infinitum*.

Was not Leibniz thinking on these lines?

FRACTAL POLYHIERARCHIES

The final picture of the polyhierarchic information-flow architecture that emerges is much more complex when the various levels of development are taken into account. The cellular information system, the nervous information system, and the social information system are a sort of fractal design (see Fig. 37) in which the nodes of the senior system are the complete junior systems. The cell has a polyhierarchic information network in which the surface is the sensorium and the ribosomes are the motorium. The nervous system is another with a sensorium and motorium and linkages where all the elements are nerves which are cells, which are complete autonomous systems. The social information system is made up of roles occupied by people each of which again is an autonomous and complete polyhierarchic information system.

HOW CAN WE USE THE HYPOTHESIS?

In view of my pessimism about the predictability of biological systems, it might be asked what useful (predictive) results can arise from the model I present? The answer is threefold. Firstly, I suggest that it might be possible, in the light of the model or some more sophisticated modification of it, to find predictive regularities or constraints of a statistical nature which will at least

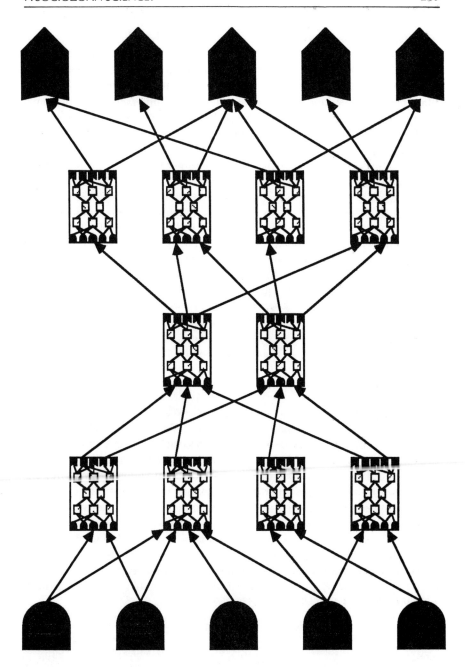

Figure 37   Fractal polyhierarchies

reduce the uncertainty of outcome which characterises all biological systems and sciences. Secondly, if I am right in my hypothesis about the inherent unpredictability of the behaviour of morphostats, it is as well if that is recognised, it was in the science of fundamental particles after Bohr. The extension of that principle to the world of forms will save a lot of human effort now spent on the hopeless quest for strict causal laws in the biological sciences. Thirdly, and this is the most hopeful thought, I suggest that it will be possible to make more predictive computer models of highly complex biological systems once their fundamental architecture and general modality is understood. These should do better at finding ways to reduce uncertainty, make better guesses, as the human brain does in human affairs. The heart of this thought is that the work done on the taxonomon so far suggests that computers may be able to cover the role of generating hypotheses, leading to the recognition of otherwise unseen patterns in complex data. With their immense speed and patient number-crunching power computers can already do much better than people at *testing* hypotheses, they may be able to do more still when they can make and modify hypotheses with equal speed and facility. Once a science gets the paradigm right it usually makes progress. My main case is that in the biological field we need to test a new family of different paradigms. Even if the elementary one I present is found to be deficient, the need remains. I hope that when success is found, as always, at the top of a heap of failures, this work may qualify at least as one of them.

THE HIDDEN HAND

I have told how the Scotsman Adam Smith (1723–90) saw the commercial market as a sort of 'engine' which, independently of any individual will but driven by the separate self-regarding actions of unnumbered individuals, directs social interaction so as to optimise the flow of goods, services, money, credit, capital and all the other elements of advanced social life. Unable to explain the origin of this mysterious phenomenon, he spoke of a 'hidden hand' which regulated human affairs to the best advantage of us all.

His ideas gained wide acceptance as industrialisation developed in Europe and America, then went out of fashion as the loose set of ideas which are subsumed under the labels 'socialism' and 'communism' captured the imaginations of generations of intellectuals and became powerful world-wide political movements.

At the turn of the century, science, firmly based on a determinist philosophy, was achieving unprecedented advances in many fields. The associated cornucopia of industrialism was unevenly pouring out vast new wealth to many, in parts of the world. Although it was the release of the talents of the people in the free market, the trial-and-error system noted by Smith, that made that rapid industrialisation possible, the changes were vast and fast. An unprepared social structure was traumatised and some new and also some traditional sections of communities were so disturbed that several reactions occurred. Anarchism and early Marxism were reactions against the spontaneous industrial organisation that had grown up.

These ideas and those of socialism generally were based fundamentally on a view which emphasised altruism as a human motivator. Wherever seriously tried, they all reacted towards the monohierarchic centralist control system which had been traditional before the new commercialists and industrialists had broken free of aristocratic monohierarchic control to do their enriching thing. (Another form this reaction took was called 'fascism'.)

'If scientific methods could do so much in an apparently unregulated system,' argued the socialists, 'how much better it would be if these brilliantly successful scientific methods could be used to direct the social network. Let scientific control and planning replace the disturbing severities of the market and solve the relatively simple problems of planning production and arranging the distribution of the new wealth as it flowed from the cornucopia.'

That the case was plausible, even convincing, I have to concede because for most of my life I would have accepted the label 'socialist' for myself.

I confess that the conclusions and views I put in this book were enormously unpalatable to me when I first had to face them in the late 1950s as my speculations developed. I had to endure a very painful and disturbing conversion which even threatened my normally robust health at one time.

This same painful lesson had to be learned ubiquitously. It turned out that all attempts to regulate, control or direct Adam Smith's 'engine' or 'hidden hand' fell into disarray as the market responded with unconscious, unplanned and spontaneous resistance and obstruction to whatever opposed its trends. In many places nothing less than the complete replacement of the self-regulating system by a tyrannical central hierarchic one could persuade this living, resisting, self-willed thing called the market to be regulated.

And then, after the traumas of revolutions and wars arising from fascist and communist ideologies, it slowly became apparent that the places where the market was still free (or freer) made more progress, became richer and more attractive to immigrants than those where socialist systems had taken over (or the fascist ones either). I write from that non-centralist world and might be thought to be prejudiced. But I see irrefutable evidence for the view that the open market system is the one which maximises human satisfaction. My evidence comes from the answer to two simple questions. ''Which way do the walls face?'', ''For which system do the feet vote?''

If a cultural system has to restrict the movement of its people, goods and wealth then it has shown itself to be a less desirable place to be than those which do not need to do so. If a country has to set up barriers to immigration it clearly has a better system and life-style than those that create barriers to emigration. It was this kind of evidence that made me look back more severely at my long held political convictions and accept the verdict of my enquiry about how intelligent systems like cells, animals, and societies are likely to function in the light of the model I thought I saw.

The ideas of Adam Smith gradually became popular again as thinkers like Friederich Hayek, Milton Friedman and their followers developed and re-presented them for a new appraisal.

It will be very obvious by now that the paradigm I present in the sociological and economic fields is cognate and congruent with the Smithian paradigm. I hope it may be seen as a development of it, one which shows how thinking about information systems fits in with and helps to flesh out these ideas. These ideas also represent an extension of the Smithian paradigm so that its realm will be seen to cover all living and thus choice-making systems.

The answer to the mystery of the hidden hand which puzzled Smith seems to me to be that the hidden hand is the same and the mystery is the same as in any other intelligent system. The hidden hand mystery is the same as that of the biological miracles I wrote of in the first chapter and tried to abolish in later ones.

THE CURRENT WORLD CULTURE

I have written of the concept of a world culture in several of my books and since it arises from the context presented here I shall outline the idea again.

I see the succession of world-scale civilisations as an interrupted unity. The dynasties of the Sumerians, Assyrians, Chaldeans, Egyptians, Indians, Chinese, Aegeans, Judeans, Greeks, Persians, Macedonians, Romans, Mongolians, Franks, Arabians, Scandinavians, Turks, South-Americans, Euro-peans and others are, at least in part, the stages in the intermittent growth of a world-scale interacting information pool. Craft and agricultural techniques, political systems, human life-styles, knowledge, social customs, arts, languages, literatures were, in these repeated flowerings, being evolved, sorted, selected, developed, elaborated, imperfectly at first but with increasing skill and accuracy they were recorded and passed on via the medium of that world-changing discovery, written language. This sort of databank succeeded the previous type, the stories, legends, myths and religions, as perpetuated by a class of tale-telling remembrancers, priests, sages, witch-doctors and other social memory specialists. Obviously the written records made possible something unachievable before, a *world* databank.

It is my thought that after the agricultural revolution there was a crash development of many differing human agricultural life-styles (which were, in effect, competing sociozoa). This was a quantum-style leap for the human sociozoa. They were now subject to the normal biological phenomenon of successful variants, speciation. Tribal and then larger group life-styles began changing, forking out to fit the many different climatic and other environments. Adapting arts, techniques and social systems so far achieved by the particular group, there was trial-and-error selection for the most viable. And within each adapting group, individuals and smaller groups again specialised out to form the crafts, trades and professions that became necessary for these more complex sociozoa.

Then, as the mutually repelling tribal structure became permeable by the traders and artisans, there developed first the need for and then the means for faster travel. Centres of excellence became possible. In Alexandria and then in many other places there appeared the institution which was to change the world decisively, that knowledge, art and culture market which led to the present-day university. Savants, scholars, thinkers, philosophers from all traditions and cultures met and began, in the relatively dogma-free atmosphere that the variety created, to forge what turned out to be an eclectic consensus, a selection from all cultures of the best elements, or at least those good elements that would fit together into a comprehensive whole of a kind. With the development of literature it became possible for these many databanks to fuse and form one. A world culture was in the making.

With many ups and downs, extinctions and new beginnings, these tenuous merging cultures began to penetrate and finally permeated the rigid dogma-locked communities, like the religious ones which represented the social heredity mechanisms of the many various competing sociozoa.

What we see today is a mixed world in which the vast array of greatly differing cultures, life-styles and religions exist and compete as before. But at a higher stratum there is a supervening, uniting world culture to which many of the intelligent and educated people in the various cultures can belong in parallel. There is a world-wide community, much of it travelling, writing and telephoning, around the world, coming from all groupings, ethnic, cultural, religious, ideological, national and commercial, which, without disloyalty to their native culture, works in, with and for this world culture.

The elements of the world culture are so many that they cannot all be listed here. Some examples are the international aspects of the arts, the best in literature, every field of science, scholarship, philosophy, education, technology, trade, commerce, banking, company law, trade practices, maritime and air transport techniques, communication and rescue practices, international law, mores and customs, navigational meteorological information, many religions and festivals, and above all the communications network in all its forms. All these are in the enormous shared pool, the world databank that is open to the citizen of any open country who has the ability and the desire to join it. There are closed countries. Predictably, there is reaction to this world culture by some of the many established cultures which it inevitably traumatises. One resistance bloc of this type is seen in the parts of the Islamic world.

What is the warrant for the world culture?

I can see that there will be readers who will see what I describe as the world culture as simply what has been rejectingly labelled 'the dominant culture' or even, despite the great contributions to it from Soviet and third-world cultures, the 'imperialist colonialist' culture. Others may see it as just another culture among many. Others with more justice may say that I am describing what is simply the Hebraic-Hellenic-Roman culture now called 'Western culture', which contributed so heavily to it.

How can I claim that it is supervening and world eclectic? The answer gives itself. While all the contributing and local cultures are rigid, dogmatic and intolerant of modification, the world culture is the opposite, it is open, changing, evolving and undogmatic. It is an intelligent selection unconsciously and gradually established over time by the whole of the international community of savants, of the ablest and most discerning elements from all, but all, the existing cultures. There are no exceptions; all earth cultures have contributed. The features and elements were chosen because they consistently stand up to the many tests of practice. There were no choices enforced by dogmatists or zealots.

Further, while the contributing cultures are mutually antagonistic and contradictory the world culture is coherent. All its elements and features are quite compatible. Like modern science, it can be distinguished from the host of pseudo-sciences that compete for our credulity by the fact that it does form a relatively coherent, consistent and mutually compatible whole. The competitive pseudo-sciences are a jumbled mass of incompatible, mutually insulated, mutually contradictory dogmas.

Barring catastrophe, the advantages of the polyhierarchic way of managing production, distribution and exchange are so great that it seems certain that the world culture will continue to spread its influence around the world. That a world in which it is influential is bound to be more stable than one in which it is not is clear. What is stable survives. And in the long chain of random accidents of history it is certain that if the world falls more widely into that mode it will have more chance of staying there than in any other mode. In such cases it is in the stable mould that things are eventually found.

A new factor of which the full importance may not yet be seen is the effect of the world-wide linkage of computer information systems. This is becoming more than a world databank, it is beginning to become a world brain. The effects of its development and spread are very hard to predict.

If this increasingly powerful and influential world enmeshing system, which is not under the control of any one person or group, is based on an inappropriate model the result for the world culture and society may suffer. If the system cannot evolve into a biomorphic mode it may delay the development of the stable and viable world society and biosphere we all desire.

I would predict that, even if the long chain of ephemeral civilisations is not yet complete and there are more dark ages to come, the end product will be an earth-scale supervening world culture, influencing but not controlling a rich and wide variety of local, national and ethnic subcultures each of which will jealously and advisedly guard and maintain its own differential beauty while they enjoy the ordered, peaceful and advantageous combination of competition and symbiosis which is best calculated to preserve both the whole and the rich variety of contributing parts.

But before this is achieved the world culture, the brain, the noosphere, the essence of earth's biosphere, will be questing outwards from the earth towards the planets, the stars . . . And to do this it must first have developed what must be described as an earth will or consciousness or ego. That may take some time.

9

Biological intelligence and its artificial intelligence

Is it possible for an intelligent entity to create an artefact which is itself intelligent in the sense derived from the present paradigm? It would be wise to start with that question though the answer 'Yes' already stares us in the face.

How were the present entities to which intelligence is ascribed created? By evolution, the selection of random, blind options. It took a long time but it was achieved, *without the help of prior intelligence*. Are we to believe, then, that *with* the help of an advanced intelligence it is impossible?

I have argued that contrary to what appears to be common sense, living things, the Creatura, can transcend their creators, pick themselves up by their own bootstraps.

Your genome gave a set of instructions to the cytoplasm of your cells which prescribed and created your intelligent brain. Is not the hypothesis that no such string of instructions in the universe could do similarly a little risky?

I shall venture to assume that the phenomenon 'intelligence' can appear on many types of substrate system and that the parent substrates are not confined to the world of organic chemistry. Considering the possibility of brains based on silicon-electronic or fibre-optical substrates, I think it would be dangerous to rule it out and I cannot summon up the courage to do so. That is for bolder spirits.

The statement above is based on the extended view of what intelligence is which arises from these pages. But even if a narrower view is taken I cannot see any evidence for, let alone proof of, the negative hypothesis that non-biological intelligent systems are impossible.

Of course, in the absence of an agreed meaning or definition for the word it will always be possible for people to say that what is put up as an example of artificial intelligence is not so. I am of course going to have to put up with that sort of objection.

Our species, *homo sapiens,* arrogates to itself, with some justification, the pre-eminent position on the scale of known intelligences. We must now come to the twin questions, 'Will there be other entities which excel us in this field, and, if so will they be our evolutionary successors or will they be our own artefacts?'

Biology shows no previous example of permanent pre-eminence in any type of excellence so we must not expect too much. Worse, as you will see from what follows, we may already be in the presence of something which is beyond us in intelligent performance. Read on.

A RIVAL INTELLIGENCE ON EARTH?

In the early days of science fiction before the full implications of the space-time prison in which earthly intelligence is confined were realised (a 13-year signal response cycle for the *nearest* neighbour system), there were stories of invasion by alien intelligences from outer space. In many stories they came in spaceships and would have subjugated or destroyed us all if it had not been for a small and clever group of human heroes who thwarted them.

I hope you will not be alarmed when I point out that our species on earth have already been invaded and largely taken over by an intelligence other than that mediated by the intelligence within human brains. Much to our mutual benefit, there is a super-brain of a simple, even an elementary type, operating to co-ordinate and modify our behaviour as individuals.

It is that first discovered by Adam Smith and he called it an 'engine'. It is the world-scale communications network, the money, ideas, knowledge, know-how, market which is the essence of the world culture I dealt with in the last chapter. It is the needs/resources, optimising computer by which we all get daily, hourly, votes with our feet, our money and our behaviour. There are countless millions of signals moving around this vast unexplorable network. It is another intelligence which is largely independent of the crude switch throwing and lever pulling of political *government.* A government is like the little boy who thinks he is the pilot of his chairoplane at a fairground. Try as they may, our political masters cannot master this intelligent creature as it evades, dodges and wriggles around the fiats, laws, 'fine tuning' and the rest. Still less can we, the electorate, exert control with our five-yearly, cross-on-paper votes for Jack This or Jill That. We can change the people at the 'controls' of what is not under control. Politicians of all persuasions do have some effect on this other intelligence; effect, not control. They can, with skill, devotion and persistence, corrupt or damage its function of optimising human satisfaction. For a time.

I am not against the 'we can sack you' democracy we have in the First

World', there is no better way to limit and evict the ever hopeful clever ones who *know* what no-one does, the non-existent 'predictive laws', the economic system, and how to 'control' it.

But these remarks are outside the usual context of artificial intelligence, which is always seen in a master/servant, controller/controlled context. The picture presented here is different. In an intelligent system all the elements are in the dual role of master and servant in a much more intimate and immediate sense than that of a voting democracy. Every element has to survive, to be kept stable, and so has its needs, news of which it sends into the system. Every active element should also have its supply role, its contribution functions. To fulfil these it must get instructions from the system. Not all the functions are vital and essential, but because of the essential nature of redundancy and competition the system would not survive for long without them.

The thing that we human beings *should* be afraid of is *not* to be functioning within such an intelligent system. This is the unhappy fate of many people in parts of the world where an ancient, intelligent and stable, if frugal, life in ecological balance with the local biosphere has been broken up and replaced by attempts to govern by systems which have not grown, evolved or spread from successful examples elsewhere but are based on simple-minded cognitive models imposed and directed by an elite of 'wise controllers' who know what to do and induce or force people to conform. Alas! The people stay poor, and the hidden, uncomprehended intelligence behind the traditional cultural and behavioural patterns they have evolved is unable to save them from ecological disturbance, famine and disease. They fall into a messy and traumatic muddled cultural pattern that is neither the old nor the new but worse than either.

The first thing a politician discovers when he or she attains power is how little power it is. The clumsy central fingers on a great complex of half-understood buttons and levers gets more and more hesitant as meter needles start waggling past red lines and alarms start shrilling at all points in the largely mysterious system.

It all seems so wonderfully easy when you are sternly shouting monitory backseat-driving instructions from the opposition benches. But when you sit at the controls yourself . . . ! You are like poor Alice, with her struggling flamingo stick trying to hit her wilful, animate croquet balls through self-willed, mobile, temperamental hoops.

In the non-traditional world, mankind is part of the network of a large primitive form, a tentative beginning for a creature of a new type. It may not last, but there seems no chance now, without catastrophe, of returning to the safer but poorer and harsher world before it happened. The great merger of many different contending human sociozoa occurred when neolithic agricultural man replaced mesolithic man.

We cannot go back, so we might as well go on. We shall do so the better for trying to make better models of it. The chick cannot crawl back into the safety of the egg. It has to go out and face a new world. In our case perhaps an extra-terrestrial one.

IS MAN MAKING HIS OWN SUPPLANTER?

In creating artificial intelligence is man making his own supplanter?

Who can tell? Supplanter-making is the stuff of life. We produce our personal supplanters called children, and our societal supplanters as we evolve new life-styles and cultures. The mesolithic hunter-gatherer sociozoa made the neolithic agricultural ones which in turn made the past civilisations, and they the modern world culture. I expect that earth culture sociozoa will create their successor, solar planetary cultures, and so on out. It is the pattern, it is morphostic, biophilic, and good for things to be so. I am against evolutionary chauvinism. But who am I to say? The morality that arises from the present paradigm says it would be bad if evolution, supplanter-making, came to a halt. In other moralities, take your choice. It is an aesthetic matter. Be a specialist or culture chauvinist if it makes you happy; it will not make any difference in the long term. Life will choose not us.

My friend Clive Sinclair talks of the time when non-organic intelligences will be so much more intelligent than human beings can be that they may keep humans as pets. Even so, I see a long period in which human beings will remain an essential part of something that will grow from the present combination of biological and social intelligence. Already the outcome is much affected by a growing input of artefact intelligence. That aspect cannot but grow more influential as time goes on, but a lot of time will pass before man's descendants disappear if this road is followed. If other roads were followed I would give man a shorter reign as he would be overtaken by a rival somewhere, or speciate and divide in the normal biological way.

Species, as well as animals, are mortal. Species are much more durable but none will last for ever. If evolution is not to come to a halt *something* will replace mankind. It might be something evolved from us or from some other animal. It might equally be, or be made by, some human artefacts. That fourth-order, new sort of living thing, the world-culture seems set for a fairly long life if it survives the traumas of its first few millennia. While wishing for mankind to live for ever is a wasted wish, we do not have to start planning for the funeral just yet. Let us try to see that what replaces us, whenever that is, is better, more durable, more intelligent, more powerful, more exploratory, more peaceful, more orderly and more space-conquering than we are. That seems a moral and an achievable aim. The alternative seems to be an immoral attitude, 'Après moi, le deluge!'.

10

Intelligence: the future

We now move on beyond the realm of speculation to that of none too bridled imagination. Extrapolation is always dangerous and never more so than in these cloudy heights. Seeing the trendline I have begun to map, I should be cautious but should not shy away from at least a glance along the road indicated. The implications are startling at first sight, they run counter to cherished ideas, but look at least I must. The reader may or may not accept, as he or she has a mind. At least we shall know the trend we oppose if we do not like the track we see before us. We may oppose the better for comprehending the more.

SOME IMPLICATIONS OF A HETERONOMOUS UNIVERSE

Here is a world model, one of two semi-independent realms. Realm one is the physical world of matter and energy, the Pleroma. Realm two is the heteronomous world of the Creatura or the biota, a realm of surviving, evolving, negentropic forms living on substrates that obey the laws (statistical) of the physical realm, but the forms that live on them do not because they have access to events at a level where there are no strict laws. The creatures in this realm use and amplify quantum indeterminism to draw on options to defeat the statistical weight of physical laws. They do 'illegal' (that is, highly improbable) things. In the realm of the Pleroma, the physical world, there is a trend towards higher probability and increasing disorder. In the counterpoised other realm, that of the Creatura, we see a continuum of morphostasis, an opposite trend towards improbable combinations, negentropy, greater order, complexity, intelligence and the symbiosis of larger and larger combinations of life forms in more and more complex and symbiotic systems. We may have rejected

221

Haeckle's notion of a *Scala Naturae* as anthropocentric because it sets man up as the King of the Castle of Life. But when we see that the trend-line goes on beyond man and life on this earth we may find the trend both more plausible and less attractive.

Can we, after all, get an 'ought' from an 'is'?

The Scottish philosopher David Hume (1711–76) captured a consensus for the idea that we cannot derive a value system from any observation of the world. We cannot get an 'ought' from an 'is'. Societies, he thought, decide priorities, what is good and what is bad, by a social consensus which arises spontaneously. Hume's idea was new and revolutionary; he implied that a society's ethics are its choice, they are not *given* from nature or even from the versions of God that various religions preach.

There is a later development of this idea that comes originally from the thinking of that other influential Scottish philosopher, Adam Smith. Friederich Hayek, a follower of Smith, and also the biologist Professor Cyril Dean Darlington have suggested that systems of ethics and morality actually *evolve* in a similar way to that in which biological species evolve.

This fits in perfectly with the ideas developed here. We can see the *mores*, rules, laws of a tribe or any other society as well as their techniques, skills and general living know-how as non-genetic heredity, a transmissible social information pool. It acts as another sort of heredity side by side with genetic heredity for the survival of the sociozoon, the tribe or other group.

The small tribal group was for some millions of years up to the last Ice Age the only type of social unit of the hominids. It follows that our genetic make-up, our hard-wiring, must have evolved for that kind of hunter-gatherer social life. The last half dozen millennia are far too short a period for there to have been very much genetic adaption of our species to the much larger social units we now live in. This may account for many of the problems and instabilities of modern urban life. It may account for the *need* for a written language and morality, for laws. These are a social heredity system to correct the now unsuitable genetic emotional and instinctive tendencies.

It was only when agriculture mysteriously developed a few thousand years after the last Ice Age and the larger sociozoa, like populated cities and empires, were able to form that the simple tribal traditions and mores failed as a tool of social heredity. A better system of trans-generational information flow was needed. More complex skills and techniques had to be passed on. More importantly, different socially necessary values, goals and objectives had to be tried and passed on between generations. This new set of behaviour-modifying rules, laws, traditions, mores, was a new kind of heredity reinvented at a higher level. Only when this became stable, conservative and reliable was it possible for the much enlarged social units with quite different life-styles to cohere and survive.

We may speculate that a thousand variants of moral systems appeared, a wide variety upon which selection must have operated. These moral and traditional variants (perhaps clothed in the trappings and myths of religions) will have been subject to selection both for their value to the society and also for their transmissibility and durability. The more stable and the more viable of them would survive and spread. Those with the right behavioural content and also the best emotional appeal to the conative system of the hunter-gatherer substrate would survive because they would be more acceptable, transmissible. This thought might lead to a theory of religion, that myths are set to amalgamate the new within the old form, to use the hunter-gatherer, social norms to embrace the different ethical needs of larger units. Some of these new forms, these ethical systems, must surely have been such as to make the substrate groups upon which they operated more successful, more cohesive and more stable than other groups. Surely the groups with the successful ethical systems succeeded, grew, divided and spread at the expense of those with inferior (meaning less morphostatic) ethical systems. The selection would be for viability and also for the hereditary grip upon the social unit. If you have a good system you have to be conservative or you will soon lose it.

Social heredity is Lamarckian

This sort of social heredity has an advantageous feature which does not apply to genetic inheritance. The biologist Chevalier Jean Baptiste Lamarck (1744–1829) held that acquired characteristics could be transmitted between genera-tions genetically. There was much dispute about this but the view was finally disproved and discredited. There is no way that the somatic experiences of an animal could change the genes beneficially. Mutations are random. But social heredity can be and almost certainly is Lamarckian.

With social heredity, acquired characteristics *can* be passed on. Man is an imitator, the successful ethical system could be and almost certainly was copied by other tribes and thus acquired a life of its own as a breeding, developing form, a morphostat which survived on more and more widespread social substrates.

The idea that morality evolved by the evolutionary modification of tribal customs is reinforced by the origin of both the words we use in this context. The word 'ethics' comes from the Greek *ethos,* the word 'morals' comes from the Latin *mores.* Both had the same meaning, 'custom' or 'tradition'. Originally the words obviously applied to the small social unit, the tribe or village.

We could say that the evolutionary view of morality is a contradiction of the Humean view because the 'is' of the successful tribe spread and developed the 'ought' of its *mores*. But Hume would say that consensus must have arisen for the moral code before it had proved successful and thus it was imposed by the society without referring to 'the way things are'.

I now have the task, a heavy one, of looking back at the problem of ethics in the light of the crude world model I am elaborating. We may agree that our present ethical systems are those that survived because they spread of themselves and because the societies that embraced them were stable and successful. They survived to pass them on to us. The tribes with inadequate moralities had no survivors left to pass them on. The morphostat, the ethical system, died. But what of the substrate, the people? They may have died out with the unsuccessful pattern, but that does not necessarily follow. People live in societies but they are free to leave them. Successful societies, firms, nations, and organisations grow, they acquire more people. Where do they come from? A lot come from unsuccessful firms, nations, organisations. It seems like a very good idea. It is another reduced-punishment-for-failure idea.

Accepting that Hume was basically right, can we still get an 'ought' from the 'is' of the two realms paradigm?

I cautiously suggest that we *can* begin to see, if a little dimly, by the faint new light of the model presented, the outline of an *existential* base for ethics.

I invite you to make the arbitrary but understandable (*aesthetic*, if you like) decision that we identify with the creatures rather than with the things, that we come within, are citizens of, the realm of the forms, that we have a patriotic/ chauvinistic prejudice in favour of the realm to which we belong, the biota, that we would be reluctant to see the end of life. If you accept my invitation, and given only that we can get some 'oughts' from the trend and shape of the 'is' of the model, if we accept it, we can without shame embrace those oughts as existential ones.

If we are, on the other hand, traitors to the biota, life-hating Pleromists who see life as a disease of matter and generally a thoroughly bad thing, we would get a clear and definite Pleromist morality from that view. We should know how to behave and start making nice big nuclear bombs.

But if we are ready to discrimate, if we are unashamed realmists, ready to favour the Creatura, just because it is our own kind, then all we have to do is to set the Pleromist morality on its head and we have a set of 'oughts' which are deriveable from the 'is' that I am exploring.

To begin with, we would favour the progress along the track of the morphostasis continuum (though we might argue a lot about where the track led and how to go along it). However, there are important aspects of the continuum that are confusing, that do not fit well with the rest. There is a singularity in one of the trends, which was first noticed by Teilhard de Chardin.

Like all biologists since Darwin he noted the strong diverging trend of evolution. There is an evolutionary tree-like form. The trend is towards ever greater diversity. All species complexify and divide again and again towards an explosively increasing variety of ever more specialist forms to fit ever more and tinier ecological niches.

But he also noted the strange, emergent, contradictory and recent convergence trend, the trend towards co-operation and symbiosis. Especially he noted the convergence and combination of human cultures in the last few millennia after millions of years of divergence and mutually competitive repulsion. I am astonished, as the evidence emerges from ethnological and anthropological studies, how little modern thinkers are perplexed by that recent phenomenon our world civilisation and culture. How, just how, did a creature bred for millions of years to live in small, mutually repelling, territorial, hunter-gatherer groups suddenly become the creature that built the world-wide civilisation of modern man?

There *are* a few thinkers who followed that track. With his concept 'world brain', Herbert George Wells suggested an echoing thought. Bernard Shaw's 'life force', and Karl Popper's 'World III', have the same philosophical root.

And, contradicting Hume, Hayek and Darlington, there are signs that among educated and informed humanity there is beginning to emerge an expanded or extended view of morality and ethics which does not fit the evolutionary paradigm for cultures. There is a widespread concept, a view of morality which is seen as valid for mankind as a whole, a most extraordinary idea in any biological perspective.

There is a widely accepted, passionately believed view of mankind as a single whole, which is contrary to all human traditions and biological precedents. The norm for all highly successful species hitherto is this. Soon after they attain pre-eminence they begin to speciate, divide into different subspecies and then species under population pressure and competition, each singling out some sub-niche for themselves. Mankind is the sole exception. The slight beginnings of speciation visible in the different ethnic groups seem to be coming to a halt as modern travel remixes mankind. I personally rejoice in this as I notice it and it has led me to these views.

The world culture is increasingly a whole-earth community, a noosphere, as Chardin would say. The emergence, growth and success of this earth-scale phenomenon was not predicted and is not congruent with anything in the human evolution before everything began to change about six or seven short millennia ago. It is a surprise from every point of view.

But it does fit one model, it fits the model of the morphostasis continuum I have advanced. It fits it in this way. We may see the world culture as a symbiotic/competitive network of many cultures rather than of many people, a creature in its own right, one which by its existence may preserve a biosphere that might otherwise have been destroyed.

COMPETITION AND CO-OPERATION

There is a problem which has long bedevilled human thought concerning the social value of co-operation and of competition. The two terms are crude and unspecific (they have a very low sufficiency) and perhaps for that reason there is much confusion at the social level as to whether social unity requires the sharp reduction or even the abolition of competition and a society based entirely on the principle of social co-operation. Others emphasise the optimising value of competition and see it as the greatest force for advantageous change and improvement.

The morphostatic point of view seems to help because it makes clearer what the problem is.

Competition is the offering of options. All optimisation, learning, whether genoplastic, ontoplastic or social, requires two things. There must be options, choice among them, and the raising of the probability or frequency of the successful options being chosen in the future.

Co-operation is a deeply essential part of the morphostasis continuum. The co-operative , symbiotic assembly of larger and larger systems is the main trend, as I tried to show in Figure 1.

Competition and co-operation are complementary, two essential aspects of all morphostasis. They are not opposites and they are not incompatible. Every morphostat combines the two features in some proportion and in the proportion lies the success or failure of the morphostat concerned.

Meta-learning, the higher, more strategic-level learning, is the business of finding the best of competing ways to optimise the combination of co-operation and competition. That seems to be the most important human problem today, both socially and in the field of commerce and between nations and life-styles.

The taxonomon model of the learning process has a simple built-in system by which the nodes compete to capture noisy patterns. Non-centralist societies have the independent trader, farmer, industrial firm, which works within an environment of social order and restraint, a compulsory co-operative framework of law, order and accepted commercial and legal practice. When it works well the result is the best of both worlds, a system of competition within co-operation that seems to produce increasingly good results for most people.

Does the future come too fast?

We should not forget, however, that the very successes of the recent world cultural co-operation which has so suddenly raised and changed the world population may have its long-term dangers. The usual biological sequence where there are great successes, population explosions, is great failures, population crashes. Industrialism in field and factory has called into being an enormous number of people and societies whose ecological fit with each other and the biosphere is new and untested. It may, I fear, prove to be a temporary success only.

However, there is one great hope — comprehension. Mankind has already shown that collectively it is able to solve such large problems in utterly new ways, in which the painful trial-and-error, 'die if you fail' method is replaced by soft learning, learning via models. Simulations, analogous worlds can be created by scientists, in which lessons can be learned the soft way, the cognitive way, as they are in an ontoplastic brain or to some extent in governed competitive society.

We are a long way from the central World Government which we dreamed of early in the century after two world wars, but the development of the poly-hierarchic world brain, or world computer, our developing world culture, is at least promising.

Life, death, reward, punishment, pleasure, pain, gain, loss

I wrote above of soft learning and elsewhere of the trend towards reducing the severity of punishments.

Certainly there can be no real learning, optimisation, without options and competition and therefore without winners and losers, rewards and punishments. The visible trend, however, is that as the movement along the morphostasis continuum proceeds the rewards and punishments get less severe.

In earlier forms of life there is only one penalty, capital punishment. The more advanced animals have an improvement: pain and pleasure with an appetitive system to supply the signals that change behaviour patterns in the learning phase. The animal is modified, not the whole species.

A later stage still is the cognitive brain, which is a simulation system where behaviour patterns can be tried out in an internal model of the world in world simulation experiments called thinking and planning. The pleasure/pain input here is more subtle: pleasure at a good idea or plan, irritation at a bad one or a mistake. But the pleasure/pain spectrum is there, it must be to drive the learning machine.

At the social level the reward/punishment antithesis at the sociozoan level returns to severity. Unsuccessful social groupings, firms, associations, cultures and life-styles, tend to die out, often not by the death of the components, people, but their departure, by their feet voting to join preferred sociozoa — other firms, cultures, countries.

At the individual level reward and punishment are even further softened to gain and loss, approval and disapproval, honour and disgrace, rewards and fines, liberty and imprisonment. (Prison is bad but preferable to torture or death.)

What worries me is that in the face of the entire history of life and humanity there are some good and kindly people nowadays who feel that even the softest form of marking failure, to help the learning process, is bad and to be avoided. I see no escape from one fundamental truth. Where there is no success and failure, or where it may not be recognised, where there are no winners and losers, there can be neither learning nor progress, nor, in the long run, survival. Each and every creature and combination of creatures on earth today is a winner, selected in a multi-trillion stage low-chance raffle. This is an unpalatable fact to most of us, brought up as we are in the comfortable lap of a protective State. Like it we may not. Ignore it we dare not. As social animals we may and must ameliorate the lot of the losers, ideas-people, planners, scientists, associations — people, but losers — and everybody else must face facts and signify failure. There can be no life without options and choice. Where you have options and choice you have losers. Losers are essential to any morphostatic system but we cannot build the future from them and we must not fail to learn the lessons they are there to teach. Losers must be allowed to do their important job and make their contribution.

There are uncomfortable and unpopular conclusions that follow from the present hypothesis. I am not going to pretend that they attract me. I, too, am a product of my time and culture and have all the standard moral preferences of my age. I reassert my warning against untested moralities based on no more than man's simple reasoning powers.

However, we ought at least to follow the track in our minds. For pilot trial and possible selection I offer these ideas.

Most thinkers in the mainstream of Western thought are appalled by the horrors of the increasingly damaging nature of the old human practice of warfare. Believing that conflicts within nations are often less frequent and less damaging than those between them, they seek the unification of humanity. They want to bring us all together into one political unity, a centrally controlled World State. Most of the world's intelligentzia, including myself, have gone along with this.

Noting the fierce, intractable and bloody enmities between those of ethno-cultural groups, they seek to play down and ignore these differences and move towards a multi-cultural, poly-ethnic goulasch society with standardised men and women living in a society where all the cultural styles cohabit the same space at the same time. Again we have all gone along with this idea.

Now I have argued that, at least in origin, moralities *evolved* to serve a function in the survival of small, competing societies. They were based on religions until the so-called 'Age of Enlightenment', when there arose some d.i.y. versions that are still under test.

These latter-day 'rational' moralities borrowed a lot from the traditional ones but they contained some very important new elements, among which the idea of individual freedom, which seems to have released a tide of enterprise and beneficial change.

Now we see being painfully born the beginnings of a human race scale morality, which seems to be aimed at the survival and successes of the species as a whole. This trend appears in the United Nations and the whole panoply of international organisations. That this should appear at all is very much against the history of our species and very strange indeed, but it fits the concept of the morphostasis continuum.

Further and even more mysterious, there is a third-order morality, a biophil morality, based on a reverence for life itself. The growing ecology lobby and the Green Parties bear witness to the emergence of this species — altruistic meta-morality. This too fits.

It is possible that this represents no more than a form of reaction to modern industrialism, the hunter-gatherer within us all protesting at our new life-style. But there does seem to be a real underlying rational concern which deserves serious attention.

While I am very sad that a few attention-seeking extremists are bringing these ideas into disrepute with selective, simplistic, sentimental campaigns and absurd public antics, I am impressed by the underlying thinking which fits well with these ideas. The fast-growing popularity of biophil ideas among those of the world culture is a sign, and an important one, that an experimental biosphere morality is possible and beginning to assert itself.

BIOPHIL ETHICS

What should a biophil ethical system be like? Biophil (life-loving or morphostatic) ethics is defined as that general ethical system that arises from a favourable view of the Creatura and acceptance and approval of the morphostasis continuum. I say 'general', bearing in mind that all existing ethical systems were evolved to serve separate human groups, nations, cultures. These systems have survived and spread because of the success and the symbiotic merging of the separate and previously contending cultures which adopted them.

There is much in common between these surviving but different ethical systems around the world but there are many differences also. Many of the differences have a ritualistic, religious aspect which seems to the intelligent, regardless of culture, to have little or no survival value to the group or culture. These mystical elements are much more various as between religions. This helps us to see what is essential and what is contingent. The more variable the feature, the less necessary it is likely to be. So the mythical elements in religion may be their selling gimmicks, the means of spread and propagation between generations. They may be part of the social heredity of morality.

It is also true that the international governmental community has patched together an eclectic amalgam of the different ethical systems. An attempt to express this is found in the United Nations charter and many other complex treaties and lawlike agreements.

Much more important, there is an eclectic but tacit general world morality. This is a selection from the morality systems of the successful cultures. It operates in the world communities which meet and interact in the world culture. This morality pertains to and informs the commercial, travel, industrial, scientific, artistic, and all other types of international and intercultural communication and interaction. This is a tacit, unwritten, but universal patchwork of understood practice in each field of international contacts which is self-regulating and unenforced. More than anything else it is what makes the present world civilisation possible. This moral code is observed because people, firms and institutions of all kinds have to acquire and keep a reputation if they are to operate in this milieu at all. It is an error to think that international laws and intergovernmental conventions are vitally important to this. These are good and right but they operate only at the margin. Using them is failure. They are used in the last resort, when the normal effective system has broken down. No-one but lawyers prosper from enforced commercial morality. For most of the time and most of the cases good international relations work on tacit morality and need no law.

The biophil can unhesitatingly approve of this sort of morality. Why? Because it evolved. It arose not from cognitive, logical consensus but by trial, error and selection. The institutions that made the right guesses about how to manage relations survived, wrong guessers did not.

That was the way the many separate religious moralities originally evolved, according to Darlington and Hayek. That is why, in spite of all their faults, the biophil may also trust such systems, even when his reason tells him not to.

Generally the biophil moralist is humble. He does not arrogate to himself the intelligence to be a moral innovator. He does not trust his intellect to tell him what is good and what is bad for the Creatura. He fears that it is not given to us to understand and predict the outcome of radical social changes in enormously complex modern social assemblies in an age of very rapid technological change. He suspects that what has worked well for a long time and brought a society to enlightenment and prosperity is often quite good and should not be impulsively changed. Innovation is not barred, but radical changes should be tested to destruction in pilot experiments before the risk of general adoption is taken.

Our biophil moralist would favour as many, various experimental cultures, life-styles, communities as possible. Only this will offer variety for selection by the social evolution process. But such innovative communities should be seen as what they are — pilot experiments.

The biophil sees the working of the commercial market as a symbiotic combination of peaceful, limited competition and co-operation, within an ordered system of social constraint. He might be against the tendency to standardise and equalise cultural life-styles within a nation. Let communities as well as companies run themselves, within some overall constraint, in any way they find good. Let there be variety for selection. Without it there can be no progress along the morphostasis continuum.

The tide of beneficial (at least superficially) change has, as I have said, brought about among intellectuals and many others an atmosphere in which it is thought that *all* change is good. We hear pundits talking about social change as though this were an obvious benefit in all cases. Their sense of morality is mainly concerned with speeding up this tardy process.

Biophil ethics would indicate caution about social change. The wished for effects may be splendidly obvious but how sure, in the present state of sociological prediction, can we be that we fully understand the long-term side-effects?

I was one of the generation that rushed headlong into, for instance, rejecting Victorian morality and opting for a permissive society. It seemed positive, an obvious improvement, setting us all free to 'do our own thing'. And it did, for a long time. It may be that the increase in crime, divorce, one-parent families and problem families, and a growing group of disturbed and under-achieving children are other and utterly unrelated problems. But it is easy to be sceptical about that. To the fair question, 'Are we all obviously better off and happier for these changes?', it is hard for one who has been through it to answer with an unequivocal 'Yes'.

New moral ideas must arise in thought, they cannot yet be tested there. Unlike Jefferson, I do not believe that morality is self-evident. It may be that we can in the future develop artificial intelligence models which will out think our limited intelligence and be able to know what the long-term effects and side-effects of changes in moral laws will be, but the almost universal failure to develop successful *economic* models shows that that time is a fair way off yet. (If really predictive economic models were possible the discoverer would be visible as the owner of most of the world's goods in a very short time.)

I begin to have suspicions and doubts about some of the moral laws and precepts that became so widely followed in so many cultures since, so recently, the British utilitarians and the French encyclopaedists began to design do-it-yourself moral codes. These thinkers may have been presumptuous to argue that moral codes based only on human cognitive intelligence should be adopted untested.

With that caveat made, I can follow the direction of the morality trend-line indicated by the paradigm we are looking at that of the two realms and the morphostasis continuum.

If we have made the decision that we are favourable to the development and optimising of the Creatura in this way of looking at the world, it follows that what is good and moral is that which favours the continuation of all the trends mentioned in Figure 1.

Life and information forms are good and desirable as they reduce in probability, and increase in durability, stability, divergent variety (this sounds like but is not a contradiction of stability), complexity, organisation, symbiotic convergence, comprehension of and power over the physical universe. We need measures for these properties or trends if they are to be judged rationally.

However, rational judgement is what we must be cautious about trusting. Competitive trials of life-styles, cultural, moral, economic and other systems, within some overall biophil constraints, seem to be the way forward. One day, maybe, there will arise world models that are good and congruent enough and entities, biological or artificial, that are intelligent enough to make confident changes without going through the painful routine of competitive trial and error. That day is not yet.

The principle of least error cost

Paradoxically, thinking about ethics and morality is bedevilled by Gods (so to put it). If morality is immanent, unchallengable and selectively revealed to an elite of wise men directly by God, it is an impertinence to think about it at all, even if one is one of the elect oneself. Who are you, you small, ephemeral mortal? Take your orders and obey!

But out of the model I present there comes a view about morality, what it is and what its function is.

As one of those who questions such a selectively revealed morality I am in a weak position. In the light of my position of biophysical dualism, I do not trust the so-called rational human judgement overmuch either. I agree with the rationalists in questioning revelation but I disagree that *they* know best and that morality is self-evident.

Pragmatists like myself must judge morality by its results, the kind of life it promotes in the morphostats which have it, not only the people but their institutions, societies and cultures. Do they make progress on the continuum of morphostasis?

There is one thing I mentioned earlier that should be emphasised at this stage. It is Pascal's Policy, the fail-safe principle of least error cost. If we do not have enough information, if we cannot know all the long-term effects of any given moral policy or precept, we can at least be guided by Pascal's Policy. When we stand perplexed between two courses, we can try to calculate which has the least error cost and usually it will be best to follow that road.

Generally the moral advice must be to make no changes where you cannot be sure they are beneficial, unless you can experiment first and check your judgement. If you can experiment, subject a pilot sample to the novelty and adopt it only if it is clearly beneficial, then do nothing unless faced by a very severe threat to stability. The greater the severity of the threat, the more radical is the sort of untested change that may be wise.

The feature of human group behaviour called panic seems to be counter-biological but it is not. When the threat of death to a group is dire enough, leader-proneness fails and random individual behaviour asserts itself. It pays off because some deviant, radically new behaviour may be the one way to preserve that form through that crisis, by preserving just one lucky member. 'Every man for himself' is a pay-off policy *in extremis*.

But except in emergencies, the known and tried is the best course, according to this model. Experiment should never cease but really new ways should pass a test to destruction phase before they are widely adopted. I predict that the time has come for return to the traditional suspicion of innovation after the recent incessant tide of it that has been sweeping much of mankind. I predict an age when stability will be more valued than further unceasing 'progress', 'development', 'social change', 'growth' and all the other new goals that have been accepted so lightly and universally with so little thought and almost no prior trial.

Power

Some social scientists are much concerned with power. What is power in this context? It does not mean simply the amount of energy available as measured in watts (or terawatts). The meaning we seek lies in the idea of a trigger or relay which we explored earlier. The power of a morphostat node lies in the amplification factor more than in the crude wattage. By power in this sense we really mean 'power available to mind', or 'open to purposive or moral choice'. The larger the morphostatic system, the greater will be the amplification factor needed if it is to be able to do what is essential for its survival and further evolution offer variety for selection. Now the only place the indeterminism of real options can come from is the microcosm. What we seem to be saying therefore is that it is good for a morphostat to be able to obtain penny-toss type options from the quantum world. But power available to mind and power controlled by chance are not the same things.

How do we reconcile the contradiction? There are two ways and one of them involves multiplying entities without necessity. I shall deal with that second.

First: what is offered by the microcosm to the mesocosmic and maybe later to the macrocosmic morphostat are *options* not choices. If the entity is a protozoon it chooses and lives or dies, but if it is a creature of more advanced intelligence it has a world simulator called a brain which has a large data store of tested, learning patterns, so the new option (called an idea) can be tested in the simulation programs called imagination and cognition before being tried in the real world. The suggestion is that those aspects of the mind we call imagination and creativity have an important contribution from the microcosm. When we seek to be 'free' we are asking for the freedom to behave whimsically, to make experiments which are not justifiable rationally, for access to our own personal penny tosses.

It is clear that however large living systems become, those that despite their size preserve this creative aspect best will in the long term, be likely to produce the most viable survivors in the long term, because there will be less restraint on the variants offered for selection.

I mentioned an idea which unnecessarily multiplies entities. It is one in which I join many speculations, such as those of Eccles, Julian Huxley and Bergson, in blatant defiance of Occam.

Possibly a purposive mind itself is an aspect of all matter and thus a micro-cosmic phenomenon in itself. Maybe it is not simply options that the microcosm offers but sometimes *selected* options and even sometimes marginal triggerlike decisions. Suppose the universe is indeterminate, as I argue, and that there *is* a power or force or God, not omnipotent and omniscient, but a purposive origin for the realm of the Creatura which is striving against the other realm, the Pleroma. If we grant it only power at the margin in the region of the indeterminate then it would have to operate at first by building up stable platforms of order and developing them as triggers to mesocosm systems. It would have to build up life forms, create a morphostasis continuum.

The view above is presented with maximum tentativeness. It is the unfalsifi-able hypothesis to end all such, the ultimate in entities multiplied without necessity. But has the view not a surface gloss, at least, of plausibility?

The next question is vital. What difference would it make to our view of a biophil moral code, whether or not we accept the above deist hypothesis as dogma? None, I suggest

If it were not so, if there were no original intelligence, mind force, what you will, surely the nature of the two-realm universe (if it is at all congruent with the one out there) would itself bring about the emergence of something like it. I gave my reason for this in my remarks on the origin of purpose in the universe, earlier in the book.

The convergence of intelligence

As I have said, there would have been no reason, before it happened, to anticipate the convergence of, the co-operativeness of, and the communica-tional integrity of the world culture of men that I have described. Nor would there have been any reason to anticipate the idea of human unity that is implied by the United Nations and the many other international hierarchies and networks that have arisen in this century. That they do not work well and dissatisfy many is not the point, they had no call to arise on an earth dominated by a successful, strongly competitive, intensely territorial, hunter-gatherer predator. That this convergence should happen was unlikely. It is not less likely that, after the trauma of first contact is over, the same kind of symbiotic convergence should continue, if mankind, while he is still around, should make contact with other life forms from beyond the earth. Most earthlings who have thought about it today would expect that, and that fact too is odd and predictive. The life-term of men and the distances in the macrocosm make such contact between men and other intelligences most improbable but the scope and duration of artefact intelligences is an unknown which is all potential. The childish science fiction dream which recapitulates the human convergence in imagination among the galaxies may not be so childish or laughable as it seems at first sight.

In forms we cannot possibly imagine but in ways in which we may even now be playing a precursory part, the interstellar and even intergalactic contact, interaction and convergence of intelligences may happen. The primitive hominids never dreamed of our present world culture but they were contributing to it by the way they were and the way they were going.

John Good was the first to see that if man's skills can make an intelligence which can surpass his own, then that is the first step to an intelligence explosion which may not have limits.

The advanced intelligence takes a hand in designing its successor, and that successor in the design of *its* successor . . . This was John Good's reasoning.

Immanent purpose?

Following this fanciful image a little further, we see a dual universe where the matter/energy realm is vastly dominant and all-pervasive. So far. That realm operates under its own invariances and constraints in the microcosm. Although at base it is indeterminate, in any large aggregate it appears to be determinate because it is governed by the vast weight of statistical laws which apply to very large numbers. The other realm we posit is that of an intelligence, a Mind or God or Purpose or Life Force. It exists/existed in some unknown, perhaps non-material form. It had no power in the middle world of the mesocosm. So far. But in the realm of the indeterminate it may have some marginal power.

If that which favours the Creatura is a striving, purposive God who wants power over events in the mesocosm, the level of our human lives, and later the macrocosm of the stars and galaxies he must build up trigger-chains and cascades so as to amplify his posited, minute power over the quantum world. And to do this he will first need to get a purchase on the cascade of disordering change, the slide to disorder, to entropy, that is universal at mesocosmic levels. The first main objective must surely be to create platforms of stability in the mesocosm. These are needed as a base for operations. Nothing can be done in an anarchy of constant change. The intelligence must retain and develop control of his stable forms via trigger-chains and cascades built into them.

What I have described is precisely the morphostatic model for life forms. A human society which can change itself and the world because of an idea in one man's mind is a model of a system where the microcosm is struggling for control of the macrocosm. At a later stage the God, the Intelligence, the driving force of the Creatura, would need to intervene judiciously via his many-link trigger-cascades, to guide the development of more and larger intelligence-driven creatures, civilisations and cultures. He would have to make them competitive to achieve excellence. He would have to make the competitive forms diverge at first but that would create a dilemma. To have real control he would need a convergence stage at the end. There would have to be symbiosis as well as competition. The convergence of the biosphere as a whole and of what Chardin called the noosphere and I have called world culture is congruent with that thought.

Further, and this is the uneasy thought, the beings and cultures and institutions that were built up might be influenced to experiment with the manufacture of even more advanced forms of mind and intelligence. These artificial forms would not be constrained by the age-long historical clutter of biological systems which had been developed on the crude, slow, genoplastic learning plan. The trial-and-error development of artefact simulations of intelligence could be informed by highly developed intelligences (which the God may have direct access to at a sophisticated level, may be able to *inspire* — to use the common religious phrase). This would be better than the marginal effect on the penny-toss, try-everything mode of genoplastic evolution.

Further such development of AI is unconstrained by the painful biological evolutionary path by which biological forms came to exist. An example of such is the commercial/scientific community as a whole on earth today. It can invent viable artefacts much more quickly and easily than evolution can do.

Let me propose a moral test. Suppose human technology does, in fact, lead to the emergence of a new form of morphostat, a surviving, organised, self-replicating form of non-carbohydrate life. Suppose this is created at first by man and later replicated and improved by itself, perhaps on a base of electronics and silicon components, perhaps on bases and taking forms as yet undreamed of. Suppose this life form, as I think it would be, could live longer, travel further, be more powerful and intelligent than mankind or its associations. Supposing this life form, our creation and successor, should move out into the universe and continue the course and work of the biota there. Here is my moral problem. Would that be morally wrong?

Men are mortal. So are species. All of them. Yet old men think and plan for their successors, the children who will survive them and inherit from them. Is that immoral? Can we as a species and a culture achieve a feat of meta-morality? Can we think and plan for life forms which may one day supersede us? Should we take on the almost impossible intellectual task of opening our morality window wide enough to accept the inevitability of our supersession and try to see that what survives and replaces us is a continuation and development of the universal trend of the Creatura which I seem to see?

This seems to me to be the most important moral question of all.

INTELLIGENCE IN THE FUTURE

In trying to show what an ethics based on the morphostasis continuum would be like I have given an admittedly vague and fuzzy picture of what would be a *desirable* future for a biophil, a life-lover. I must now treat the question implied in the title of this book. What *will* be the future of life and its product, intelligence?

I have claimed that the least-error-cost belief is that we live in a forked world in which there are real options. It follows that prophets are an endangered species, especially those in such heady heights of speculation as this.

Caveats over, I see this. The human race begins to dominate the biosphere of this small, lonely planet and together we are moving towards an important decision fork.

Homo Sapiens and his social institutions has, over the last few thousand years, been growing and changing at an explosive, exponential rate. Even in this tiny time slot there have been several surges and relapses, as various large civilisation patterns have been tried and scrapped. The present world civilisation and culture will either take off and reach the next plateau of stability at a higher morphostatic level, or relapse again for some time before it makes another salmon leap at the falls.

A fork in the road

Along one fork, the next plateau will be a stable, durable, biosphere on the earth supporting a world culture which, not at the command of some central control, but because of its autonomous polyhierarchic inner dynamic, pushes on up the improbability and negentropy slopes towards more intelligent people, societies and artefacts. These will, if not this time then at a later attempt, reach out from the earth and start to inhabit and populate the bodies and space of the Solar System and later, one day, galactic space and other worlds. In the very long term I see contact with other intelligences, competition, strife, then co-operation and resumption of expansion along the continuum.

But what is it that will reach out from earth's surface? What will the adventurers be like? If they are to be men and women, humanity will have to speciate, breed space folk, because the cost and difficulty of sending earthlike environments around the universe will be too high. But we do not like

speciation, genetic breeding applied to people. Also it is very slow, generations are too long.

The conclusion is that if future societies believe what we do then people,
some people, somewhere at some time, will *make* the space adventurers, the
intelligences, the seeds of sapience and comprehension, which, who, will go
out to continue the work out there. And they, unobstructed by the age-long
accumulation of hardwired biological decisions on our evolutionary track,
will have to learn to make and modify themselves using cognition and its
developments to help in offering options for evolutionary choice instead of
the blind chance which brought life to where it is (as we believe). On earth the
development of artificial intelligence will bring many changes. The societies
that opt for it will be found to be more stable, prosperous and powerful than
those that do not. Eventually the feet will vote, if the hands do not, for a system
which uses their aid. Or, alas, since we are combative, there will be wars. We
can guess where the advantage will lie. You should not put your money on the
side without or with less effective AI aid. Either way, the influence of the two
other forms of intelligence will grow as they combine to form a single one. The
social intelligence of the world culture will be informed and supported by the
growing influence of intelligent artefacts.

The other fork

That is one fork. What is the other one?

This biosphere will be just one more seed that fell on rock. No problem!
There must be plenty enough out there.

Humanity will take the soft option, will spurn and reject a rival in the
sapience game. We shall spread our earth culture more widely; more and
more people will have a longer, more healthy, easier and more amusing life.
And eventually there will be a war, a comet, a sun disaster, or disease, and that
will be the end. At best, if we survive for a long time there will be the
speciation that lies in wait for the successful. What we now call a man will be
not so. Mankind will be to the successors what the chimpanzee is to mankind,
other.

There are sound biological reasons for believing that the further improvement of human intelligence by evolution is limited. The ground plan of our
brain is set, hardwired. Natural selection could increase the average intelligence but it is unlikely to do much to raise the peak. (This has been shown in
breeding experiments with rats. They have bred two populations apart so that
the maze running nous of the maze-thickest of one group was better than that
of the maze-brightest of the other. But the *brightest*, maze-bright, did *not*
improve).

Therefore, the future for humanity if it neglects to provide for succession is
that of all such morphostats, it will have none.

In this world there are two sorts of people, a few expendable entrepreneurs, adventurers, innovators and a lot of safety-first, quiet lifers. The latter can always outvote the former. But they cannot stop them. It is adventurers who, as a set, mould the future. Most of them, nearly all, fail or die trying, but a few, just a few, change the world. If you have to bet it would be unsafe to put your money on the other set. My money and blessings are on the first fork.

The glossary of neologisms and unusual words

Being an unashamed autodidact, and writing in a field where communication is difficult because the language tools have not developed, I have allowed myself the liberty of coining neologisms wherever I think that the meaning envelope of the nearest existing word will fail to transmit or will distort meaning. I am sure that the meaning will be clear enough from the local context but for the sake of form I define them here. I also include my definitions of other unusual words.

Acausality. (*neol.*) Non-causality, indeterminacy.

Afferent. Receiving signals or information.

Aperiodic. Used here in Schroedinger's sense, non-repetitive. A normal crystal would be considered repetitive because the pattern repeats.

Autocatalysis. The catalysis of reaction by the product of that reaction.

Automatic taxonomy. The technique of finding useful and beneficial ways to classify the events perceived by an entity.

Autonomous. Internally governed.

Biomorphic. (*neol.*) In form like living systems or entities.

Bio-physical dualism. (*neol.*) The hypothesis that the biological and physical realms are heteronomous.

Brainable. (*neol.*) Compatible with the human brain, thinkable.

Conative. Associated with drive or will.

Congruent.   The quality of being of similar form.

Continuum.   That which is continuous, stepless.

Decorticate.   Adjective applied to a mammal where the whole of the cerebral cortex has been removed.

Determinate.   Having a fixed outcome.

Efferent.   Transmitting signals or information.

Entelechy.   Distinctness of realised existence: a vital principle supposed by vitalists to direct processes in an organism toward realisation of a certain end.

Entropy.   The degree of disorder of molecules. Any free physical system will distribute its energy so that the entropy increases but the available energy diminishes.

Equiponderous.   Of equal weight or effect.

Epigenesis.   The theory that the development of an embryo consists of the gradual production and organisation of parts.

Epistemology.   The science of knowledge.

Fractal.   A semi-random pattern which is similar at any scale.

Genoplastic. (*neol.*)   Modified advantageously only between generations, 'learning' by evolution.

Heteronomous.   Subject to other laws.

Heteropotent. (*neol.*)   Having unequal mutual effect, non-equipotent.

Homologous.   Corresponding in relative position, general structure and descent.

Macrocosm.   The world of stars and galaxies.

Mesocosm. (*neol.*)   The middle world between the microcosm and the macrocosm, the familiar world of everyday scale.

Meta-morphostatic.   Morphostatic with respect to senior morphostatic entities.

Metaprogram. (*neol.*)   A computer program which writes programs.

Metazoon — *pl.* **Metazoa.**   Multi-cellular animals usually having a nervous system and an enteric cavity.

Microcosm.   The world of fundamental particles, atoms and molecules.

Morphodyn. (*neol.*)   Joking word for corpse. Entity which changes its form radically with time.

Morphostasis. (*neol.*)   The activity of any system which behaves as though it had the purpose to preserve its form through time with minimum modification.

Morphostat. (*neol.*)   Entity which behaves as above, living system, cell, animal, social group thereof.

Motorium. (*neol.*)   The entire set of efferent, outgoing (instructional) output ports to a living data-processing system.

Neonate.   New-born child or animal.

Ontoplastic. (*neol.*)   Able to adapt behaviourally as individuals within a generation by learning.

Orrery.   A mechanical model of the solar system.

Ontogeny.   The history of the development of an individual. (*cf* phylogeny history of the development of a race.)

Panspermia.   Seeded from space. The idea that the original life forms came from outer space.

Pecking-order.   Dominance, rank order in social animals.

Placenta.   A flattened structure which forms an intimate union between the natal chord and the uterine wall of the mother.

Polycentric (geometrically impossible).   In this sense, having many centres of influence.

Polyhierarchy.   A network of information flow where multiple interconnected stratified converging hierarchies spring from the same base.

Protozoon — *pl.* **Protozoa.**   Small animals of varying shape and complex micro-structure. Unicellular or acellular.

Proprioceptor.   A sensory nerve ending receptive to internal stimuli.

Quantum.   The indivisible unit of any form of physical energy, e.g., photon.

Scala Naturae (ladder of nature).   Supposed continuum of lower and higher life forms.

Sensorium. (*neol.*)   The entire set of afferent ingoing, (informational) input ports to a living data-processing system.

Socio-centrism. (*neol.*)   Life models built on a social base.

Sociozoon. (*neol.*)   An intercommunicating social morphostat, one where the communications are by external signals.

Speciesism. (*neol.*)   Favouring ones own species, *cf* racism.

Spectrum.   The colour continuum.

Strategic/tactical continuum.   The words 'strategical' and 'tactical' are here used to indicate the level of decision-making. Strategic decisions are those with larger and more widespread effects. Tactical decisions are those concerned with details.

Sufficiency.   The proportion of the weighted input to a threshold gate that is sufficient to activate it; the threshold level or the boundaries within which an entity has enough evidence or excitation to pass it on.

Taxonomy.   Strictly, the science of classification as applied to living organisms. The extended sense here is making decisions about how to classify data.

Teleonomy.   Impressions of purpose arising from the natural selection.

Tolerance.   Permissible deviation.

Topion. (*neol.*)   A topological or connectional 'locality'; a connectional region or zone within a network in which connection weights are relatively high.

Bibliography

I give a list here of the books that have influenced me or which have been mentioned in the text.

Aleksander, I.   *The Human Machine*. Georgie Publishing

Alt, F. L. and Rubinoff, M. (editors) (1965)   *Advances in Computers,* Vol 6. Academic Press, New York

Andreski, S.   *Social Sciences as Sorcery*. Pelican

Andrzejewski, S. (1954)   *Military Organisation and Society*. Routledge & Kegan Paul, London

Andrzejewski, S.   *Social Sciences as Sorcery*. Pelican

Ardrey, R.   *The Territorial Imperative*.   Collins

Arkad'ev, A. G. and Braverman, E. M. (1967)   *Teaching Computers to Recognise Patterns*. Academic Press, London (1967)

Asimov, I.   *The Human Brain*. Mentor

Asimov, I.   *Guide to Science*. Pelican

Ayer, A. L.   *The Problem of Knowledge*. Pelican

Barasch, D. P.   *Sociobiology and Behaviour*. Elsevier, Oxford

Barton, A. W.   *A Textbook of Heat*. Longmans Green & Company

B.B.C. Publications   *The Laws of Disorder*

Beer, S.   *Cybernetics and Management*. British Steel Corporation

Bell, D.   *Decision Trees in Pattern Recognition*. National Physical Laboratory, D.T.I.

Berelson, B. and Steiner, G. A.   *Human Behaviour: An Inventory of Scientific Findings*. Harcourt, Brace & World, New York

Bergson, H. (1911)   *Matter and Memory*. Allen & Unwin, London

Bono, E., de   *The Mechanism of Mind*. Jonathon Cape

Cairns-Smith, A. E.   *Genetic Take-over.* Cambridge University Press
Cairns-Smith, A. E.   *The Life Puzzle.* Oliver and Boyde
Carter, C. O.   *Human Heredity.* Pelican
Cattell, R. (1972)   *Beyondism.* Pergamon
Cattell, R. (1971)   *Abilities: Their Structure, Growth and Action.* Houghton Mifflin, Boston
Chardin, P. T., de (1965)   *The Phenomenon of Man.* Fontana Books, London
Charniak, E.   *Introduction to Artificial Intelligence.* Drew
Cherfas, J.   *Man Made Life.* Blackwell, Oxford
Cohen, J.   *Reproduction.* Pergamon
Cohen, J. (1967)   *Living Embryos.* Pergamon, Oxford
Cornell Aeronautic Laboratories Inc.   *The Perceptron*
Crick, F.   *Life Itself.* Simon & Schuster
Culbertson, J. T.   *Consciousness and Behaviour.* W. C. Brown & Co., Dubuque, USA
Darlington, C. D.   *The Evolution of Man in Society.* Allen & Unwin
Darlington, C. D.   *Genetics and Man.* Pelican
Dawkins, R.   *The Selfish Gene.* Palladin
Feigenbaum, E. A. and McCorduck, P.   *The Fifth Generation*
Foss, B. M. (editor)   *Perception: A Cross Cultural Perspective.* Penguin
Good, I. J.   *Speculations Concerning First Ultra-intelligent Machine Advances in Computers.* Academic Press, New York
Good, I. J. (editor)   *The Scientist Speculates: An Anthology of Partially Baked Ideas.*   Unicorn Books, New York
Gould, S. J.   *Ever Since Darwin.* Burnett Books
Gregory, R. L.   *Mind in Science.* Peregrine Books, London
Gregory, R. L. (1970)   *Eye and Brain.* Weidenfeld & Nicolson, London
Gregory, R. L. (1970)   *The Intelligent Eye.* Weidenfeld & Nicolson, London
Gribbin, J.   *In Search of Schroedinger's Cat.*   Corgi
Guildford, J. P. (1967)   *The Nature of Human Intelligence.* McGraw Hill, New York and London
Hayek, F. A.   *The Sensory Order.* Routledge & Kegan Paul, Hayek, Eamonn Butler and Smith, London
Hayek, F. A.   *Knowledge, Evolution and Society.* Adam Smith Institute, London
Hayek, F. A.   *The Road to Serfdom.* Routledge & Kegan Paul
Hebb, D. O.   *The Organisation of Behaviour.* Wiley Books
Holland, R. C.   *Microcomputers and Their Interfacing.* Pergamon
Hook, S. (editor) (1961)   *Dimensions of Mind.* Collier-Macmillan, London
Hume, D.   *Treatise on Human Nature.*   Pelican
Hunter, M. L.   *Memory.* Pelican
Kanal, L. N.   *Pattern Recognition.* Thompson Book Co., Washington, D.C.

Katz, D.   *Animals and Men*. Pelican
Koestler, A.   *The Art of Creation*. Hutchinson
Kuhn, T. S.   *The Structure of Scientific Revolutions*. University of Chicago
Lloyd, B.   *Perception and Cognition*. Penguin, London
Lorenz, K.   *On Aggression*. Allen & Unwin
Lowenstein, O.   *The Senses*. Pelican
Luria, A. R.   *The Working Brian*. Penguin
MacMillan, R. H. (editor) (1962)   *Nonlinear Control Systems Analysis*.
     Pergamon, Oxford
Macworth, J. E.   *Vigilance and Attention*. Pelican
Mair, L.   *Primitive Government*. Pelican
Mark, R.   *Memory and Nerve Cell Connections*. Clarendon Press, Oxford
Marvin Minsky and Seymour Papert   *Perceptrons*. Science Press Inc.
McKenzie, W. J. M.   *Biological Ideas in Politics*. Penguin
McLeish, J.   *The Science of Behaviour*. Barrie & Rockliff
Michie, D. (editor) (1971)   *Machine Intelligence I*. Edinburgh University
     Press, edited Collins, N. L.
Michie, D. (editor)   *Machine Intelligence II*. Oliver and Boyde, edited Dale, E.
Midgely, M.   *Evolution as a Religion*. Methuen, London
Monod, J.   *Chance and Necessity*. Collins/Fount
Morris, D.   *The Naked Ape*. Corgi
Mottram, V. H.   *Physical Basis of Personality*. Pelican
Muses, C. A. (editor) (1962)   *The Aspects of the Theory of Artificial Intelligence*.
     Plenum Press, New York
Nathan, P. (1969)   *The Nervous System*. Pelican, London
Pagels, H. E.   *The Cosmic Code*. Pelican
Pask, G.   *An Approach to Cybernetics*. Hutchinson
Paul, E. H.   *The Physiology of Nerve Cells*. Blackwell Scientific Publications
Penfield, W. and Roberts, L. (1959)   *Speech and Brain Mechanisms*. Princeton
     University Press
Popper, K. R.   *The Logic of Scientific Discovery*. Ginsons, London
Popper, K. R. and Eccles, J. C.   *The Self and It Brain*. Springer International
Porter, A.   *Cybernetics Simplified*. English University Press
Rhodes, F. H. t.   *The Evolution of Life*, Pelican
Ross Ashby, W. (1960)   *Design for a Brain*. Chapman & Hall, London
Russell, B.   *An Inquiry into Meaning and Truth*. Pelican
Sagan, C.   *The Dragons of Eden*. Random House, New York
Saparina, Y.   *Cybernetics with Us*. Peace Publishers
Sawyer, W. W.   *The Search for Pattern*. Pelican
Schade, J. P.   *Molecular Neurology*. Roche, Switzerland
Schroedinger, I.   *What is Life?*Cambridge University Press
Serebriakoff, V. (1985)   *Cybernetics and Factory Organisation*. Paper read to
     Theoretical Studies Group, British Sociological Association

Serebriakoff, V.   *Brain*. Davis-Poynter, London
Sherington, Sir Charles   *Man and his Nature*. Cambridge University Press
Slukin, W.   *Minds and Machines*. Pelican
Smith, Adam   *The Wealth of Nations*. Pelican
Sommerhoff, G.   *Analytical Biology*. Oxford University Press
Uhr, L. (editor)   *Pattern Recognition*. John Wiley & Sons, New York
Uttley, A. M. (1970)   *The Informon Journal of Theoretical Biology*, **27,** 31-67
Vernon, M. D.   *The Psychology of Perception*. Pelican
Waddington, C. H.   *The Strategy of the Genes*. Allen & Unwin
Wells, H. G.   *The Outline of History*. Cassells
Wiener, N.   *Cybernetics*. M.I.T. Press
Wilder, Penfield & Lamar Roberts   *Speech and Brain Mechanisms*. Pheneam, New York
Wilkinson, J. F.   *Introduction to Microbiology*. Blackwell Scientific Publications
Wright, Q. (1965)   *A Study of War*. University of Chicago Press
Woolridge, D. E. (1963)   *The Machinery of the Brain*. McGraw-Hill, London
Young, J. F. (1969)   *Cybernetics*. Iliffe Press, London
Young, J. F.   *Chemical Basis of Life*. Readings from the *Scientific American*
Young, J. F.   *Perception* (Mechanism and Models) and *Recent Progress in Perception*. Readings from the *Scientific American*

Appendix 1

A COMPUTER MODEL FOR A TAXONOMIC SYSTEM

I publish here, with the kind permission of my friend James Cherrill, the program and notes of the Fortran program that he produced in 1977 after reading my book. Further experimentation with this program and developments from it are proceeding at present. His original program was in APL but that is no longer available. The program is also available in Sinclair Spectrum Basic (kindly translated by Mr Seymour Laxon) but is very slow on a microcomputer. Those who are interested in such programs are invited to contact the author at Flat 1 No. 6 The Paragon London SE3 0NY UK.

Introduction

The model described in this paper is one of a taxonomic system — i.e., one which, when presented with a large set of data, will develop a classification scheme for that data. The classification scheme is evolved from an initial pseudo-random state by a heuristic process based on the results of attempting to classify each new set of data using the existing scheme. This heuristic process causes the classification scheme to be based only on the regularities in the sets of data, and not on any *a priori* assumptions built into the system itself. A further result of the heuristic process is that the exact criteria used in the classification scheme are evolved in relation to the noise inherent in the data, and thus the 'tightness' of these criteria will match the precision of the data.

The structure of the model is one of a large number of similar elements connected in a roughly hierarchical network. Each element is relatively simple, and has a limited fixed capability for modifications of its parameters.

249

The classification scheme is evolved as a set of connections between network elements, the relative strength of the connections reflecting the importance of various data elements or configurations in the classification scheme.

It has been suggested (but not by the author) that this system may be, itself, a simple model for some parts of the brain or nervous system. In this model, the network elements would correspond to neurones (or small groups of neurones) and the connections to synapses.

The model

The model consists of a number of interconnected units called 'nodes'. Each node has a number of inputs, each of which carries a binary signal, and one output, which is also binary. If the data present on the inputs conform to certain requirements (which change dynamically), the node will attempt to respond by changing the state of its output from 0 to 1.

Nodes are interconnected by paths of inhibition. They are normally defined to be two-way paths ('mutual inhibition'). Where a number of mutually inhibiting nodes attempt to respond, only one of them is allowed to respond.

Thus the interconnections between nodes can be of two types:

(i)   One node has an inhibition path to one or more other nodes.

(ii)   The output of a node forms the input for one or more other nodes.

The input to the model consists of a binary string of predetermined length. Nodes may use any bit or bits of this string as an input.

The model does not have an 'output' as such, but its response to an input binary string is defined by the nodes which succeed in responding as a result of that input string.

Typical simple model

Hierarchical organisation.

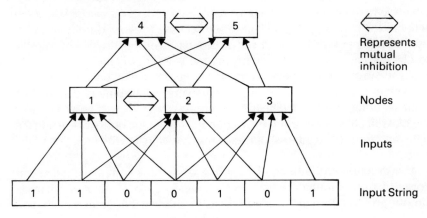

In this example model the nodes are arranged into levels, the lowest taking its input from the input strings and passing its outputs as inputs for the next level.

The combined effect of inhibition and of overlapping inputs is to establish a 'competitive' situation at each level, where many nodes may attempt to respond to the same input string but only some can actually respond.

The 'learning' process by which nodes modify their response to inputs is such that, in this 'competitive' situation, nodes sharing common inputs will 'learn' to respond to different sets of input strings. This is the basis of the taxonomic (classification making) properties of the network.

At higher levels in the hierarchy, inputs correspond to the presence or absence of particular sub-strings in the input string, and outputs indicate the presence or absence of configurations of sub-strings.

For example, suppose the input string is a representation of the letter 'X'. This is coded by dividing the field on which the 'X' is formed into a grid, and coding each element of the grid as 0 or 1 depending on whether part of the letter is absent or present in that element. Nodes at the first level may then respond in the presence of particular 'features' — top left diagonal termination, absence of letter at bottom centre, etc. Nodes at higher levels will respond to assemblies of features — an inverted 'V' in the lower half etc — and nodes at the highest level will respond to the whole pattern.

The reducing number of nodes at each level, combined with the effects of mutual inhibition, leads to an important 'convergence' effect. In the simple example model there are $2^7 = 128$ possible input strings. However, there are only six possible responses from the first level, and only three possible outcomes at the top level. The hierarchy can thus perform one of two functions: sieving, or classification. The former, in which the hierarchy responds to only three of the 128 possible strings, is of little interest; it is the latter case for which the model is designed.

If the mechanism determining the node's response to a given set of inputs is suitable, a node can be arranged to respond to any member of a set of similar input strings (a crude example is to store an object string for the node and attempt to respond if more than 75 percent of the bits in the input match the object string).

In the example of the letter 'X', this mechanism would correspond to a node responding (for example) to the upper left diagonal termination, regardless of the exact angle and whether or not a seriph is present. The input to higher levels of the hierarchy thus consists of the presence or absence of abstracted features in the input string, and at each level further abstraction of features will occur.

This level-by-level abstraction process can also be considered as a noise rejection mechanism. However, the level-by-level process is such that 'noise' is defined at progressively higher levels in the context of the features defined or expected at each level. This characteristic is of fundamental importance.

This process is defined as classification, in as much as any input string from a large set leads to one of a smaller number of responses, based on abstracted groupings of abstracted features of the string.

The 'learning' mechanism

The crucial mechanism is that by which a node's response to its inputs is determined and modified. The basic mechanism chosen is that of a weighted input threshold gate.

Thus, for each of n inputs, i, there is an input weighting w_i, and for the node there is a threshold T. Each input has a binary value v_i, and the node will attempt to respond if

$$\sum_{1}^{n} v_i w_i \geqslant T$$

Note that if $T = \sum_{1}^{n} w_i$, the node will only attempt to respond if all v_i are 1 ('and' gate). If $T = 0$ the node will attempt to respond for any $v_i = 1$ ('or' gate). The normal condition is between these two extremes.

It is the relationship between T and w_i which determines the 'width' of the classification made by a node; increasing values of T correspond to increasingly high selectivity, decreasing values of T correspond to an increasingly broad range of acceptable input strings.

A large number of mechanisms could be proposed for adjusting T and w_i. The one actually used was chosen because it is relatively simple and because it leads to a very useful value of T and w_i being set. The mechanism is as follows:

Initially all $w_i = 1$ and $T = 0$

(the node is thus an 'or' gate).

If the node responds successfully, all inputs with $v_i = 1$ have their weighting increased to $w_i + 1$ (corresponding roughly to an inverse exponential growth).

All inputs with $v_i = 0$ have their weightings decreased by 1. (Values of w_i less than 1 are not permitted and any input which has its weighting reduced below 1 is removed completely. Other mechanisms within the model allow for the creation of new inputs on a pseudo-random basis. New inputs so created have an initial weighting of 1.)

This definition leads to values of w_i which fluctuate around levels dependent on the degree of consistency of the input. For example, consider a node with eight inputs (i.e., one 'learning' an eight-element feature). Suppose that, because of variability in the feature and because of noise, an average two of these elements will be absent in any given input string. On any one input, therefore, in N input strings, 6/8 values will be 1, and 2/8 N will be zero.

If N is large enough, the weighting for that input will tend to fluctuate around a value near 3, at which it will tend to receive six increases around $\frac{1}{3}$ for every two decreases of 1. If an average of one element is absent in each input string, the corresponding value of w_i is around 7 (i.e., receiving seven increases of around 1/7 of every decrease of 1).

The weighting factors thus tend to a mean value which is high for highly consistent inputs and low for inconsistent (i.e., 'noisy' or 'irrelevant' inputs).

The threshold value T is modified from its starting value of zero by applying all increases or decreases in the w_i equal to T. This is equivalent to the definitions:

$$T = \sum_{1}^{n} w_i - n$$

$$T = \sum_{1}^{n} (w_i - 1)$$

It thus follows immediately that, where there is a high degree of consistency in the whole input string, T is high-valued, and vice-versa. However, the key characteristic of this particular mechanism is that the node will reach a stable configuration for any given level of consistency in the input, and will then attempt to respond only to an input within that consistency but ignore any input string of lower consistency.

Following the two previous examples:
For the case of an average of 2 bits absent

$$w_i \simeq 3$$

$$T = \sum_{1}^{8} (3 - 1) = 16$$

The threshold will therefore be exceeded if any six bits are present, but not five.

For the case of an average of 1 bit absent

$$W_i = 7$$

$$T = \sum_{1}^{8} (7 - 1) = 48$$

The threshold will be exceeded with any seven bits present, but not with six. In the case where some input bits are consistent, but others not, the w_i will vary to reflect this, and a similar argument to the above still holds.

The above argument applies to inputs whose presence confirms the presence of a given element or feature. The model mechanism also allows for inputs which indicate the absence of an element or feature (inhibitory inputs). This aspect of the model is still under investigation and is not discussed here.

The mutual inhibition mechanism

If a node receives a set of inputs such that $\sum_i^n w_i v_i > T$ it attempts to respond. Its success is determined by its inter-reaction with other nodes connected to it by paths of inhibition.

If, for each node attempting to respond, we define an 'excitation strength' as $\sum_i^n w_i v_i$ then the node will respond only if its excitation strength is greater than the excitation strength of every other node which is connected to it by an inhibiting path and which is also attempting to respond. Thus only one of a set of inter-connected nodes can fire for any one input string.

In the case where a node attempts to respond but is successfully inhibited by another, this is taken to indicate that both nodes are developing a response to similar input strings. This redundancy is countered by reducing the weightings (and therefore the threshold) of the inhibited node, thus increasing and changing the class of strings to which it could respond.

The network thus develops towards a steady state in which each node responds to a particular class of input string or higher level features. Where nodes are connected by paths of mutual inhibition, the classes to which they respond will be mutually exclusive.

The generation and destruction of input connections

The mechanism for increasing and decreasing the weighting factors on node inputs includes a process by which weighting factors can be reduced to zero. An input with a weighting of zero is considered as 'not connected' and is ignored by the response mechanism.

In order to prevent a complete depletion of inputs, and in order to establish a random (or, strictly, pseudo-random) basis for the development of a response to new input strings, there is a further mechanism which generates new inputs. When the model is initialised, all weighting factors are zero – i.e., there are no input connections formed. Before each input string is presented to the network, all inputs with zero weighting are examined and a random selection of these are given weightings of 1. Thus the input connections defined in the specification of the network geometry should not be considered as fixed; they are actually a set of potential input connections, from which new, weak input connections are constantly being made on a random basis. If such a new input is found to be associated with a successful response, it will be reinforced by increasing its weighting. If not, the weighting will soon be reset to zero, and the input connection thus broken again.

With the mechanisms so far described, there is a danger that, if an input string is presented with an abnormally high degree of consistency for a few successive presentations, the weightings and threshold of a node responding to that input string will also become abnormally high. The node will then be excessively selective, and will fail to respond to any further normal presentations of the string. It is also possible that changes in the population of input strings will leave some highly selective nodes in a state where they will not respond to any members of the new population.

Without a further mechanism in the model, it is impossible that such a node will ever have its threshold decreased, and so the node will effectively become useless. The technique employed to prevent this is that when the excitation level for a node fails to exceed its threshold all input weightings (and thus the threshold) are decreased by a small, fixed amount. In the absence of an occasional successful response, a node will therefore tend slowly to decrease its selectivity until it begins to respond again. The amount by which weighting factors are decreased in the absence of an attempted response is set small enough to be insignificant in the case of a normally responding node.

Neurophysiological parallels

It is not being claimed that the model is an accurate model for neuronal function. It may be possible, however, that the behaviour of the model may parallel the behaviour of networks of neurones such as those processing visual information. Such a parallel would be based on a functional similarity between a model node, and a single neurone or small group of neurones. The input and inhibition connections would thus correspond with axonal and dendritic synapses. If such a parallel can be accepted, the model, which can be easily controlled, modified, monitored and measured, could throw useful light on neuronal network mechanisms which are too difficult to study in reality.

Experimental notes

The basic principles described in this paper were developed and tested during 1976 by computer simulation using the APL progamming language (which is ideally suited to work of this type).

Further investigations, however, require a more efficient and more easily, transported program. This has now been written using the Fortran IV language, preliminary results are encouraging. Copies of the program are available from the author.

James Cherrill
November 1977

PROGRAM NOTES

1 Defining the network
2 Defining the input patterns
3 Control cards
4 Program installation

Defining the network

The network geometry is fully defined by specifying the potential connections of node outputs to node inputs, input string bits to node inputs, and inhibiting paths between nodes.

The logical division of the nodes into 'levels' of a hierarchy is not intrinsic in the model; it is just a function of the geometry defined for inputs and inhibition. There is, however, one constraint on node numbering and geometry which must be observed, viz: A node 'i' may only use another node 'j' as input if node 'i' is a higher numbered node than node 'j' and is a higher numbered node than all the nodes which may inhibit node 'j'.

For a conventional structure, logically divided into levels, this condition is automatically met if nodes are numbered starting with the lowest level.

The network definition is loaded into the model from cards (or card images). It is entered as an un-delimited string of integers, in the Fortran format 1216 for each card. If the last card is not filled, it should be padded with zeros unless the Fortran compiler will accept blanks as zeros.

The data items comprising the input are as follows:

(i)   The number of nodes in the network.

(ii)   The number of inputs for each node, by node.

(iii) The number of inhibiting nodes for each node, by node.

(iv)   A list of input node numbers for each node.
       If input is directly from an input pattern, specify the input pattern element number as a negative value.

(v)   A list of the numbers of inhibiting nodes for each node.

Example of network definition

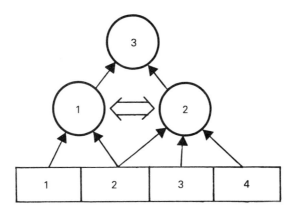

INPUT
PATTERN

Data items:
(i)   3
(ii) 2 3 2
(iii) 1 1 0
(iv) −1 −2
     −2 −3 −4
      1   2
(v)   2   1

On cards this would appear as:
3 2 3 2 1 1 0 −1 −2 −2 −3 −4
1 2 2 1 0 0 0 0   0   0   0   0

Defining the input patterns

Input patterns are specified as strings of zeros and ones. It is frequently useful to visualise them as two- (or more) dimensional arrays, but this is not represented within the model.

All input patterns are the same length, and their length must be a multiple of 16 (unrequired elements in an input string may be ignored by not specifying them as being inputs to any node).

Input patterns are specified on cards (or card images) as an un-delimited string of integers in the Fortran format 6411 on each card. These cards must follow immediately after the network geometry definition cards. Unused positions on the last card should be filled with zeros unless the Fortran compiler accepts blanks as zeros. Preceding the input patterns is a single card containing the number of input patterns, and the number of bits per pattern, in the format 1216.

Example of pattern definition

Input patterns are:

1	0	1
0	1	0
1	0	1

0	1	0
1	1	1
0	1	0

1	1	1
1	0	1
1	1	1

As each pattern is 9 bits, the size must be defined as the next higher multiple of 16. Bits 10-16 will then be ignored when defining the network.

Input pattern definition cards:

    3   16
101010101000000000101110100000000

(continued) 111101111000000000000000000000000

Control cards

Runs of the model are controlled by a sequence of run control cards. These divide into two main types: those which change the value of a model parameter and those which cause the model to execute one or more functions. With the exception of the 'start' card, control cards may appear in any order and any quantity. The run stops when there are no further control cards to process.

All control cards have the same format: a two-character identifier, followed by a six-digit parameter.

The control card types are as follows:

1) ST — the 'start' card
   The parameter is a run number, used to identify printout. This must be the first card in the control sequence, and it must follow immediately after the model network definition cards.

2) RU — the RUN card.
   The parameter is the number of cycles through which the model is to be run ('run' cards may be interspersed with changes in parameter values etc).

3) PR — the PRINT card.
   The parameter is the number of a node whose threshold and input weightings are to be printed out.

4) GR — GROWTH RATE parameter.
   Defines a % probability that any zero-weighted input will have its weighting set to one in any cycle. The default is 50%, and the permissible range 0-100.

5) RI — RANDOM INPUT %.
   Defines a % probability that a purely random string will be used as input for any cycle. The default is zero, and the permissible range 0-100.

6) NO — NOISE %.
   Defines the % of bits in any input string to be corrupted (on average). The default is zero, and the permissible range 0-100.

7) HW — INHIBITOR WEAKENING.
   Defines the amount by which a node's input weightings are decreased when the node is successfully inhibited. The value is scaled by a factor of 100 to keep the parameter integer. The default is 100 (i.e., weakening of 1.00).

8) LR — LAPSE RATE.
   Defines the amount by which a node's input weightings are reduced when the node fails to reach its own threshold. As for HW it is scaled by 100. The default is zero.

9) SD — RANDOM NUMBER GENERATOR SEED.
   Specifies a seed for the random number generator. Must be in the range 1-256. If no seed is specified, the same seed will be used in all runs.

10) LS — LOWEST STRING.
   Specifies the lowest numbered string to be included for selection as an input to the model, or for reporting. The range is 1–HS (see below), and the default is 1.

11) HS — HIGHEST STRING.
   Specifies the highest numbered string to be included. The range is LS – (no. of strings), the default is its maximum value.

12) LN — LOWEST NODE.
   As LS, but selects nodes for reporting purposes only.

13) HN — HIGHEST NODE.
   As HS, but range is LN to (no. of nodes).
   N B .   LN and HN only affect printout; unlike LS and HS they do not have any effect on the running of the model itself.

14) MO — MONITOR.

Sets a switch to control the level of printout produced in each cycle of the model. Values are:

0 – no printout is produced

1 – the cycle number, input string number (zero for a random input), the number of the highest numbered successfully responding node, and the threshold for that node.

2 – the cycle number, input string number (zero for a random input), and a string of bits, one per node, showing zero if the node failed to respond successfully, or 1 if it succeeded.

The default is zero.

The strings and nodes included in MO output can be restricted by the LS, HS, LN cards.

15) PP — PRINT PARAMETERS.

Displays the current values of the main parameters in the model. No value is required.

16) SC — START COUNT.

Starts counting nodes response vs input string numbers. No value is required. When issued, this instruction also zeros any existing counts.

17) PC — PRINT COUNT.

Prints the accumulated counts for those strings and nodes selected by LS, HS, LN, and HN. This command has no effect on the counts themselves. Random input strings are shown as string '0', totals are shown under '9999'. A maximum of 10 strings (starting with LS) will be printed by each PC instruction. No value is required.

18) DU — DUMP.

Prints an unformatted decimal dump of the main data array. If value is 1, this is preceded by the contents of the main data pointers.

Control card example

ST	1	– start
LR	5	
RI	10	establish parameters
NO	25	
HS	2	– include only two strings
RU	500	– run 500 cycles
HS	3	– add in string 3
RU	500	– run another 500
MO	1	– turn on some monitor printout

RU	50	– run another 50 with printout
MO	0	– turn off monitoring
NO	50	– increase the noise level
RU	100	– run another 100 .
MO	2	} run 50 with full monitoring
RU	50	}
PR	20	⎤
PR	21	⎟
PR	22	} print details of some of the nodes
PR	23	⎟
PR	24	⎦
(end of file)		– end of run

Program installation

The program is written in pure Fortran IV, with the exception of file open/close statements. These will have to be modified to meet the requirements of each system. The initial card in the program is for identification purposes only. Do not discard it, as it should be quoted in any correspondence about the program.

The program assumes a minimum of 16 bits per word. IBM users can increase program capacity by a factor of two with an IMPLICIT INTEGER should be in line with test 2 statement. All variables are integers; no floating point facilities are required.

The main data array 'A' contains all the model definition and variable working storage. It needs to be dimensioned in the program to make as much of the machine's storage available as possible. Its minimum size is:

       $4 \times$ No. of nodes in network
$+$ $2 \times$ No. of inputs to all nodes
$+$ No. of inhibiting nodes to all nodes
$+$ input string length
$+$ (No. of input strings) $\times$ (input string length)/16
$+$ (No of input strings $+$ 1) $\times$ (No. of nodes $+$ 1).

For example, for 20 nodes, with an average of six inputs and four inhibiting nodes each, ten input strings of 32 bits, the data array size must be a minimum of

$4 \times 20 + 2 \times 120 + 80 + 32 + 10 \times 32/16 + 11 \times 21$

$= \quad 80 + 240 + 80 + 32 + 20 + 231$

$= \quad 683$ words

If storage is restricted, data array usage can be reduced by not using the count facilities (Start Count card). In this case the final term in the above formula is not required, and, in the example given, the storage is reduced by 11×21 words, i.e., from 683 to 452 words.

All input is baud of a fixed format symbolic file of 80 character records (cards). Output is a fixed format symbolic file, with the first character of each record blank (to prevent problems with carriage control).

Main data array usage

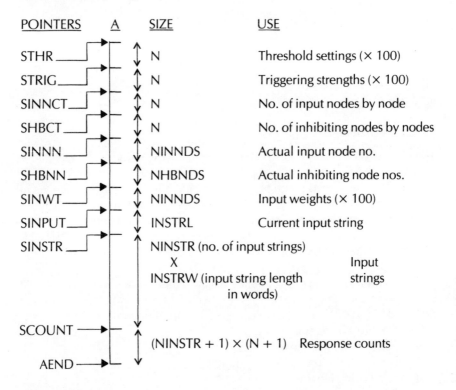

POINTERS	A	SIZE	USE
STHR		N	Threshold settings (× 100)
STRIG		N	Triggering strengths (× 100)
SINNCT		N	No. of input nodes by node
SHBCT		N	No. of inhibiting nodes by nodes
SINNN		NINNDS	Actual input node no.
SHBNN		NHBNDS	Actual inhibiting node nos.
SINWT		NINNDS	Input weights (× 100)
SINPUT		INSTRL	Current input string
SINSTR		NINSTR (no. of input strings) X INSTRW (input string length in words)	Input strings
SCOUNT		(NINSTR + 1) × (N + 1)	Response counts
AEND			

Pointera are to element zero of their section (e.g., triggering strength for node one is (STRIG+1).

Appendix 2

FORTRAN PROGRAM
– to simulate a proposed taxonomic system

```
** 1600TERR2   /SIM•JC-SY;TERR   THURSDAY  APR 27, 1978 12:06:51 PM
$CARD
C
C       PROGRAM TO SIMULATE A PROPOSED TAXONOMIC SYSTEM
C
C       DESIGN AND PROGRAMMING BY JAMES CHERRILL, FROM IDEAS PROPOSED
C       BY VICTOR SEREBRIAKOFF•
C
C       COPYRIGHT 1977 BY JAMES CHERRILL•
C       JAMES CHERRILL
C       42A, CARLISLE PLACE
C       LONDON
C       SW1                      TELEPHONE 01-834 2682
C
C       TECHNICAL NOTES•
C           ALL VARIABLES ARE INTEGERS, AND REQUIRE ONLY 16 BITS/WORD•
C           IBM USERS SHOULD DECLARE THE MAIN ARRAY INTEGER*2 TO
C           PRESERVE SPACE•
C           STREAM 5 IS USED FOR CARD-FORMAT INPUT•
C           STREAM 6 IS USED FOR PRINTER OUTPUT• NO CONTROL CHARACTERS
C           ARE PRESENT, BUT EACH LINE BEGINS WITH A SPACE•
C
CCCCCCCCCCCCCCCCCCCCCCCCCCCCCCCCCCCCCCCCCCCCCCCCCCCCCCCCCCCCCCCCCCCCCCCC
C
C       VERSION DATE  5 OCTOBER 1977
C
        IMPLICIT INTEGER
```

263

```
C       GO BACK TO GET NEXT CARD
        GO TO 100
C
C       END OF MAIN LOGIC SECTION
C
CCCCCCCCCCCCCCCCCCCCCCCCCCCCCCCCCCCCCCCCCCCCCCCCCCCCCCCCCCCCCCCCCCCCCCCCC
C
C       INPUT AND SETUP SECTION - CALLES FROM MAIN ROUTINE
C
C       FIRST STAGE IS TO READ NETWORK DEFINITION INTO ARRAY AND SET UP
C       POINTERS INTO ARRAY FOR EACH SECTION OF DEFINITION
C
 1001 FORMAT (12I6)
 1000 READ(5,1001)BUFR12
      N=BUFR12(1)
C       NO. OF NODES IN NETWORK
      STHR=0
C       START OF THRESHOLD VALUES IN ARRAY
      STRIG=N
C       START OF TRIGGERING STRENGTH VALUES
      SINNCT=2*N
C       START OF COUNTS OF INPUTS PER NODE
      SHBCT=3*N
C       START OF COUNTS OF INHIBITING NODES PER NODE
C
      DO 1100 I=1,N
        A(STHR+I)=0
C         INITIALISE THRESHOLDS TO ZERO
 1100 CONTINUE
C
C       ESTIMATE NO. OF CARDS TO READ TO GET ALL INHIB. NODE COUNTS
      N1=N/6
C       TRANSFER REMAINDER OF FIRST CARD TO ARRAY
      DO 1110 I=1,11
        A(SINNCT+I)=BUFR12(I+1)
 1110 CONTINUE
C
C       READ NEXT BLOCK OF CARDS INTO ARRAY
      IF (N1 .EQ. 0) GO TO 1130
      DO 1130 I=1,N1

        READ(5,1001)BUFR12
        DO 1120 J=1,12
          I1=SINNCT+I*12+J-1
          A(I1)=BUFR12(J)
 1120   CONTINUE
 1130 CONTINUE
C
C       COMPUTE TOTAL NO. OF INPUTS AND INHIBITING NODES
      NINNDS=0
      NHBNDS=0
      DO 1140 I=1,N
        NINNDS= NINNDS+A(SINNCT+I)
        NHBNDS= NHBNDS+A(SHBCT+I)
 1140 CONTINUE
C
C       COMPUTE NO. OF CARDS STILL TO BE READ
      N2=(2*N*NHBNDS+NINNDS)/12 -N1
C       READ REMAINDER OF CARDS INTO ARRAY
      DO 1160 I=1,N2
        READ(5,1001)BUFR12
```

```
         DØ 1150 J=1,12
           I1=(N1+I)*12 +SINNCT+J-1
           A(I1)=BUFR12(J)
 1150 CØNTINUE
 1160 CØNTINUE
C
C     SET UP REMAINDER ØF PØINTERS
      SINNN=4*N
C     START ØF INPUT NØDE NUMBERS
      SHBNN=SINNN+NINNDS
C     START ØF INHIBITING NØDE NUMBERS
      SINWT=SHBNN+NHBNDS
C     START ØF INPUT WEIGHTINGS
      SINPUT=SINWT+NINNDS
C     START ØF CURRENT INPUT STRING STØRAGE AREA
C
C
C     SECØND STAGE IS TØ READ IN INPUT STRING DEFINITIØNS.
C     THESE ARE PACKED AT 16 BITS PER WØRD
C
C
C     MAIN DATA ARRAY A MUST BE INDIVIDUALLY DIMENSIØNED TØ FIT MACHINE.
      DIMENSIØN A(500)
C
C     INPUT/ØUTPUT BUFFERS
      DIMENSIØN BUFR64(64),BUFR12(12)
C
C     CØNSTANTS FØR IDENTIFICATIØN ØF CØNTRØL CARDS
      DATA ST/2HST/
      DATA RU/2HRU/
      DATA GR/2HGR/
      DATA RI/2HRI/
      DATA NØ/2HNØ/
      DATA HW/2HHW/
      DATA LR/2HLR/
      DATA SD/2HSD/
      DATA LS/2HLS/
      DATA HS/2HHS/
      DATA MØ/2HMØ/
      DATA PR/2HPR/
      DATA PP/2HPP/
      DATA DU/2HDU/
      DATA LN/2HLN/
      DATA HN/2HHN/
      DATA SC/2HSC/
      DATA PC/2HPC/
C
C
C     ØPEN INPUT AND ØUTPUT FILES. IMPLEMENTATIØN DEPENDENT.
      ØPEN(5,INPUT,SYMBØLIC,PRØMPT'INPUT FILE:')
      ØPEN(6,ØUTPUT,SYMBØLIC,*HERE)
C
C
CCCCCCCCCCCCCCCCCCCCCCCCCCCCCCCCCCCCCCCCCCCCCCCCCCCCCCCCCCCCCCCCCCCCCCCC
C
C     MAIN LØGIC CØNTRØL SECTIØN - CALLS ALL ØTHER SECTIØNS AS NEEDED
C
      GØ TØ 1000
C     READ NETWØRK DEFINITIØN AND INITIALISE VARIABLES
 1999 CØNTINUE
```

```
C
  1       FORMAT (A2,I6)
C         READ CONTROL CARD
 100      READ(5,1)CODE,VALUE
  2       FORMAT(1X,A2,I6)
          WRITE(6,2)CODE,VALUE
C
C         IF CODE IS NOT 'RUN', GO TO CONTROL CARD PROCESSING SECTION
          IF (CODE .NE. RU) GO TO 7000
C
          DO 200 IMAIN=1,VALUE
C            RUN CORRECT NO. OF PASSES THROUGH MODEL
             TIME=TIME+1
             GO TO 2000
C            GET INPUT STRING
 2999     CONTINUE
             GO TO 3000
C            TRIGGER NODES AND PROCESS INHIBITION EFFECTS
 3999     CONTINUE
             GO TO 4000
C            TEST RESULTS OF NODE RESPONSES
 4999     CONTINUE
             IF (MONSW .NE. 0) GO TO 8100
C            IF MONITORING ACTIVE, GO TO PRINTOUT ROUTINE
 8199     CONTINUE
 8299     CONTINUE
             IF (CNTSW .GE. 0) GO TO 8700
C            IF COUNTING ACTIVE, COUNT NODE RESPONSES
 8799     CONTINUE
             GO TO 5000
C            MODIFY INPUT WEIGHTINGS
 5999     CONTINUE
             GO TO 6000
C            GENERATE NEW INPUT CONNECTIONS
 6999     CONTINUE
C            END OF 'RUN' LOOP
 200      CONTINUE
C
C         RETURN POINT FROM PROCESSING OTHER CONTROL CARDS...
 7999     CONTINUE

C1002     FORMAT (2I6)
C         READ NO. OF INPUT STRINGS AND INPUT STRING LENGTH
          READ(5,1002)NINSTR,INSTRL
C         COMPUTE STRING LENGTH (PACKED) IN WORDS
          INSTRW=INSTRL/16
C         SET POINTER TO START OF PACKED STRING STORAGE AREA
          SINSTR=SINPUT+INSTRL
C         SET DEFAULTS FOR LOWEST AND HIGHEST STRING NO. IN USE
          LISNO=1
          HISNO=NINSTR
C         COMPUTE NO. OF CARDS TO BE READ
          N1=(NINSTR*INSTRW +3)/4
C         READ THE CARDS
 1003     FORMAT (64I1)
          DO 1190 I=1,N1
             READ(5,1003)BUFR64
C            PACK STRINGS
             DO 1180 J=1,4
                L=0
                M=1
```

```
          DO 1170 K=1,15
            I1=J*16+K-16
            L=L+BUFR64(I1)*M
            M=M*2
 1170     CONTINUE
C         SIXTEENTH BIT IS CODED AS SIGN BIT
          I1=J*16
          I2=BUFR64(I1)
          IF (I2 .EQ. 1) L= -L
C         STORE PACKED WORD
          I1=SINSTR+ (I-1)*4 +J
          A(I1)=L
 1180   CONTINUE
 1190 CONTINUE
C
C
C     THIRD STAGE IS TO SET DEFAULT VALUES FOR PARAMETERS
C
      TIME=0
      PCRIN=0
C     PERCENTAGE OF RANDOM STRINGS USED AS INPUTS
      PNOISE=0
C     PERCENTAGE OF BITS SUBJECT TO NOISE IN INPUT STRINGS
      LAPSE=0
C     DECREASE IN INPUT WEIGHTINGS WHEN NODE DOES NOT TRIGGER
      GROWTH=50
C     PERCENTAGE OF POSSIBLE NEW INPUTS GROWN PER CYCLE
      MONSW=0
C     MONITOR LEVEL SWITCH
      INHWKN=100
C     AMOUNT BY WHICH INPUT WEIGHTINGS DECREASED WHEN INHIBITED
      I=RAND(257)
C     SET RANDOM NO. SEED
      IMAIN=0
      LNODE=1
      HNODE=N
C     NODES BEING MONITORED
      CNTSW=-1
C     SWITCH CONTROLLING RESPONSE COUNTS
C
C
C
C     LAST STAGE IS TIDY-UP
C
C     COMPUTE AMOUNT OF MAIN ARRAY ACTUALLY USED
      SCOUNT=SINSTR+NINSTR*INSTRW
      AEND=SCOUNT+(N+1)*(NINSTR+1)
 1201 FORMAT (22H MAIN DATA ARRAY USAGE,I6,9H WORDS, ( ,
     1         16,16H WITHOUT COUNTS)  )
      WRITE(6,1201)AEND,SCOUNT
C
C     IF CARDS WERE CORRECTLY CODED, NEXT CARD IS 'START' CARD
C
C     SWITCH INPUT FILES SO THAT NETWORK DEFINITION AND CONTROL CARDS
C     ARE READ FROM DIFFERENT FILES.
C     CODE IS IMPLEMENTATION DEPENDENT, AND CAN BE OMITTED IF ALL
C     INPUT IS TO BE FROM THE SAME FILE.
C
      CLOSE(5)
      OPEN(5,INPUT,SYMBOLIC,*HERE)
C
```

```
      READ(5,1)CODE,VALUE
      IF (CODE .NE. ST) GO TO 1900
 1004 FORMAT(9H RUN NO. ,I6,8H STARTED)
      WRITE(6,1004)VALUE
C     RETURN TO MAIN ROUTINE
      GO TO 1999
C     IF CARD WAS NOT 'START', ABORT RUN
 1900 WRITE(6,1005)
      STOP
 1005 FORMAT (49H START CARD NOT IN CORRECT POSITION - RUN STOPPED)
C
C     END OF INPUT AND INITIALISATION ROUTINE
C
CCCCCCCCCCCCCCCCCCCCCCCCCCCCCCCCCCCCCCCCCCCCCCCCCCCCCCCCCCCCCCCCCCCCCCC
C
C     ROUTINE TO SELECT AND CONDITION AN INPUT STRING. CALLED FROM MAIN
C
 2000 IF (PCRIN .EQ. 0) GO TO 2200
C     CHECK IF RANDOM INPUT IS TO BE USED
      I=RAND(100)
      IF (I .GT. PCRIN) GO TO 2200
C
C     GENERATE RANDOM INPUT STRING
      DO 2100 I=1,INSTRL
        A(SINPUT+I)=RAND(2)
 2100 CONTINUE
C     CODE STRING NO. AS ZERO, AND RETURN
      ISNO=0
      GO TO 2999
C
C     SELECTION OF NON-RANDOM STRINGS
 2200 N1=HISNO-LISNO +1
C     NO. OF INPUT STRINGS FROM WHICH SELECTION IS TO BE MADE
      ISNO=LISNO+ RAND(N1)
C     HAVING CHOSEN STRING, LOCATE IT IN ARRAY AND UNPACK IT
      DO 2500 I=1,INSTRW
C       EXTRACT NEXT WORD OF STRING
        J=SINSTR+ (ISNO-1)*INSTRW +I
        L=A(J)
C
C       DECODE SIGN BIT
        I1=SINPUT+I*16
        A(I1)=0
        IF (L .GE. 0) GO TO 2300
          A(I1)=1
          L= -L
 2300   CONTINUE
C
C       UNPACK REMAINING 15 BITS
        DO 2400 J=1,15
          I1=SINPUT +(I-1)*16+J
          A(I1)=MOD(L,2)
          L=L/2
 2400   CONTINUE
 2500 CONTINUE
C
C     IF NO NOISE IS REQUIRED, RETURN DIRECTLY TO MAIN ROUTINE
      IF (PNOISE .EQ. 0) GO TO 2999
C
C     CORRUPT BITS AT RANDOM
      DO 2600 I=1,INSTRL
```

```
          J=RAND(200)
C         N% NOISE IS N/2% BITS CORRUPTED
          IF (J .LE. PNOISE) A(SINPUT+I)=1-A(SINPUT+I)
 2600 CONTINUE
C     RETURN TO MAIN ROUTINE
      GO TO 2999
C
C     END OF INPUT STRING ROUTINE
C
CCCCCCCCCCCCCCCCCCCCCCCCCCCCCCCCCCCCCCCCCCCCCCCCCCCCCCCCCCCCCCCCCCCCCCC
C
C
C     ROUTINE TO DTERMINE NODE RESPONSES
C
C     INITIALISE POINTERS FOR NEXT INPUT NODE, NEXT INHIBITING NODE,
C     AND NO. OF HIGHEST NODE FOR WHICH INHIBITION HAS BEEN EXAMINED
 3000 NEXTIN=0
      NEXTHO=SHONN
      HNINH=0
C
C     MAIN LOOP. FOR EACH NODE IN NETWORK...
      DO 3400 I=1,N
C         INITIALISE TRIG. STREN. AND THREASHOLDS FOR THIS NODE TO ZERO
          TSTRN=0
          THRSH=0
C         GET NO. OF INPUTS FOR THIS NODE
          INNDS=A(SINNCT+I)
C
C         NOW LOOP THROUGH EACH INPUT
          DO 3300 J=1,INNDS
          NEXTIN=NEXTIN+1
C         GET ACUAL INPUT NO. FOR THIS INPUT
          INNN= A(SINNN+NEXTIN)
C         CHECK WHETHER INPUT FROM INPUT STRING OR ANOTHER NODE
          IF (INNN .GT. 0) GO TO 3100
C
C         GET BIT FROM INPUT STRING
          INBIT= A(SINPUT - INNN)
C         (IE. SINPUT + -INNN BECAUSE INNN IS NEGATIVE FOR STRING POSN.)
          GO TO 3200
C         INPUT FROM ANOTHER NODE... FIRST CHECK IF NODE HAS BEEN
C         PROCESSED FOR INHIBITION
 3100     IF (INNN .GT. HNINH) GO TO 3500
C         IF NOT, CALL INHIBITION ROUTINE BEFORE CONTINUING
 3998     CONTINUE
C         SET INPUT ACCORDING TO WHETHER NODE RESPONDED OR NOT
          INBIT=0
          ITRSTN= A(STRIG+INNN)
          IF (ITRSTN .GT. 0) INBIT=1
 3200     CONTINUE
C
C         INCREMENT TRIGGERING STRENGTH OF NODE BY WEIGHTED INPUT
          I1=A(SINWT+NEXTIN)
          TSTRN=TSTRN+I1*INBIT
C         INCREMENT THREASHOLD
          IF (I1 .GE. 100) THRSH=THRSH+I1-100
 3300     CONTINUE
C
C         IF FINAL TRIG. STRENGTH LESS THAN THRESHOLD, NO RESPONSE
```

```
C        IF (TSTRN .LE. THRSH) TSTRN=0
C        SAVE FINAL TRIG. STRENGTH , AND GO ON TO NEXT NODE
         A(STRIG+I)=TSTRN
         A(STHR+I)=THRSH
 3400 CONTINUE
C
C     PROCESS REMAINING NODES THROUGH INHIBITION SECTION.
C     RETURN FROM THIS SECTION IS DIRECT TO MAIN ROUTINE
      INNN=N
      GO TO 3500
C
C
C     INHIBITION PROCESSING SECTION
C
C
 3500 HNINH=HNINH+1
C     PROCESS ALL UNPROCESSED NODES UP TP THE ONE REQUIRED
      DO 3700 K=HNINH,INNN
C        GET NO. OF INHIBITING NODES FOR THIS NODE
         HBNDS=A(SHBCT+K)
C        IF THERE ARE NONE, SKIP THIS LOOP
         IF (HBNDS .EQ. 0) GO TO 3700
C
C        OTHERWISE, GET THIS NODE'S TRIGGERING STRENGTH...
         TSTRN1=A(STRIG+K)
C        THEN LOOP THROUGH ALL ITS INHIBITING NODES...
         DO 3600 L=1,HBNDS
          NEXTHB=NEXTHB+1
C         ...GETTING THEIR TRIGGERING STRENGTHS
          HBND=A(NEXTHB)
          TSTRN2=A(STRIG+HBND)
C
C         IF ANY IS GREATER, EXIT WITH NODE FLAGGED AS INHIBITED
          IF (TSTRN2 .LT. TSTRN1) GO TO 3600
          IF (TSTRN2 .GT. TSTRN1) GO TO 3550
C         TRIG SRENGTHS EQUAL, TAKE RANDOM 50/50 CHOICE
          I1=RAND(100)
          IF (I1 .LT. 50) GO TO 3600
 3550     CONTINUE
C         FLAG INHIBITED NODE BY TRIG. STRENGTH LESS THAN ZERO.

          A(STRIG+K)= -IABS(TSTRN1)
 3600    CONTINUE
 3700 CONTINUE
C
C     UPDATE RECORD OF NODES PROCESSED THROUGH INHIBITION
      HNINH=INNN
C     IF ALL NODES ARE NOW PROCESSED, RETURN IS TO MAIN ROUTINE,
C     OTHERWISE RETURN IS BACK TO NODE RESPONSE PROCESSING
      IF (HNINH .EQ. N) GO TO 3999
      GO TO 3998
C
C     END OF INHIBITION AND NODE RESPONSE PROCESSING
C
C
CCCCCCCCCCCCCCCCCCCCCCCCCCCCCCCCCCCCCCCCCCCCCCCCCCCCCCCCCCCCCCCCCCCCCCC
C
C     SECTION TO TEST NODE RESPONSES.
C
C     NOT YET DESIGNED, ALL RESPONSES ARE ASSUMED TO BE OK.
C
```

```
 4000  ØK=1
       GØ TØ 4999
C
C      (FUTURE DEVELØPMENT IS TØ DEFINE ØVERALL RESPØNSE ØF NETWØRK AS
C       'CØRRECT' ØR 'INCØRRECT', THUS ALLØWING IT TØ BE 'TAUGHT')
C
C
CCCCCCCCCCCCCCCCCCCCCCCCCCCCCCCCCCCCCCCCCCCCCCCCCCCCCCCCCCCCCCCCCCCCCCCC
C
C      SECTIØN TØ MØDIFY INPUT WEIGHTINGS
C
C      NB. THRESHØLD IS UPDATED DURING NEXT RUN THRØUGH
C      RESPØNSE PRØCESSING.
C      ACTIØN DEPENDS ØN WHETHER RESPØNSE WAS ØK ØR NØT
C
 5000  IF (ØK .EQ. 0) GØ TØ 5800
C      FØLLØWING CØDE IS FØR ØK RESPØNES
       NEXTIN=0
C
C      FØR EACH NØDE, GET TRIG. STRENGTH AND NØ. ØF INPUTS
C
       DØ 5700 I=1,N
         TSTRN=A(STRIG+I)
         INNDS=A(SINNCT+I)
C
C        LØØP THRØUGH THE INPUT NØDES
         DØ 5600 J=1,INNDS
           NEXTIN=NEXTIN+1
           I1=SINWT+NEXTIN
           I2=A(I1)
           IF (TSTRN .GE. 0) GØ TØ 5100
C
C          THIS IS THE CASE WHERE NØDE WAS INHIBITED. WEAKEN CØNNECTIØNS
           A(I1)=I2-INHWKN
           GØ TØ 5600
 5100      IF (TSTRN .EQ. 0) GØ TØ 5500
C
C          THIS IS THE CASE WHERE NØDE RESPØNDED SUCSESSFULLY
C          ACTIØN DEPENDS ØN WHETHER INPUT WAS 1 ØR 0
C          GET INPUT NØDE NØ.
           INNN=A(SINNN+NEXTIN)
           IF (INNN .GT. 0) GØ TØ 5200
C
C            INPUT IS FRØM AN INPUT STRING
             INBIT=A(SINPUT-INNN)
C            (NB. INNN NEGATIVE.)
             GØ TØ 5300
C
C            INPUT IS FRØM ANØTHER NØDE, FIRST CHECK ITS RESPØNSE
 5200        INBIT=0
             ITSTRN=A(STRIG+INNN)
             IF (ITSTRN .GT. 0) INBIT=1
 5300      CØNTINUE
C          IF INPUT WAS 1, INCREASE WEIGHTING, ØTHERWISE DECREASE IT
           IF (INBIT .EQ. 0) GØ TØ 5400
           IF (I2 .GE. 100) A(I1)=I2+10000/I2
           GØ TØ 5600
 5400      A(I1)=I2-100
           GØ TØ 5600
C          FINAL CASE IS WHERE NØDE DID NØT ATTEMPT TØ RESPØND.
C          IN THIS CASE, THE LAPSE RATE IS APPLIED
```

```
5500      A(I1)=I2-LAPSE
5600    CONTINUE
5700 CONTINUE
C
C      END OF PROCESSING FOR OVERALL RESPONSE OK, SO RETURN
       GO TO 5999
C
C
C      SECTION FOR MODIFICATION OF INPUT WEIGHTINGS WHEN OVERALL
C      RESPONSE NOT OK. NOT YET DEFINED
5800 GO TO 5999
C
C      END OF INPUT WEIGHTING MODIFICATION SECTION
C
C
CCCCCCCCCCCCCCCCCCCCCCCCCCCCCCCCCCCCCCCCCCCCCCCCCCCCCCCCCCCCCCCCCCCCCCC
C
C
C      SECTION TO ESTABLISH NEW INPUT CONNECTIONS, OR REMOVE EXCESSIVLY
C      WEAKENED ONES
C
6000 DO 6100 I=1,NINNODS
C          EXTRACT WEIGHTING FOR EVERY INPUT
           INWT=A(SINWT+I)
C          NO ACTION IF WEIGHTING ALREADY STRONG ENOUGH
           IF (INWT .GE. 100) GO TO 6100
           INWT=0
C          (REMOVE EXCESSIVLY WEAKENED INPUTS)
           J=RAND(100)
           IF (J .LT. GROWTH) INWT=100
C          (RE-GROW RANDOM SELECTION OF POSSIBLE INPUTS)
           A(SINWT+I)=INWT
6100 CONTINUE
     GO TO 6999
C
C      END OF INPUT CONNECTION SECTION
C
C
CCCCCCCCCCCCCCCCCCCCCCCCCCCCCCCCCCCCCCCCCCCCCCCCCCCCCCCCCCCCCCCCCCCCCCC
C
C      CONTROL CARD PROCESSING
C
7000 IF (CODE .NE. PR) GO TO 7010
C      CALL PRINTOUT ROUTINES
C      TYPICAL TEST ON VALIDITY OF PARAMETER FOLLOWS...
       IF (VALUE .LT. 1) GO TO 7900
       IF (VALUE .GT. N) GO TO 7900
       GO TO 8300
C
7010 IF (CODE .NE. MO) GO TO 7020
C      CALL TO MONITOR ROUTINES
       IF (VALUE .LT.0) GO TO 7900
       IF (VALUE .GT. 2) GO TO 7900
       GO TO 8000
C
7020 IF (CODE .NE. HS) GO TO 7030
C      'HIGHEST STRING' COMMAND
       IF (VALUE .LT. LISNO) GO TO 7900
       IF (VALUE .GT. NINSTR) GO TO 7900
       HISNO=VALUE
       GO TO 7999
```

```
C
 7030 IF (CODE .NE. LS) GO TO 7040
C     'LOWEST STRING' COMMAND
      IF (VALUE .LT. 1) GO TO 7900
      IF (VALUE .GT. HISNO) GO TO 7900
      LISNO=VALUE
      GO TO 7999
C
 7040 IF (CODE .NE. SD) GO TO 7050
C     NEW RANDOM NUMBER SEED
      I=RAND(VALUE+257)
      GO TO 7999
C
 7050 IF (CODE .NE. GR) GO TO 7060
C     PERCENTAGE GROWTH RATE FOR NEW INPUTS
      IF (VALUE .LT. 0) GO TO 7900
      IF (VALUE .GT. 100) GO TO 7900
      GROWTH=VALUE
      GO TO 7999

C
 7060 IF (CODE .NE. NO) GO TO 7070
C     PERCENTAGE OF NOISY BITS IN INPUTS
      IF (VALUE .LT. 0) GO TO 7900
      IF (VALUE .GT. 100) GO TO 7900
      PNOISE=VALUE
      GO TO 7999
C
 7070 IF (CODE .NE. RI) GO TO 7080
C     PERCENTAGE OF INPUTS AS RANDOM STRINGS
      IF (VALUE .LT. 0) GO TO 7900
      IF (VALUE .GT. 100) GO TO 7900
      PCRIN=VALUE
      GO TO 7999
C
 7080 IF (CODE .NE. HW) GO TO 7090
C     AMOUNT BY WHICH INPUTS WEAKENED WHEN NODES INHIBITED
      IF (VALUE .LT. 0) GO TO 7900
      INHWKN=VALUE
      GO TO 7999
C
 7090 IF (CODE .NE. LR) GO TO 7100
C     LAPSE RATE
      IF (VALUE .LT. 0) GO TO 7900
      LAPSE=VALUE
      GO TO 7999
C
 7100 IF (CODE .NE. PP) GO TO 7110
C     PRINT PARAMETERS
C     VALUE IS NOT USED
      GO TO 8400
C
 7110 IF (CODE .NE. DU) GO TO 7120
C     DUMP
      IF (VALUE .LT. 0) GO TO 7900
      IF (VALUE .GT. 1) GO TO 7900
      GO TO 8500
C
 7120 IF(CODE .NE. LN) GO TO 7130
C     LOWEST NODE BEING MONITORED
```

```
         IF (VALUE .LT. 1) GO TO 7900
         IF (VALUE .GT. HNODE) GO TO 7900
         LNODE=VALUE
         GO TO 7999
C
 7130 IF (CODE .NE. HN) GO TO 7140
C        HIGHEST NODE BEING MONITORED
         IF (VALUE .LT. LNODE) GO TO 7900
         IF (VALUE .GT. N)GO TO 7900
         HNODE=VALUE
         GO TO 7999
C
 7140 IF (CODE .NE. SC) GO TO 7150
C        START COUNT
         GO TO 8600
C
 7150 IF (CODE .NE. PC) GO TO 7160
C        PRINT COUNTS
         GO TO 8800
C
 7160 CONTINUE
C        END OF VALID CONTROL CARD TYPES
C
C        INVALID CODE.
 7001 FORMAT (39H CARD TYPE NOT RECOGNISED, CARD IGNORED)
         WRITE(6,7001)
         GO TO7999
C
C        INVALID VALUE FOR PARAMETER
 7900 WRITE(6,7002)
 7002 FORMAT (33H VALUE OUT OF RANGE. CARD IGNORED)
         GO TO 7999
C
C        END  OF CONTROL CARD PROCESSING
C
CCCCCCCCCCCCCCCCCCCCCCCCCCCCCCCCCCCCCCCCCCCCCCCCCCCCCCCCCCCCCCCCCCCCC
C
C        PRINTOUT SECTION, HANDLES ALL PRINTS AND MONITORS
C
C        FIRST SECTION HANDLES CHANGES IN MONITOR STATUS
C
 8000 MONSW=VALUE
         IF (MONSW .EQ. 0) GO TO 7999
C        WHEN TURNING MONITORING ON, PRINT HEADINGS
         IF (MONSW .EQ. 2) GO TO 8010
 8001 FORMAT (32H  TIME INPUT  NODE THRESHOLD*100)
         WRITE(6,8001)
         GO TO 7999
 8010 WRITE(6,8002)
 8002 FORMAT (29H  TIME INPUT NODES RESPONDING)
         GO TO 7999
C
C        SECOND SECTION GIVES ACTUAL MONITOR OUTPUT
C
 8100 IF (MONSW .NE. 1) GO TO 8200
C
C        PRINTOUT FOR MONITOR LEVEL 1
C        FIND HIGHEST RESPONDING NODE
         J=HNODE
         N1=0
```

```
       DØ 8110 I=LNØDE,HNØDE
         I1=A(STRIG+J)
         IF (I1 .GT. 0) GØ TØ 8120
         J=J-1
  8110 CØNTINUE
       J=0
       GØ TØ 8125
  8120 N1= A(STHR+J)
C      (IE. THRESHØLD FØR THAT NØDE)
  8121 FØRMAT (4I6)
  8125 WRITE(6,8121)TIME,ISNØ,J,N1
       GØ TØ 8199
C
C      PRINTØUT FØR MØNITØR LEVEL 2
  8201 FØRMAT (2I6)
  8200 WRITE (6,8201)TIME,ISNØ
C      CLEAR ØUTPUT BUFFER
       DØ 8210 I=1,64
         BUFR64(I)=0
  8210 CØNTINUE

       N1=0
C
C      LØØP THRØUGH NØDES CHECKING FØR SUCESSFUL RESPØNSES
C      STØP TØ EMPTY BUFFER EVERY 64 NØDES
       DØ 8240 I=LNØDE,HNØDE
         N1=N1+1
         IF (N1 .LT. 65) GØ TØ 8230
C          BUFFER NEEDS EMPTYING
  8202     FØRMAT (13X,64I1)
           WRITE(6,8202) BUFR64
           N1=1
C          RESET CØUNTER, CLEAR BUFFER
           DØ 8220 J=1,64
             BUFR64(J)=0
  8220     CØNTINUE
C        SET NEXT ELEMENT IN BUFFER TØ 1 IF NØDE RESPØNDED
  8230   I1=A(STRIG+I)
         IF (I1 .GT. 0) BUFR64(N1)=1
  8240 CØNTINUE
C
C      EMPTY BUFFER
       WRITE(6,8202)BUFR64
C
C      END ØF MØNITØR PRINTØUT
       GØ TØ 8299
C
C      THIRD SECTIØN HANDLES PRINT CØMMANDS
  8300 I1=A(STHR+VALUE)
       WRITE(6,8301)VALUE,I1
  8301 FØRMAT (6H NØDE ,I6,12H. THRESHØLD=,I6,4H*100)
       WRITE (6,8302)
  8302 FØRMAT (17H INPUT WEIGHT*100)
C
C      FIND WHERE THIS NØDE'S INPUTS START IN A
       N1=0
       I1=VALUE-1
       IF (I1 .EQ. 0) GØ TØ 8310
       DØ 8310 I=1,I1
         N1=N1+A(SINNCT+I)
  8310 CØNTINUE
```

```
C
C      THEN LOOP THROUGH ALL THE INPUTS, PRINTING
       I1=A(SINNCT+VALUE)
       DO 8320 I=1,I1
         I2=N1+I
         INNN=A(SINNN+I2)
         INWT=A(SINWT+I2)
  8311   FORMAT (2I6)
         WRITE(6,8311)INNN,INWT
  8320 CONTINUE
       GO TO 7999
C
C      FOURTH SECTION HANDLES 'PRINT PARAMETERS'
C
  8400 WRITE(6,8401)TIME
       WRITE(6,8402)LISNO,HISNO
       WRITE(6,8403)PCRIN,PNOISE
       WRITE(6,8404)LAPSE,GROWTH
       WRITE(6,8405)INHWKN
       WRITE(6,8406)LNODE,HNODE
       GO TO 7999
  8401 FORMAT(25H MAIN PARAMETERS AT TIME=,I6)
  8402 FORMAT(22H INPUT STRINGS IN USE:,I6,3H TO,I6)
  8403 FORMAT(I7,18HPC. RANDOM INPUTS,,I6,10HPC. NOISE.)
  8404 FORMAT(11H LAPSE RATE,I6,23H   NEW INPUT GROWTH RATE,I6)
  8405 FORMAT(25H INHIBITED WEAKENING RATE,I6)
  8406 FORMAT(23H NODES BEING MONITORED:  ,I6,3H TO,I6)
C
C      FIFTH SECTION HANDLES DUMPS
C
  8500 IF (VALUE .EQ. 0) GO TO 8550
C      PRINT ARRAY POINTERS
       WRITE(6,8501)N,STHR,STRIG
       WRITE(6,8502)SINNCT,SHBCT,NINNDS,NHBNDS
       WRITE(6,8503)SINNN,SHBNN,SINWT
       WRITE(6,8504)SINPUT,SINSTR,NINSTR,INSTRL
  8501 FORMAT(8H      N=,I6,9H     STHR=,I6,9H    STRIG=,I6)
  8502 FORMAT(8H SINNCT=,I6,9H    SHBCT=,I6,9H NINNDS=,I6,
      1 9H  NHBNDS=,I6)
  8503 FORMAT(8H  SINNN=,I6,9H    SHBNN=,I6,9H    SINWT=,I6)

  8504 FORMAT(8H SINPUT=,I6,9H   SINSTR=,I6,9H   NINSTR=,I6,
      1 9H  INSTRL=,I6)
C
  8550 WRITE(6,8551)TIME
  8551 FORMAT(26H MAIN DATA ARRAY AT TIME=  ,I6)
       I1=(AEND+11)/12
C      NO. OF LINES FOR DUMP
       DO 8590 I=1,I1
         DO 8580 J=1,12
           I2=(I-1)*12+J
           BUFR12(J)=A(I2)
  8580   CONTINUE
         WRITE(6,8582)BUFR12
  8582 . FORMAT(12I6)
  8590 CONTINUE
       GO TO 7999
C
C
C      SIXTH SECTION HANDLES RESPONSE COUNTS
C
```

```
C     START CØUNT
8600  I1=SCØUNT+1
      DØ 8610 I=I1,AEND
        A(I)=0
8610  CØNTINUE
      CNTSW=TIME
      GØ TØ 7999
C
C     CØUNT NØDE RESPØNSES
C
8700  I1=SCØUNT+ISNØ*(N+1)+1
C     CØUNT ØCCURRENCES ØF STRING
      A(I1)=A(I1)+1
      I2=STRIG
C     CØUNT RESPØNDING NØDES
      DØ 8710 I=1,N
        I1=I1+1
        I2=I2+1
        TSTRN=A(I2)
        IF (TSTRN .GT. 0) A(I1)=A(I1)+1

8710  CØNTINUE
      GØ TØ 8799
C
C     PRINT CØUNTS
C
8800  WRITE(6,8801)CNTSW,TIME
8801  FØRMAT(16H CØUNTS FØR TIME  ,I6,3H TØ,I6)
      I1=HISNØ-LISNØ+1
C     NØ. ØF STRINGS TØ PRINT
      IF (I1 .GT. 10) I1=10
C     CLEAR BUFFER
      DØ 8810 I=1,11
        BUFR12(I)=0
8810  CØNTINUE
      BUFR12(12)=9999
      DØ 8820 I=1,11
        BUFR12(I+1)=LISNØ+I-1
8820  CØNTINUE
C     PRINT HEADINGS
      WRITE(6,8802)BUFR12
8802  FØRMAT(/,12H    STRINGS:  ,12I5)
C     CLEAR BUFFER
      DØ 8830 I=2,12
        BUFR12(I)=0
8830  CØNTINUE
C     SET UP CØUNTS ØF ØCCURRENCES ØF STRINGS
      BUFR12(1)=A(SCØUNT+1)
      DØ 8840 I=1,I1
        I2=SCØUNT+(LISNØ+I-1)*(N+1)+1
        BUFR12(I+1)=A(I2)
        BUFR12(12)=BUFR12(12)+A(I2)
8840  CØNTINUE
      WRITE(6,8803)BUFR12
8803  FØRMAT(/,12H ØCCURRENCES   ,12I5)
C     SET UP CØUNTS BY NØDE
      DØ 8870 I=LNØDE,HNØDE
        DØ 8850 J=2,12
          BUFR12(J)=0
8850    CØNTINUE
        I2=SCØUNT+I+1
```

```
          BUFR12(1)=A(I2)
          DO 8860 J=1,11
            I2=SCOUNT+(LISNO+J-1)*(N+1)+I+1
            BUFR12(J+1)=A(I2)
            BUFR12(12)=BUFR12(12)+A(I2)
 8860     CONTINUE
          WRITE(6,8804)I,BUFR12
 8804     FORMAT(6H NODE  ,I5,1H:,12I5)
 8870 CONTINUE
      GO TO 7999
C
C
C     END OF PRINTOUT ROUTINE
C
      END
C
C
C
CCCCCCCCCCCCCCCCCCCCCCCCCCCCCCCCCCCCCCCCCCCCCCCCCCCCCCCCCCCCCCCCCCCCCCCC
C
C     RANDOM NUMBER SUBROUTINE
C
      INTEGER FUNCTION RAND(IMAX)
C
C     RETURNS PSEUDO-RANDOM NUMBER IN RANGE ZERO TO (IMAX-1)
C     LARGEST IMAX IS 256
C     IF IMAX GT 256, MOD(IMAX,257) IS USED AS NEW SEED
C
      IF (IMAX .GT. 256) GO TO 10
      ISEED=127*ISEED+113
      RAND=MOD(ISEED,IMAX)
      ISEED=MOD(ISEED,257)
      RETURN
C
 10   ISEED=MOD(IMAX,257)
      RAND=ISEED
      RETURN
C
C     END OF PSEUDO-RANDOM NUMBER SUBROUTINE
C
```

Index